taste of home
Christmas

taste of home
BOOKS

A TASTE OF HOME/READER'S DIGEST BOOK

© 2012 Reiman Media Group, LLC
5400 S. 60th St., Greendale WI 53129

EDITORIAL

Editor-in-Chief: **Catherine Cassidy**

Executive Editor, Print and Digital Books: **Stephen C. George**
Creative Director: **Howard Greenberg**
Editorial Services Manager: **Kerri Balliet**

Senior Editor/Print and Digital Books: **Mark Hagen**
Editor: **Janet Briggs**
Associate Editor: **Amy Glander**
Craft Editor: **Shalana Frisby**
Associate Creative Director: **Edwin Robles Jr.**
Art Director: **Rudy Krochalk**
Content Production Manager: **Julie Wagner**
Layout Designers: **Catherine Fletcher, Nancy Novak**
Contributing Layout Designer: **Holly Patch**
Copy Chief: **Deb Warlaumont Mulvey**
Copy Editor: **Mary C. Hanson**
Recipe Editors: **Mary King, Tina Bellows, Irene Yeh**
Recipe Content Manager: **Colleen King**
Assistant Photo Coordinator: **Mary Ann Koebernik**
Food Editor: **Wendy Stenman**
Test Kitchen Manager: **Karen Scales**
Recipe Testing: **Taste of Home Test Kitchen**
Food Photography: **Taste of Home Photo Studio**
Editorial Assistant: **Marilyn Iczkowski**

BUSINESS

Vice President, Publisher: **Jan Studin, jan_studin@rd.com**
Regional Account Director: **Donna Lindskog, donna_lindskog@rd.com**
Eastern Account Director: **Joanne Carrara**
Eastern Account Manager: **Kari Nestor**
Account Manager: **Gina Minerbi**
Midwest & Western Account Director: **Jackie Fallon**
Midwest Account Manager: **Lorna Phillips**
Western Account Manager: **Joel Millikin**
Michigan Sales Representative: **Linda C. Donaldson**
Southwestern Account Representative: **Summer Nilsson**

Corporate Integrated Sales Director: **Steve Sottile**
Digital Sales Planner: **Tim Baarda**

General Manager, Taste of Home Cooking Schools: **Erin Puariea**

Direct Response Advertising: **Katherine Zito, David Geller Associates**

Vice President, Creative Director: **Paul Livornese**
Executive Director, Brand Marketing: **Leah West**
Senior Marketing Manager: **Vanessa Bailey**
Associate Marketing Manager: **Betsy Connors**

Vice President, Magazine Marketing: **Dave Fiegel**

READER'S DIGEST NORTH AMERICA

President: **Dan Lagani**

Vice President, Business Development: **Jonathan Bigham**
President, Books and Home Entertaining: **Harold Clarke**
Chief Financial Officer: **Howard Halligan**
Vice President, General Manager, Reader's Digest Media: **Marilynn Jacobs**
Chief Content Officer, Milwaukee: **Mark Jannot**
Chief Marketing Officer: **Renee Jordan**
Vice President, Chief Sales Officer: **Mark Josephson**
Vice President, Chief Strategy Officer: **Jacqueline Majers Lachman**
Vice President, Marketing and Creative Services: **Elizabeth Tighe**
Vice President, Chief Content Officer: **Liz Vaccariello**

THE READER'S DIGEST ASSOCIATION, INC.

President and Chief Executive Officer: **Robert E. Guth**

For other **Taste of Home books** and products, visit us at **tasteofhome.com**.

International Standard Book Number: (10): 0-89821-990-6
International Standard Book Number: (13): 978-0-89821-990-6
Library of Congress Control Number: 2011937184

COVER PHOTOGRAPHY
Photographers: **Dan Roberts, Jim Wieland**
Food Stylists: **Kaitlyn Besasie, Shannon Roum**
Set Stylists: **Melissa Haberman, Dee Dee Jacq**

Pictured on the front cover (plated): Tiramisu Nanaimo Bars (p. 129), Classic Cherry Pie Cookies (p. 124), Blue Ribbon Carrot Cake Cookies (p. 128), Apple Crisp Crescents (p. 130), Raspberry Cheesecake Bars (p. 125), Lemon Meringue Pie Cookies (p. 127).

Across the Top: Simple Turtle Cheesecake (p. 97), Glazed Cornish Hens with Pecan-Rice Stuffing (p. 29), Felt Trees (p. 228), Deb's Oysters Rockefeller (p. 9).

Pictured on the back cover: Brandy & Date Cheese Ball Pops (p. 20), Maple-Pecan Glazed Ham (p. 23), Tangerine Tuiles with Candied Cranberries, (p. 112).

Additional Photography Used: Ornaments, Subbotina Anna/Shutterstock.com (endpapers), Ornament, kuleczka/Shutterstock.com (back cover), Ornament and Lights, Kati Molin/Shutterstock.com (p. 177), Christmas Lights, Artistic Endeavor/Shutterstock.com (p. 177), Christmas Tree, nikkytok/Shutterstock.com (p. 177).

Printed in U.S.A.
1 3 5 7 9 10 8 6 4 2

Contents

Celebrate this *Special* Season with Everything from *Easy* Crafts and *Fun* Decor to *Scrumptious* Meals and *Buttery* Cookies!

With Taste of Home Christmas, you'll discover hundreds of recipes for memorable meals, must-try appetizers and divine sweets—most shared by family cooks who made these dishes traditions in their homes. You'll also find more than 50 crafts, decorating ideas and gifts, turning this collection into a heartwarming keepsake you're sure to treasure.

Party Starters & Beverages. Nothing brings family and friends together like food...particularly an assortment of savory bites and seasonal beverages. See this chapter for all of your holiday party needs.

Christmas Dinners. Creating a comforting menu is a snap with the meals in this colorful section. Turn here for a complete dinner featuring Cornish hens, a feast centered around mouthwatering ham and an entire meal where golden Beef Wellingtons take center stage.

Holiday Bread Basket. Whether you prefer dinner accompaniments such as Sun-Dried Tomato Provolone Bread or sweet specialties like Chocolate-Apricot Coffee Cake, this is one section you'll turn to time and again.

Seasonal Get-Togethers. Hoping to enjoy a cozy Christmas Eve with your family? Want to throw a delightful New Year's brunch? You'll find menus and hostess ideas for both of these parties as well as recipes for a Feliz Navidad event friends won't soon forget!

Two Takes. Family cooks know the benefits of beating the kitchen clock during the busy yuletide season...and they share their time-saving secrets here. These large-yield recipes allow you to turn leftovers into two or more incredible dishes, shaving minutes off prep work.

Almost Homemade. Enjoy time with family and friends this holiday by giving homemade flair to everyday convenience items. From appetizers and soups to main courses and desserts, the ideas in this chapter promise to help you set incredible food on the table without much effort—no matter how busy your schedule becomes!

Perfectly Sized Desserts. Ideal for everything from dessert buffets to formal sit-down dinners, individually sized treats make any gathering special. Turn here for Gingerbread Souffles, Molten Chocolate Cherry Cakes, Petite Pear Purses and more!

Cookies with a Classic Twist. It's nearly impossible to have your fill of Christmas cookies, particularly when presented with these change-of-pace options! Here, popular desserts are made into bite-size delights such as Boston Cream Pie Cookies and Baklava Rounds.

Sweet Sensations. Special gatherings just aren't complete without impressive desserts that round out holiday menus. Here, you'll enjoy more than 2 dozen luscious favorites guaranteed to satisfy any sweet tooth.

Novel Gifts. Favorite books and homemade goodies always make wonderful hostess gifts. So much so, that the two are paired in this chapter. Package a copy of "A Christmas Carol" with Sugar Plum Kringles or bag some Herbed Nut Mix with the popular "Nutcracker" book. See this section for these ideas and more!

Deck the Halls. Turn your home into a wonderland with these easy decorating ideas. From tree skirts and ornaments to centerpieces and advent calendars, look for simple solutions to your decor dilemmas here.

Gifts to Give. You'll warm hearts, impress friends and save money this year when you craft your own gifts to give. No matter what your skill level may be, you're sure to find the perfect surprise for everyone on your Christmas list.

Turn the page and enjoy all of the magic this wonderful time of year has to offer. After all, with Taste of Home Christmas at your fingertips, your holiday promises to be merry and bright...and as memorable as ever.

Party Starters
& BEVERAGES

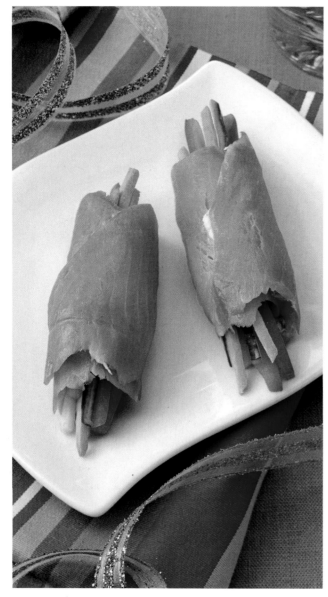

In a large bowl, beat the cream cheese, parsley, chives, lemon peel and garlic until blended.

Spread some of the cream cheese mixture over a salmon slice. Arrange a small amount of carrot, cucumber and pepper across the short side of the salmon, about 1 in. from the edge. Roll up tightly.

Repeat with remaining salmon, cream cheese mixture and vegetables.

Mini Mushroom Tarts

PREP: 40 MIN. **BAKE:** 10 MIN. **YIELD:** 45 TARTS

These little tarts are filled with a fabulous vegetable mixture that promises to get compliments. They're an ideal nosh to munch while circulating around a party.

Jacki Milazzo ★ Bonita, California

2-1/2 cups chopped baby portobello mushrooms
1-3/4 cups chopped fresh mushrooms
1/3 cup chopped carrot
1/3 cup chopped celery
1/4 cup finely chopped onion
3 tablespoons chopped sweet red pepper
2 tablespoons olive oil
1 garlic clove, minced
1/4 cup ricotta cheese
2 tablespoons minced fresh parsley
2 tablespoons minced fresh basil
1/2 teaspoon salt
1/8 teaspoon pepper
3 tablespoons seasoned bread crumbs
3 packages (1.9 ounces *each*) frozen miniature phyllo tart shells

In a large skillet, saute the mushrooms, carrot, celery, onion and red pepper in oil until crisp-tender. Add garlic; cook 2 minutes longer. Drain, reserving 2 tablespoons of the cooking liquid.

Remove from the heat; stir in the cheese, parsley, basil, salt and pepper. Stir in bread crumbs and the reserved cooking liquid.

Fill each tart shell with 2 teaspoons of filling. Place on ungreased baking sheets.

Bake at 350° for 6-8 minutes or until golden brown. Serve warm or at room temperature. Refrigerate leftovers.

Smoked Salmon Roulades

PREP/TOTAL TIME: 20 MIN. **YIELD:** 2 DOZEN

You're sure to impress guests with these colorful bites. Not only are they as elegant as they are scrumptious, but they're also easy, which makes them a plus for any busy hostess!

Taste of Home Test Kitchen

1 package (8 ounces) reduced-fat cream cheese
2 tablespoons minced fresh parsley
1 tablespoon minced chives
1 tablespoon grated lemon peel
1 garlic clove, minced
4 packages (3 ounces *each*) sliced smoked salmon *or* lox
1 medium carrot, peeled and julienned
1 small cucumber, julienned
1 small sweet red pepper, julienned

Lemon Meringue Pie Cocktail

PREP/TOTAL TIME: 5 MIN. **YIELD:** 1 SERVING

Don't let the light lemon flavor and rich, creamy texture fool you. This cool concoction is an adults-only indulgence. Make your own limoncello (recipe on page 164) or purchase in the liquor section of your supermarket. For a family-friendly version see the recipe variation below.

Taste of Home Test Kitchen

    1 lemon wedge
Coarse yellow and white sugar
1-1/2 to 2 cups ice cubes
    3 ounces limoncello
    1 ounce half-and-half cream
    1 tablespoon lemon sorbet
    2 teaspoons lemon juice

Rub lemon wedge around the rim of a martini glass; dip rim in coarse sugar. Set aside.

Fill a shaker three-fourths full with ice. Add the limoncello, cream, sorbet and lemon juice to shaker; cover and shake for 10-15 seconds or until condensation forms on outside of shaker. Strain into prepared glass.

Lemon Meringue Pie Mocktail: Substitute 1/3 cup of lemonade for the limoncello.

This sparkling centerpiece will be an eye-catching addition to your table. Best of all, you can complement your holiday decor by using matching metallic tones and shimmering beads.

Purchase a metallic vase about 10-in. tall and a piece of Styrofoam for the inside. You will also need a variety of beads, thin metal wire, wire cutters, sand, metallic spray paint and a few artificial or dried real branches.

Fill the bottom of the vase with a 2-in. layer of sand for a stabilizer. Trim the Styrofoam to fit snugly in the vase leaving about an inch of open space at the top. Fill this area with a layer of beads or even glass gemstones.

Spray paint the branches with metallic paint and let dry. Arrange branches as desired and insert ends a few inches into the Styrofoam base to secure in place.

Cut several 6- to 12-in. lengths of wire. Bend one end of each wire into a small curl. Add beads to the other end, leaving a couple of inches of open wire at the top. Wrap open wire of each beaded strand around the branch a few times to secure in place. Trim excess wire. Randomly place beaded strands on branches a few inches apart.

Deb's Oysters Rockefeller

PREP: 1 HOUR **BAKE:** 15 MIN. **YIELD:** 2-1/2 DOZEN

Every November, family and friends gather at our home for an annual "Oyster Party." My sons and some of their friends shuck between 300 and 400 oysters throughout the day, and I prep and bake them for the guests. Then, I spread forks out over the platter, and everyone just starts grabbing the baked oysters off the tray. To me, the most important part of this recipe is the easy hollandaise sauce that is put over the top of the finished oysters.

Deb Holt ★ Baltimore, Maryland

- 30 fresh oysters in the shell, washed
- 1 package (10 ounces) frozen chopped spinach, thawed and squeezed dry
- 1/2 pound bacon strips, cooked and crumbled
- 1/3 cup finely shredded cheddar cheese
- 1 envelope hollandaise sauce mix
- 4 pounds rock salt

Shuck oysters, reserving bottom shell; set aside. Spread rock salt into two ungreased 15-in. x 10-in. x 1-in. baking pans. Lightly press the oyster shells down into the salt. Place one oyster in each shell; top each with spinach, bacon and cheese.

Bake, uncovered, at 400° for 14-16 minutes or until the oysters are plump. Meanwhile, prepare the hollandaise sauce according to package directions. Drizzle over oysters and serve immediately.

Dirty Martini Deviled Eggs

PREP: 10 MIN. + CHILLING **YIELD:** 1 DOZEN

I wanted to offer some classic appetizers for my mother's 92nd birthday, so I made deviled eggs with an added adult flavor twist. I suggest chilling these for 2-3 hours before serving to allow the flavors to blend and the filling to firm.

Linda Foreman ★ Locust Grove, Oklahoma

- 6 hard-cooked eggs
- 1/4 cup mayonnaise
- 1 tablespoon green olive juice
- 1 teaspoon dry vermouth
- 1-1/2 teaspoons minced fresh parsley *or* 1/2 teaspoon dried parsley flakes
- 1/4 teaspoon cayenne pepper
- 1/8 teaspoon pepper

Sliced green olives

Cut eggs in half lengthwise. Remove yolks; set whites aside. In a small bowl, mash yolks. Add the mayonnaise, olive juice, vermouth, parsley and peppers; mix well. Stuff or pipe into egg whites.

Refrigerate until serving. Garnish with olive slices.

Shucking Oysters

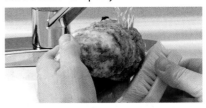

1. Scrub the oysters under cold running water with a stiff brush. Place oysters on a tray and refrigerate for 1 hour. (They will be easier to open.)

2. Protect your hands by wrapping the oyster, bigger shell down, in a clean kitchen towel with the hinge facing out or by wearing an oyster shucking glove. Keep oyster level to avoid losing any juice. Insert an oyster knife next to hinge.

3. Twist the knife until you hear a snap to pry shells open.

4. Slide the knife along the top shell to cut the oyster loose.

5. Slide knife between oyster and the bottom shell to release it. If serving in the shell, discard any bits of shell particles. If cooking shucked oysters, strain juice.

Szechuan Pork Tacos

PREP: 25 MIN. **BAKE:** 1-1/2 HOURS **YIELD:** 5 DOZEN

East meets Southwest in these savory, full-flavored Chinese tacos. The recipe makes a big batch so be sure to use it for an appetizer buffet or as a potluck dish.

Taste of Home Test Kitchen

2	tablespoons Cajun seasoning
1	teaspoon brown sugar
1/4	teaspoon Chinese five-spice powder
2	pounds boneless pork shoulder butt roast
60	wonton wrappers

Cooking spray

1/3	cup hoisin sauce
2	tablespoons rice vinegar, *divided*
2	teaspoons plus 1 tablespoon lime juice, *divided*
1/2	teaspoon hot pepper sauce
1	teaspoon honey
1/2	teaspoon grated lime peel
4	cups Chinese *or* napa cabbage, finely shredded
1/4	cup shredded carrot
2	green onions, thinly sliced
1	jalapeno pepper, seeded and minced

Combine the Cajun seasoning, brown sugar and five-spice powder; rub over pork. Place roast in a shallow baking pan. Bake, uncovered, at 350° for 1-1/2 to 2 hours or until meat is tender.

Spray 10 wonton wrappers with cooking spray. Fold each wrapper in half diagonally and place over the edge of a 13-in. x 9-in. baking pan. Bake at 350° for 5-7 minutes or until golden brown. Remove from the pan and immediately spread wrappers apart gently, forming taco shells; set aside. Repeat with remaining wrappers.

When pork is cool enough to handle, shred meat with two forks; place in a large bowl. Combine the hoisin sauce, 1 tablespoon rice vinegar, 2 teaspoons lime juice and pepper sauce; add to pork and toss to coat.

In a large bowl, combine the honey, lime peel and remaining rice vinegar and lime juice. Add the cabbage, carrot, onions and jalapeno; toss to coat. Spoon pork mixture into taco shells; top with coleslaw.

TO MAKE AHEAD: The taco shells and pork filling can be made a day ahead. Store cooled shells in an airtight container. Cover and refrigerate pork filling. To serve, heat through.

Making a Wonton Taco Shell

1. Spray wonton wrappers with cooking spray. Next, fold each of the wrappers in half diagonally and drape over the edge on a 13-in. x 9-in. x 2-in. baking pan, leaving space between each wrapper.

2. Bake as directed, and quickly remove from pan after baking. While wrappers are still warm, gently spread the sides, forming a taco shell. Cool.

Cranberry-Fig Goat Cheese Crostini

PREP: 30 MIN. **BROIL:** 7 MIN. **YIELD:** 2 DOZEN

The sweet-tart blend of flavors in my crostini makes for an absolutely scrumptious appetizer!

Barbara Estabrook ★ Rhinelander, Wisconsin

    1/2 cup balsamic vinegar
      1 tablespoon honey
CROSTINI:
     24 slices French bread baguette (1/2 inch thick)
      3 tablespoons olive oil
CRANBERRY-FIG TOPPING:
    1/2 cup coarsely dried cranberries
    1/3 cup coarsely chopped dried figs
    1/3 cup coarsely chopped unblanched almonds
    1/3 cup coarsely chopped pitted Greek olives
      1 tablespoon olive oil
      2 teaspoons balsamic vinegar
    1/8 teaspoon freshly ground pepper
CHEESE SPREAD:
      2 logs (4 ounces *each*) spreadable goat cheese
      1 teaspoon grated lemon peel
Dash freshly ground pepper
Minced fresh mint

In a small saucepan, combine vinegar and honey. Bring to a boil; reduce heat and simmer until mixture is reduced by half, about 5 minutes. Set aside to cool.

Lightly brush both sides of baguette slices with oil; place on an ungreased baking sheet. Broil 3-4 in. from the heat for 1-2 minutes on each side or until golden brown. Set aside.

In a small bowl, combine the topping ingredients; toss to coat. In another bowl, beat the goat cheese, lemon peel and pepper until blended.

To serve, spread goat cheese mixture over toasts. Stir cranberry mixture; spoon over tops. Drizzle with balsamic glaze and sprinkle with mint.

White Jamaican

PREP/TOTAL TIME: 5 MIN.   **YIELD:** 1 SERVING

A tropical twist on the classic white Russian, my frosty cocktail blends the flavors of coffee with vanilla and coconut.

Mark Brown ★ Irvine, California

Crushed ice
- 1-1/2   ounces vanilla vodka
- 1-1/2   ounces coconut rum
- 1-1/2   ounces coffee liqueur
- 3/4   ounce heavy whipping cream

Fill a shaker three-fourths full with ice. Add the vodka, rum, coffee liqueur and cream; cover and shake for 10-15 seconds or until condensation forms on outside of shaker. Strain into glass if desired or serve over ice.

Balsamic-Cranberry Potato Bites

PREP: 30 MIN.   **BAKE:** 20 MIN.
YIELD: 1-1/2 DOZEN (1-1/4 CUPS SAUCE)

Here's a delicious new take on rumaki. It requires only a few ingredients, and your guests will adore the flavor!

Kelly Boe ★ Whiteland, Indiana

- 12   small red potatoes, quartered
- 12   bacon strips
- 1/2   teaspoon salt
- 1/4   teaspoon pepper
- 1   can (14 ounces) jellied cranberry sauce
- 1/4   cup balsamic vinegar

Place potatoes in a large saucepan and cover with water. Bring to a boil. Reduce heat; cover and simmer for 3-5 minutes or until almost tender.

Meanwhile, cut bacon strips widthwise into fourths. Drain potatoes and sprinkle with salt and pepper. Wrap a piece of bacon around each potato quarter; secure with toothpicks. Place in an ungreased 15-in. x 10-in. x 1-in. baking pan. Bake at 400° for 20-25 minutes or until bacon is crisp.

In a small saucepan, combine cranberry sauce and vinegar. Bring to a boil. Reduce heat; simmer, uncovered, until slightly thickened, about 15 minutes. Serve warm with potato bites.

Pepper Shooters

PREP/TOTAL TIME: 30 MIN.   **YIELD:** 2 DOZEN

Looking for a colorful new appetizer to add to your holiday party buffet? We think these are different, delicious and definitely special. Just pop one of the savory peppers into your mouth for a tantalizing array of tastes and textures. It's like an antipasto platter all in one bite!

Taste of Home Test Kitchen

24	pickled sweet cherry peppers
4	ounces fresh mozzarella cheese, finely chopped
2-3/4	ounces thinly sliced hard salami, finely chopped
3	tablespoons prepared pesto
2	tablespoons olive oil

Cut tops off peppers and remove seeds; set aside. In a small bowl, combine the cheese, salami and pesto; spoon into peppers. Drizzle with oil. Chill until serving.

Cranberry-Orange Cordials

PREP/TOTAL TIME: 15 MIN. **YIELD:** 6 SERVINGS

Quick but elegant recipes are ideal for me. Sometimes I place the fixings for these cordials on a tray and let friends assemble their own. It's fun and saves me even more time!

Suellen Calhoun ★ Des Moines, Iowa

- 1   can (14 ounces) whole-berry cranberry sauce
- 1   cinnamon stick (3 inches)
- 1   whole star anise
- 1/3 cup orange liqueur
- 3/4 cup plain Greek yogurt
- 2   ounces cream cheese, softened
- 2   tablespoons honey
- 6   small mint sprigs

In a saucepan, combine the cranberry sauce, cinnamon stick and star anise. Bring to a boil. Reduce heat; simmer, uncovered, for 2 minutes, stirring constantly. Stir in liqueur. Set aside to cool; discard cinnamon and star anise.

In a small bowl, beat the yogurt, cream cheese and honey until blended. Divide among six shot or cordial glasses. Top with cooled cranberry mixture. Save any remaining sauce for another use. Garnish with mint sprigs.

Editor's Note: If Greek yogurt is not available in your area, line a strainer with a coffee filter and place over a bowl. Place 1-1/2 cups plain yogurt in prepared strainer; refrigerate overnight. Discard liquid from bowl; proceed as directed.

TO MAKE AHEAD: Cranberry mixture can be made the day before serving. Cover and refrigerate.

BLT Meatball Sliders

PREP: 25 MIN. **BAKE:** 30 MIN. **YIELD:** 1-1/2 DOZEN

Take sliders to an all new level with the addition of bacon and ground pork. Mayonnaise gets a bit of zip from ranch dip mix. Your guests will devour these in no time flat!

Damali Campbell ★ New York, New York

- 1   pound uncooked bacon strips
- 1   cup 2% milk
- 1   egg
- 1   cup dry bread crumbs
- 1   small onion, finely chopped
- 1   tablespoon fennel seed, crushed
- 1   teaspoon salt
- 1   teaspoon pepper
- 1/2 teaspoon crushed red pepper flakes
- 3/4 pound ground pork
- 1/2 pound lean ground beef (90% lean)
- 2/3 cup mayonnaise
- 1-1/2 teaspoons ranch dip mix
- 18   dinner rolls, split
- 3   cups spring mix salad greens
- 3   plum tomatoes, sliced

Place bacon in a food processor; cover and process until finely chopped. In a large bowl, combine the milk, egg, bread crumbs, onion and seasonings. Crumble the bacon, pork and beef over mixture and mix well. Shape into 2-in. meatballs.

Place in an ungreased 15-in. x 10-in. x 1-in. baking pan. Bake at 425° for 30-35 minutes or until a thermometer reads 160°.

Combine mayonnaise and dip mix; spread over rolls. Layer each with salad greens, a tomato slice and a meatball; replace tops.

In the same skillet, saute mushrooms and shallots in remaining oil until tender. Add garlic; cook 1 minute longer. Add sherry, stirring to loosen browned bits from pan. Stir in the cream, salt and pepper. Bring to a boil; cook until liquid is almost evaporated, about 7 minutes. Stir in beef and parsley; set aside and keep warm.

On a lightly floured surface, unfold puff pastry. Roll each sheet into a 12-in. square. Cut each into 16 squares.

Place 2 tablespoonfuls of beef mixture in the center of half of the squares. Top with remaining squares; press edges with a fork to seal. Place on parchment paper-lined baking sheets. Cut slits in top; brush with egg. Bake at 400° for 14-16 minutes or until golden brown.

In a small bowl, combine the horseradish cream ingredients; serve with appetizers. Garnish with additional chives if desired.

TO MAKE AHEAD: Freeze unbaked pastries on baking sheets until firm, then wrap and store in the freezer for up to 2 months. When ready to use, bake frozen appetizers at 400° for 16-18 minutes or until golden brown.

Beef en Croute Appetizers

PREP: 45 MIN.   **BAKE:** 15 MIN.
YIELD: 16 APPETIZERS (1-1/2 CUPS SAUCE)

Flaky puff pastry, savory beef tenderloin and tangy horseradish cream come together in this recipe for a positively holiday-worthy hors d'oeuvre.

Joan Cooper ★ Sussex, Wisconsin

- 2   beef tenderloin steaks (8 ounces *each*), cut into 1/2-inch cubes
- 2   tablespoons olive oil, *divided*
- 1-1/4   cups chopped fresh mushrooms
- 2   shallots, chopped
- 2   garlic cloves, minced
- 1/3   cup sherry *or* chicken broth
- 1/3   cup heavy whipping cream
- 1/2   teaspoon salt
- 1/8   teaspoon pepper
- 1   tablespoon minced fresh parsley
- 1   package (17.3 ounces) frozen puff pastry, thawed
- 1   egg, beaten

HORSERADISH CREAM:
- 1   cup sour cream
- 1/2   cup mayonnaise
- 2   tablespoons prepared horseradish
- 1   tablespoon minced chives
- 1/4   teaspoon pepper
Additional minced chives, optional

In a large skillet, brown beef in 1 tablespoon oil. Remove and keep warm.

Chive & Curry Cheese Straws

PREP: 20 MIN.   **BAKE:** 40 MIN.
YIELD: ABOUT 10-1/2 DOZEN

Here's a classic Southern cheese straw recipe with a delightful twist. Give it a try and taste the wonderful difference that adding a little curry powder and fresh chives can make!

Angela Spengler ★ Clovis, New Mexico

- 2-1/2   cups all-purpose flour
- 1   teaspoon curry powder
- 3/4   teaspoon salt
- 1   cup cold butter, cubed
- 1   cup (4 ounces) shredded sharp cheddar cheese
- 1   cup grated Parmesan cheese
- 2   tablespoons minced fresh chives
- 3   tablespoons cold water

In a large bowl, combine the flour, curry powder and salt; cut in the butter until crumbly. Add the cheeses and chives. Gradually add the water, tossing with a fork until dough forms a ball.

Divide dough in half. On a lightly floured surface; roll each portion into a 16-in. x 5-in. rectangle. Cut into 5-in. x 1/4-in. strips. Gently place strips 1 in. apart on ungreased baking sheets.

Bake at 350° for 15-20 minutes or until lightly browned. Cool for 5 minutes before removing from pans to wire racks to cool completely. Store in an airtight container.

TO MAKE AHEAD: Package baked cheese straws in an airtight container, separating layers with waxed paper and freeze for up to 1 month. Reheat at 350° for 5 minutes before serving.

Place chocolate almond milk in a small saucepan; heat through. Add the vodka and raspberry liqueur; transfer to a mug.

Pour vanilla almond milk into a small bowl. With a frother, blend until foamy. Spoon foam into mug. Sprinkle with cocoa if desired.

Sausage and Swiss Mini Quiches

PREP: 20 MIN.   **BAKE:** 15 MIN.   **YIELD:** 4 DOZEN

I created my heavenly little morsels for a holiday party. They were so enjoyable that family and friends now ask for them by name. I find that mascarpone makes these quiches extra rich, but you can substitute cream cheese if you like.

Lisa Renshaw ★ Kansas City, Missouri

1	package (17.3 ounces) frozen puff pastry, thawed
1	package (16 ounces) bulk pork sausage
4	green onions, finely chopped
1/2	cup finely chopped sweet red pepper
1	garlic clove, minced
4	eggs
1	carton (8 ounces) mascarpone cheese
1	teaspoon salt
1	teaspoon crushed red pepper flakes
1	teaspoon Worcestershire sauce
1/2	teaspoon dried sage leaves
1/2	teaspoon dried thyme
1/4	teaspoon ground mustard
1/2	cup shredded Swiss cheese

Roll out puff pastry to 1/8-in. thickness. Cut out twenty-four 2-1/2-in. circles from each sheet. Press onto the bottoms and up the sides of greased miniature muffin cups.

In a large skillet, cook the sausage, onions, red pepper and garlic over medium heat until meat is no longer pink; drain. Spoon into pastry cups.

In a small bowl, combine the eggs, mascarpone cheese, salt, pepper flakes, Worcestershire sauce, sage, thyme and mustard. Spoon over tops and sprinkle with Swiss cheese.

Bake at 400° for 10-12 minutes or until a knife inserted near the center comes out clean. Serve warm.

TO MAKE AHEAD: Prepare and bake as directed. Cool completely and freeze in a single layer on a waxed paper-lined baking sheet. Once frozen, package in freezer bags and freeze for up to 1 month. Place frozen quiches on an ungreased baking sheet. Bake at 350° for 15-20 minutes or until heated through.

Raspberry Truffle Cocktail

PREP/TOTAL TIME: 10 MIN.   **YIELD:** 1 SERVING

This adults-only hot chocolate will make a decadent addition to any holiday gathering. It can easily be adapted to dairy lovers' tastes by substituting chocolate milk and heavy cream for the almond products.

Melanie Milhorat ★ New York, New York

1	cup chocolate almond milk *or* 2% chocolate milk
1	ounce vodka
1/2	ounce raspberry liqueur
1/4	cup cold vanilla almond milk *or* fat-free milk

Baking cocoa, optional

Steak Crostini with Roasted Tomatoes

PREP: 30 MIN.   **COOK:** 15 MIN.   **YIELD:** 16 SERVINGS

We love having appetizers for dinner, so these mini open-face steak sandwiches are perfect for us. My husband went nuts over this recipe and actually said it was the best thing I have ever made for him!

Amy Chase ★ Vanderhoof, British Columbia

- 16 slices sourdough baguette (1/2 inch thick)
- 1 tablespoon olive oil
- 1 garlic clove, halved
- 1-1/2 cups grape tomatoes, halved
- 1 tablespoon balsamic vinegar
- 1/2 teaspoon salt, *divided*
- 1/4 teaspoon pepper, *divided*
- 1 boneless beef top loin steak (1 inch thick and 10 ounces)

BLUE CHEESE SAUCE:
- 1/4 cup finely chopped onion
- 2 teaspoons olive oil
- 1 garlic clove, minced
- 3 tablespoons whiskey
- 1 cup heavy whipping cream
- 1/4 cup crumbled blue cheese
- 2 tablespoons minced fresh parsley
- 1 tablespoon prepared horseradish
- 1/4 teaspoon salt
- 1/4 teaspoon pepper

Place baguette slices on an ungreased baking sheet; brush with oil. Broil 3-4 in. from the heat 1-2 minutes or until golden brown. Rub the toasted sides with garlic halves and set aside.

Place tomatoes in a greased 15-in. x 10-in. x 1-in. baking pan. Drizzle with vinegar and sprinkle with 1/4 teaspoon salt and 1/8 pepper; toss to coat. Bake at 400° for 5-7 minutes or until softened, stirring once.

Sprinkle steak with 1/8 teaspoon each salt and pepper. In a large skillet over medium heat, cook steak for 6-7 minutes on each side or until meat reaches desired doneness (for medium-rare, a thermometer should read 145°; medium, 160°; well-done, 170°). Remove from the pan and keep warm.

In the same skillet, saute onion in oil until tender. Add garlic; cook 1 minute longer. Remove from the heat. Add whiskey; cook over medium heat until liquid is evaporated.

Stir in cream. Bring to a boil; cook until the liquid is reduced by half. Add the blue cheese; cook and stir until cheese is melted. Remove from the heat. Stir in the remaining ingredients.

Thinly slice beef; arrange over baguette slices. Top with tomatoes and drizzle with sauce.

stand each dumpling on an even surface; press to flatten bottom. Curve ends to form a crescent shape. Repeat with remaining wrappers and filling.

In a large skillet, heat 1 tablespoon oil over medium-high heat. In batches, arrange pot stickers flat side down in pan; cook for 1-2 minutes or until bottoms are lightly browned.

Add 1/2 cup broth; bring to a simmer. Cover and steam for 6-10 minutes or until the broth is almost absorbed. Uncover; cook for 1 minute or until the bottoms are crisp and broth is evaporated. Serve with additional soy sauce if desired.

Sweet Potato Pot Stickers

PREP: 20 MIN.   **COOK:** 20 MIN.   **YIELD:** 2 DOZEN

I put a slightly Southern spin on these scrumptious pot stickers. Ginger-flavored sweet potatoes make a surprising filling, but it's savory and so delicious!

Mary Marlowe Leverette ★ Columbia, South Carolina

1-1/2	cups finely grated peeled sweet potatoes
1	medium onion, finely chopped
1	cup finely shredded cabbage
1	tablespoon sesame oil
1	tablespoon reduced-sodium soy sauce
2	teaspoons grated fresh gingerroot
1	teaspoon pepper
24	pot sticker or gyoza wrappers
2	tablespoons canola oil, *divided*
1	cup chicken broth, *divided*

Additional reduced-sodium soy sauce, optional

In a small bowl, combine the first seven ingredients. Place 1 teaspoon of filling in the center of one wrapper. (Until ready to use, keep remaining wrappers covered with a damp paper towel to prevent them from drying out.)

Moisten entire edge with water. Fold wrapper over filling to form a semicircle. Press edges firmly to seal, pleating the front side to form three to five folds. Holding sealed edges,

Shaping a Pot Sticker

1. Fill the pot sticker wrappers according to recipe directions. Lightly moisten the edge with water. Fold dough over filling, creating a half moon.

2. Press edges firmly to seal. Starting at one end, pleat the front side only to form 4 to 5 folds. While still holding edges, stand dumpling on a even surface; press to flatten the bottom.

3. Curve ends to form a crescent shape.

Roasted Vegetable Spread

PREP: 10 MIN. **BAKE:** 30 MIN. **YIELD:** 2-1/2 CUPS

Being a nutritionist, I find this recipe to be a great alternative to those fatty packaged dips so common at parties. Best of all, it tastes really fresh and is bursting with vitamins A and C.

Sherri Shields ★ Missouri City, Texas

- 1 medium yellow summer squash, sliced
- 1 medium zucchini, sliced
- 1 medium sweet red pepper, sliced
- 1 medium red onion, thinly sliced
- 2 garlic cloves, peeled
- 1/2 teaspoon salt
- 1/4 teaspoon cayenne pepper

Baked pita chips

Place the vegetables and garlic in a greased 15-in. x 10-in. x 1-in. baking pan. Sprinkle with the salt and cayenne; toss to coat. Bake at 400° for 30-35 minutes or until tender. Cool slightly.

Place in a food processor. Cover and process until blended. Serve warm with chips.

Gingered Citrus Punch

PREP: 10 MIN. + FREEZING **YIELD:** 4-1/2 QUARTS

I enjoy cooking and trying out new recipes on my personal tasting panel of family and friends. This refreshing punch was a winner with the whole gang!

Sharon Delaney-Chronis ★ South Milwaukee, Wisconsin

- 10 cups cold water, *divided*
- 2-1/4 cups frozen lemonade concentrate, thawed, *divided*
- 1-1/2 cups fresh whole cranberries
- 1 can (12 ounces) frozen grapefruit juice concentrate, thawed
- 1 liter ginger ale, chilled

In a small bowl, combine 3 cups water and 3/4 cup lemonade concentrate. Pour into a 5-cup ring mold. Freeze for 2-3 hours or until slushy. Arrange cranberries in slush mixture; push berries to bottom of mold. Freeze until solid.

In a 5-qt. punch bowl, combine grapefruit concentrate and remaining water and lemonade concentrate. Refrigerate until chilled.

Just before serving, stir in ginger ale. Unmold ice ring by wrapping the bottom of the mold in a damp hot dishcloth; invert onto a baking sheet. Place ice ring, fruit side up, in the punch bowl.

Pimiento Cheese-Stuffed Artichoke Bottoms

PREP: 30 MIN. **BAKE:** 20 MIN. **YIELD:** ABOUT 2 DOZEN

When your friends take a look at this vibrant appetizer, they'll know they're at a party! There's just nothing better than nibbling on one of these snacks while watching fall football. They are cheesy, bacony and so comforting.

Elizabeth Bennett ★ Mill Creek, Washington

- 3 cans (14 ounces *each*) artichoke bottoms, rinsed and drained
- 3/4 cup shredded sharp cheddar cheese
- 1/2 cup shredded Monterey Jack cheese
- 1 jar (4 ounces) diced pimientos, drained
- 1/4 cup mayonnaise
- 3 cooked bacon strips, chopped, *divided*
- 1 garlic clove, minced
- 1 teaspoon Worcestershire sauce
- 1/8 teaspoon salt
- 1/8 teaspoon pepper
- 1/8 teaspoon cayenne pepper
- 2 green onions, chopped

Cut a thin layer from bottom of the artichokes to level if necessary. Place in a greased 13-in. x 9-in. baking dish. In a small bowl, combine the cheeses, pimientos, mayonnaise, half of the bacon, garlic, Worcestershire sauce, salt, pepper and cayenne.

Spoon 1 tablespoon cheese mixture into each artichoke; top with remaining bacon. Bake at 350° for 15-18 minutes or until golden brown. Sprinkle with onions.

Brandy & Date Cheese Ball Pops

PREP: 30 MIN. + CHILLING **YIELD:** 2 DOZEN

Forget that same old cheese ball, and give my fun cheese pops a try! The brandy and dates add sweetness, while the almonds and bacon make for a crunchy finishing touch.

Ginger Kohutek ★ Weslaco, Texas

- 2 cups (8 ounces) shredded cheddar cheese
- 1/2 cup butter, softened
- 1 package (3 ounces) cream cheese, softened
- 1 tablespoon brandy
- 1 cup finely chopped dates
- 1 package (2-1/4 ounces) sliced almonds, chopped and toasted
- 12 bacon strips, cooked and finely crumbled
- 24 lollipop sticks

Assorted crackers

In a small bowl, beat the cheddar cheese, butter, cream cheese and brandy until well blended. Stir in dates. Shape into twenty-four 1-in. balls. Place the almonds and bacon in separate shallow bowls. Roll half of the cheese balls in almonds; roll the remaining balls in bacon. Cover and refrigerate for 2 hours or until firm.

Insert the lollipop sticks into the cheese balls. Serve with crackers.

Christmas
DINNERS

Ham Dinner

Greens with
Blue Cheese and Fruits
pg. 23

Maple-Pecan Glazed Ham
pg. 23

Cheese & Garlic Biscuits
pg. 24

Portobello & Green Bean Saute
pg. 26

Sweet & White
Scalloped Potatoes
pg. 25

Apple Jack Crumb Pie
pg. 27

Maple-Pecan Glazed Ham

PREP: 10 MIN. **BAKE:** 2-1/2 HOURS + STANDING
YIELD: 15 SERVINGS

Maple syrup is reduced to concentrate its lovely flavor, then spiced up to create a delicious glaze that browns ham to a rich color. This is a wonderful variation on the usual pineapple and brown sugar glaze.

Nancy Mueller ★ Menomonee Falls, Wisconsin

- 1 fully cooked bone-in ham (7 to 9 pounds)
- 1 cup maple syrup
- 1/3 cup finely chopped pecans
- 1 tablespoon Dijon mustard
- 2 teaspoons grated orange peel
- 1/2 teaspoon ground allspice

Trim off the skin of the ham and about 1/4 in. of the fat. Score the surface of the ham, making diamond shapes 1/4 in. deep. Place the ham, fat side up, on a rack in a shallow roasting pan. Bake, uncovered, at 325° for 2 hours.

Meanwhile, in a small saucepan, bring syrup to a boil. Reduce heat; simmer, uncovered, until reduced to 3/4 cup. Remove from the heat. Stir in the pecans, mustard, orange peel and allspice.

Baste ham with some of the glaze; bake 30-60 minutes longer or until a thermometer reads 140°, basting occasionally with remaining glaze. Let stand for 15 minutes before slicing.

Greens with Blue Cheese and Fruits

PREP/TOTAL TIME: 20 MIN. **YIELD:** 8 SERVINGS

Your guests will love the festive variety of fruits in this colorful salad. It makes a delightful addition to the menu!

Marie Rizzio ★ Interlochen, Michigan

- 1/2 cup olive oil
- 1/2 cup pomegranate *or* cranberry juice
- 1/4 cup lemon juice
- 2 teaspoons minced fresh tarragon *or* 1/2 teaspoon dried tarragon
- 1 garlic clove, minced
- 1 teaspoon honey
- 1/2 teaspoon salt
- 1/4 teaspoon pepper

SALAD:
- 12 cups spring mix salad greens
- 1 cup crumbled blue cheese
- 1 small red onion, thinly sliced
- 2 clementines, sectioned
- 1/2 cup green grapes, halved
- 1/2 cup chopped peeled mango
- 1/2 cup pomegranate seeds
- 1/4 cup minced fresh chives

In a small bowl, whisk the first eight ingredients. Chill until serving.

Divide salad greens among eight serving plates. Sprinkle with blue cheese and onion. Divide the fruits among salad plates; drizzle with dressing. Garnish with the pomegranate seeds and chives.

TO MAKE AHEAD: Dressing can be prepared up to 3 days ahead. Store in the refrigerator.

Cheese & Garlic Biscuits

PREP/TOTAL TIME: 20 MIN.   **YIELD:** 2-1/2 DOZEN

My wonderful biscuits won the division Best Quick Bread at my county fair. One of the judges liked them so much, she asked for the recipe! These buttery, savory biscuits go with just about anything.

Gloria Jarrett ★ Loveland, Ohio

      2-1/2   cups biscuit/baking mix
        3/4   cup shredded sharp cheddar cheese
          1   teaspoon garlic powder
          1   teaspoon ranch salad dressing mix
          1   cup buttermilk
TOPPING:
        1/2   cup butter, melted
          1   tablespoon minced chives
        1/2   teaspoon garlic powder
        1/2   teaspoon ranch salad dressing mix
        1/4   teaspoon pepper

In a large bowl, combine the baking mix, cheese, garlic powder and salad dressing mix. Stir in the buttermilk just until moistened. Drop by tablespoonfuls onto greased baking sheets.

Bake at 450° for 6-8 minutes or until golden brown. Meanwhile, combine topping ingredients. Brush over biscuits. Serve warm.

Carving a Butt Half Ham

The butt half of a ham is very meaty, but can sometimes be a challenge to carve since part of the bone is buried within the meat. Here are some tips that will have you carving like a pro.

1. Position the ham with cut surface flat on the cutting board. Insert a bamboo skewer from top to bottom along the bone. Using the skewer as a guide, cut the largest side from the ham.

2. Cut the piece across the grain into slices.

3. Continue using the skewer as a guide to cut sections of ham from the bone, and cut each section into slices.

Sweet & White Scalloped Potatoes

PREP: 20 MIN. **BAKE:** 45 MIN. **YIELD:** 8 SERVINGS

Since I love both sweet and scalloped potatoes, I decided to try my hand at making scalloped sweet potatoes. This easy recipe is a great way to change up your holiday table.

Yvonne Starlin ★ Hermitage, Tennessee

- 3 medium sweet potatoes, peeled and thinly sliced
- 3 medium russet potatoes, peeled and thinly sliced
- 3-1/2 cups heavy whipping cream
- 2 tablespoons all-purpose flour
- 4 teaspoons minced fresh thyme
- 3 small garlic cloves, minced
- 1 teaspoon salt
- 1/4 teaspoon pepper

Arrange potatoes in a greased 13-in. x 9-in. baking dish. In a small saucepan, combine the cream, flour, thyme, garlic, salt and pepper. Bring to a gentle boil. Remove from the heat; pour over potatoes.

Cover and bake at 400° for 20 minutes. Uncover; bake 25-30 minutes longer or until potatoes are tender and the top is golden brown.

Portobello & Green Bean Saute

PREP/TOTAL TIME: 20 MIN. **YIELD:** 10 SERVINGS

I think the key to tasty veggies is simplicity, and that's the way I like to cook—combining simple everyday ingredients for fantastic flavor. If cremini mushrooms are not available, white button mushrooms work equally well in this recipe.

Elaine Shoemaker ★ Sedgewickville, Missouri

1   pound fresh green beans, trimmed and halved
1   pound baby portobello mushrooms, quartered
1   medium onion, finely chopped
1/4   cup butter, cubed
2   garlic cloves, minced
1   teaspoon chicken bouillon granules
4   plum tomatoes, peeled and chopped
1   teaspoon dried marjoram
1/4   teaspoon pepper
1/4   cup minced fresh parsley

Place beans in a large saucepan and cover with water; bring to a boil. Cover and cook for 3-5 minutes or until beans are crisp-tender.

Meanwhile, in a large skillet, saute mushrooms and onion in butter until tender. Add garlic and bouillon; cook 1 minute longer. Drain green beans; add to skillet and toss to coat. Remove from the heat. Stir in the tomatoes, marjoram and pepper. Sprinkle with parsley.

Apple Jack Crumb Pie

PREP: 1 HOUR + SOAKING   **BAKE:** 50 MIN.
YIELD: 8 SERVINGS

I serve this apple pie at my monthly bridge club meetings and it always gets a thumbs up. You don't need to serve it with a slice of cheese, since there's cheese right in the streusel.

Mary June Donovan ★ Clinton, Massachusetts

- 1/3 cup golden raisins
- 3 tablespoons brandy
- Pastry for single-crust pie (9 inches)
- 1/2 cup packed brown sugar
- 2 tablespoons all-purpose flour
- 1-1/2 teaspoons ground cinnamon
- 1/4 teaspoon ground nutmeg
- 1/8 teaspoon white pepper
- 5 cups sliced peeled tart apples
- 2 tablespoons lemon juice

TOPPING:
- 1/2 cup all-purpose flour
- 1/2 cup sugar
- 6 tablespoons cold butter, cubed
- 3/4 cup grated aged Jack cheese
- 1/4 cup blanched almonds
- Vanilla ice cream

In a small bowl, combine raisins and brandy; cover and let stand at room temperature overnight.

Roll out pastry to fit a 9-in. pie plate. Transfer pastry to pie plate. Trim pastry to 1/2 in. beyond edge of plate; flute edges. In a large bowl, combine the brown sugar, flour, cinnamon, nutmeg and pepper. Add the apples, lemon juice and raisin mixture; toss to coat. Transfer to pastry.

Combine flour and sugar in a food processor. Add butter; cover and pulse until coarse crumbs form. Add cheese and almonds; pulse just until combined. Sprinkle over the filling.

Bake at 375° for 50-60 minutes or until apples are tender and topping is golden brown. Cover edges with foil during the last 30 minutes to prevent overbrowning if necessary. Serve warm with ice cream.

Editor's Note: You may substitute 3/4 cup grated Parmesan cheese for the aged Jack cheese.

Glazed Cornish Hens with Pecan-Rice Stuffing

PREP: 1 HOUR   **BAKE:** 1 HOUR 25 MIN. + STANDING
YIELD: 8 SERVINGS

Cornish hens bake up with a lovely golden brown luster when basted with my sweet, tangy glaze. Crunchy pecans and golden raisins add texture and taste to the rice stuffing.

Agnes Ward ★ Stratford, Ontario

- 1-1/2 cups uncooked long grain rice
- 2 teaspoons ground cumin
- 1 teaspoon curry powder
- 2 tablespoons butter
- 4 cups reduced-sodium chicken broth
- 1 cup chopped pecans, toasted
- 3 green onions, thinly sliced
- 1/2 cup golden raisins

CORNISH GAME HENS:
- 8 Cornish game hens (20 to 24 ounces *each*)
- 1/4 cup butter, softened
- 1/2 teaspoon salt
- 1/2 teaspoon pepper
- 2 cups unsweetened apple juice
- 1 tablespoon honey
- 1 tablespoon Dijon mustard

In a large saucepan, saute rice, cumin and curry in butter over medium heat for 2-3 minutes or until rice is lightly browned. Stir in broth. Bring to a boil. Reduce heat; cover and simmer for 15-20 minutes or until rice is tender. Stir in the pecans, onions and raisins.

Loosely stuff hens with stuffing. Tuck wings under hens; tie the drumsticks together. Rub skin with butter; sprinkle with salt and pepper. Place breast side up on a rack in a shallow roasting pan.

Bake, uncovered, at 350° for 1 hour. Meanwhile, place apple juice in a small saucepan. Bring to a boil; cook until reduced by half. Remove from the heat. Stir in honey and mustard. Set aside 1/2 cup for serving.

Brush hens with remaining glaze. Bake 25-35 minutes longer or until a thermometer reads 180° in the thigh for hens and 165° for stuffing, basting occasionally with pan drippings. Cover loosely with foil if hens brown too quickly. Cover and let stand for 10 minutes before serving. Serve with reserved sauce.

Ornament Vases

These glittering vases are simple to make! You can also use them as pretty take-home party favors by making one for each place setting. For each vase you'll need a 2-1/2-in. glass bulb ornament and a 1-1/2-in.-tall wooden or clay miniature pot. Cover the pot with a basecoat in your choice of acrylic paint and let dry. To add glitter, coat the pot with a layer of tacky glue and sprinkle glitter over the exterior. Shake off any excess glitter and let glue dry. To cut down on the glitter shedding, apply a coat of clear acrylic sealer and let dry. Remove metal hanger from bulb ornament. Put a thin line of tacky glue around the top edge of the pot. Set bulb ornament centered on top of pot and let glue dry. Fill ornament opening with your choice of flowers or other greenery.

Sicilian Brussels Sprouts

PREP: 30 MIN. **BAKE:** 20 MIN. **YIELD:** 12 SERVINGS

I love to make this dish because the flavors jump around in your mouth and keep you coming back bite after bite! Other nuts can be used in place of the pine nuts.

Marsha Gillett ★ Yukon, Oklahoma

- 12 ounces pancetta, diced
- 2 pounds fresh Brussels sprouts, halved
- 6 tablespoons capers, drained
- 1/4 cup olive oil
- 3 tablespoons champagne wine vinegar
- 1 teaspoon lemon juice
- 1/4 teaspoon salt
- 1/4 teaspoon pepper
- 3/4 cup golden raisins
- 1/2 cup pine nuts, toasted
- 1 teaspoon grated lemon peel

In a large ovenproof skillet, cook the pancetta over medium heat until browned. Remove pancetta to paper towels with a slotted spoon.

Add Brussels sprouts to pan; cook and stir until lightly browned. Remove from the heat. Stir in capers, oil, vinegar, lemon juice, salt and pepper.

Bake, uncovered, at 350° for 15-20 minutes or until caramelized, stirring occasionally. Add the raisins, pine nuts, lemon peel and pancetta; toss to coat.

Cranberry-Avocado Tossed Salad

PREP/TOTAL TIME: 30 MIN.   **YIELD:** 10 SERVINGS

The red and green colors in this salad make it a natural for a yuletide dinner. The dressing helps give the salad a lovely sweet-tangy flavor.

Marsha Postar ★ Albuquerque, New Mexico

1/4   cup sugar
1/4   cup white wine vinegar
1/4   cup thawed cranberry juice concentrate
4-1/2   teaspoons ground mustard
1/2   teaspoon salt
1/2   teaspoon pepper
1/2   cup canola oil

1   medium ripe avocado, peeled and cubed
1   tablespoon lemon juice
4   cups torn romaine
4   cups fresh baby spinach
1   package (6 ounces) dried cranberries
1   medium red onion, chopped
1/3   cup slivered almonds
1/3   cup sunflower kernels

In a small bowl, combine the first six ingredients. Gradually whisk in the oil; set aside.

Combine the avocado and lemon juice. In a large bowl, combine the romaine, spinach, cranberries, onion and avocado mixture; drizzle with 1/2 cup dressing. (Save remaining dressing for another use.) Sprinkle with almonds and sunflower kernels. Serve immediately.

Honey-Orange Winter Vegetable Medley

PREP: 30 MIN.   **BAKE:** 1 HOUR   **YIELD:** 9 SERVINGS

This combination of vegetables coated with a sweet-savory sauce makes a lovely addition to any holiday dinner.

Jennifer Coduto ★ Kent, Ohio

- 3   cups fresh baby carrots
- 2   cups cubed red potatoes
- 2   cups pearl onions, peeled
- 2   cups cubed peeled sweet potatoes
- 3/4 cup reduced-sodium chicken broth
- 1/2 cup orange marmalade
- 1/4 cup honey
- 2   tablespoons lemon juice
- 1-1/2 teaspoons poultry seasoning
- 3/4 teaspoon salt
- 3/4 teaspoon pepper
- 3   tablespoons butter, cubed

Place the vegetables in a greased shallow 3-qt. baking dish. In a small bowl, combine the broth, marmalade, honey, lemon juice and seasonings. Pour over vegetables and toss to coat. Dot with butter.

Cover and bake at 375° for 30 minutes. Uncover and bake 30-40 minutes longer or until vegetables are tender.

Maple-Chestnut Cheesecake

PREP: 30 MIN.   **BAKE:** 1-3/4 HOURS + COOLING
YIELD: 12 SERVINGS

Everyone at the table will want to save room for this rich cheesecake. A hint of cinnamon in the crust goes perfectly with the maple-brown sugar filling.

Taste of Home Test Kitchen

- 2   cups graham cracker crumbs
- 3   tablespoons sugar
- 1/2 teaspoon ground cinnamon
- 1/3 cup butter, melted

FILLING:

- 1-1/2 cups pure maple syrup
- 3   packages (8 ounces *each*) cream cheese, softened
- 1/2 cup packed brown sugar
- 2/3 cup sour cream
- 3   tablespoons all-purpose flour
- 2   teaspoons vanilla extract
- 1/4 teaspoon salt
- 4   eggs, lightly beaten

CANDIED CHESTNUTS:

- 1   package (7 ounces) whole cooked and peeled chestnuts, quartered
- 1/2 cup confectioners' sugar
- 1/4 teaspoon salt
- 3/4 cup pure maple syrup

Place a greased 9-in. springform pan on a double thickness of heavy-duty foil (about 18 in. square). Securely wrap foil around pan.

In a bowl, combine crumbs, sugar and cinnamon; stir in butter. Press onto bottom and 1-1/2 in. up sides of prepared pan. Place on a baking sheet. Bake at 375° for 8-10 minutes or until set. Cool on a wire rack. Reduce heat to 325°.

For filling, in a small saucepan, bring 1-1/2 cups maple syrup to a low boil; cook until reduced to about 1 cup. Cool to room temperature.

In a large bowl, beat cream cheese and brown sugar until smooth. Beat in the sour cream, flour, vanilla, salt and cooled syrup. Add eggs; beat on low speed just until combined. Pour into crust. Place springform pan in a large baking pan; add 1 in. of hot water to larger pan.

Bake at 325° for 1-1/4 to 1-1/2 hours or until center is just set and top appears dull. Remove springform pan from water bath; remove foil. Cool cheesecake on a wire rack for 10 minutes; loosen edges from pan with a knife. Cool 1 hour longer. Refrigerate overnight.

For candied chestnuts, in a small bowl, combine sugar and salt. Add chestnuts; toss to coat. Spread evenly onto a greased 15-in. x 10-in. x 1-in. baking pan. Bake at 350° for 15-19 minutes or until golden brown, stirring once after 10 minutes. Immediately transfer to a waxed paper-lined baking sheet; cool completely.

Remove rim from pan. Serve cheesecake with chestnuts and maple syrup.

Beef Wellington Dinner

My Caesar Salad
pg. 36

Gorgonzola Beef Wellingtons
pg. 35

Caramelized Port Onions
pg. 36

Olive Oil Mashed Potatoes
with Pancetta
pg. 37

Gilded Mocha-Walnut
Layer Cake
pg. 39

Gorgonzola Beef Wellingtons

PREP: 40 MIN. + CHILLING **BAKE:** 25 MIN.
YIELD: 8 SERVINGS

Guests will surely be impressed when you serve this recipe. Besides being a wonderful entree for special occasions, it's easy on the cook. That makes it ideal for the busy holidays!

Joyce Moynihan ★ Lakeville, Minnesota

- 8 beef tenderloin steaks (6 to 8 ounces *each*)
- 1/2 teaspoon plus 1/8 teaspoon salt, *divided*
- 1/2 teaspoon plus 1/8 teaspoon pepper, *divided*
- 4 tablespoons butter, *divided*
- 1 pound medium fresh mushrooms, thinly sliced
- 2 shallots, finely chopped
- 6 garlic cloves, minced
- 1 package (17.3 ounces) frozen puff pastry, thawed
- 1 cup (4 ounces) crumbled Gorgonzola cheese
- 2 eggs, beaten
- 4 cups reduced-sodium beef broth
- 1/2 cup Madeira wine *or* additional reduced-sodium beef broth
- 2 tablespoons tomato paste
- 1 teaspoon dried thyme

Sprinkle steaks with 1/2 teaspoon each salt and pepper. In a large skillet, brown steaks in 2 tablespoons butter in batches. Remove from the skillet; cool slightly and refrigerate until chilled.

In the same skillet, saute mushrooms and shallots in remaining butter until tender. Add the garlic and remaining salt and pepper; cook 1 minute longer.

On a lightly floured surface, roll each puff pastry sheet into a 14-in. square. Cut into four 6-1/2-in. squares (use scraps to make decorative cutouts if desired).

Place 2 tablespoons of cheese in the center of each square; top with 3 tablespoons mushroom mixture and a steak. Lightly brush pastry edges with egg. Bring opposite corners of pastry over steak; pinch seams to seal tightly.

Place seam side down in a greased 15-in. x 10-in. x 1-in. baking pan. Cut four small slits in top of pastry. Arrange cutouts over tops if desired. Brush with egg. Bake at 425° for 25-30 minutes or until pastry is golden brown and meat reaches desired doneness (for medium-rare, a thermometer should read 145°; medium, 160°; well-done, 170°).

Meanwhile, in a large saucepan, combine broth and wine. Bring to a boil; cook until liquid is reduced by half, about 30 minutes. Stir in tomato paste and thyme. Serve with the Beef Wellingtons.

Decorating Beef Wellingtons

1. To decorate your Wellingtons with a holly pattern as shown at left, use the leftover scraps of puff pastry. Cut out leaves with a 1- to 1-1/2-in. leaf-shaped cutter. Score veins in leaves with the tip of a sharp knife. Do not cut all the way through the dough.

2. Roll dough into small balls for berries. Using 2 leaves and 3 berries per Wellington, moisten backs with water and arrange on top. Brush tops of holly garnishes with a beaten egg.

My Caesar Salad

PREP/TOTAL TIME: 25 MIN. **YIELD:** 12 SERVINGS

Here, romaine gets a special treatment with a creamy salad dressing. It has a few veggies tossed in for color and crunch.

Julie Reynolds ★ Columbia, Tennessee

- 1 large garlic clove, minced
- 1 teaspoon salt
- 1/4 cup lemon juice
- 1/4 cup Miracle Whip
- 2 tablespoons grated lemon peel
- 1 tablespoon Dijon mustard
- 1 teaspoon coarsely ground pepper
- 1/2 cup olive oil
- 1/2 cup shredded Gruyere *or* Swiss cheese, *divided*
- 12 cups torn romaine
- 2 medium tomatoes, chopped
- 1 cup shredded carrots
- 1 cup chopped cucumber
- 2 cups garlic croutons

In a small bowl, mash garlic and salt, forming a paste. Whisk in the lemon juice, Miracle Whip, lemon peel, mustard and pepper. While whisking, gradually add oil in a steady stream until combined. Stir in 1/4 cup cheese. Refrigerate until serving.

In a large bowl, combine the romaine, tomatoes, carrots and cucumber. Whisk dressing; drizzle desired amount over salad and toss to coat. Sprinkle with croutons and remaining cheese. Serve with remaining dressing.

Caramelized Port Onions

PREP: 25 MIN. **COOK:** 35 MIN. **YIELD:** 7 SERVINGS

Whenever possible, use fresh rather than frozen pearl onions for this delicious side. Pair the sweet onions with a savory meat entree.

Erika Szymanski ★ Pullman, Washington

- 2 pounds pearl onions, trimmed
- 2 tablespoons olive oil
- 1 cup port wine *or* grape juice
- 1/4 cup balsamic vinegar
- 2 tablespoons brown sugar
- 1/2 teaspoon dried thyme
- 1/4 teaspoon salt
- 1/4 teaspoon white pepper

In a Dutch oven, bring 6 cups water to a boil. Add onions; boil for 3 minutes. Drain and rinse in cold water; peel.

In a large skillet, saute onions in oil until tender. Add wine, stirring to loosen browned bits from pan. Stir in remaining ingredients. Bring to a boil. Reduce heat and simmer until liquid is almost evaporated, about 25 minutes.

Olive Oil Mashed Potatoes with Pancetta

PREP/TOTAL TIME: 30 MIN.   **YIELD:** 8 SERVINGS

Classic American mashed potatoes get an Italian twist with the Mediterranean flavors of olive oil, garlic and pancetta.

Bryan Kennedy ★ Kaneohe, Hawaii

3   pounds Yukon Gold potatoes, peeled and cubed
3   slices pancetta *or* bacon, chopped
1   tablespoon plus 1/4 cup olive oil, *divided*
4   garlic cloves, minced
1/3   cup minced fresh parsley
1/2   teaspoon salt
1/2   teaspoon pepper

Place potatoes in a large saucepan and cover with water. Bring to a boil. Reduce heat; cover and simmer for 15-20 minutes or until tender.

Meanwhile, in a large skillet, cook the pancetta in 1 tablespoon oil over medium heat until crisp. Add garlic; cook 1 minutes longer. Remove from the heat.

Drain potatoes and transfer to a large bowl. Mash potatoes with remaining oil. Stir in the parsley, pancetta mixture, salt and pepper.

Gilded Mocha-Walnut Layer Cake

PREP: 55 MIN. + STANDING **BAKE:** 15 MIN.+ CHILLING
YIELD: 12 SERVINGS

This showstopping dessert has been in my recipe file for years and is perfect anytime that impressing your guests is a must. It does take a little time to make, but it's worth the extra effort when you hear the compliments!

Lorraine Caland ★ Shuniah, Ontario

10	eggs
1-1/2	cups ground walnuts
1	cup cake flour
2	teaspoons ground cinnamon
1/2	teaspoon salt
2	cups sugar, *divided*
2	teaspoons vanilla extract
1/2	cup chopped walnuts
3/4	teaspoon cream of tartar

MOCHA BUTTERCREAM FILLING:

1/3	cup sugar
2	tablespoons water
2	teaspoons instant coffee granules
2	egg yolks, beaten
4	ounces unsweetened chocolate, chopped
1	cup butter, softened
1-1/2	cups confectioners' sugar

WHIPPED CREAM FROSTING:

2	cups heavy whipping cream
1/3	cup confectioners' sugar
1	teaspoon vanilla extract

Gold pearl dust

Separate eggs; let stand at room temperature for 30 minutes. In a large bowl, combine the ground walnuts, flour, cinnamon and salt; set aside. Grease the bottom of four 9-in. round baking pans; line with waxed paper. Dust with flour and set aside.

In a large bowl, beat egg yolks until slightly thickened. Gradually add 1 cup of sugar, beating on high speed for 10 minutes or until thick and lemon-colored. Blend in vanilla. Gently stir 1/3 cup ground walnut mixture at a time into yolk mixture; fold in chopped walnuts.

In another bowl with clean beaters, beat egg whites and cream of tartar on medium speed until soft peaks form. Gradually beat in remaining sugar, about 1 tablespoon at a time, on high until stiff peaks form. Fold a fourth of the egg whites into the batter, then fold in remaining whites. Gently spoon into prepared pans.

Bake at 350° for 14-18 minutes or until cake springs back when lightly touched. Cool for 10 minutes before removing from pans to wire racks to cool completely.

For filling, in a heavy saucepan, bring the sugar, water and coffee granules to a boil; cook over medium-high heat until sugar is dissolved. Remove from the heat. Add a small amount of hot mixture to egg yolks; return all to the pan, stirring constantly. Cook 2 minutes longer or until mixture thickens, stirring constantly. Remove from the heat. Cool to room temperature.

In a microwave, melt chocolate; stir until smooth. Set aside. In a large bowl, cream butter until fluffy, about 5 minutes. Gradually beat in coffee mixture and chocolate. Beat in confectioners' sugar until fluffy, about 5 minutes.

For frosting, in a large bowl, beat cream until it begins to thicken. Add confectioners' sugar and vanilla; beat until stiff peaks form.

Spread mocha filling between cake layers. Frost top and sides of cake with whipped cream; dust with gold dust. Refrigerate for at least 2 hours before serving.

Holly Leaf Napkin Rings

It is easy to add a touch of elegance to your dinner party with adorable napkin rings. Choose paper or card stock scraps to go along with your party decor. For each napkin holder, you'll also need three miniature jingle bells and a 12-in. length of metallic string. First, using a holly leaf punch or cutting freehand with scissors, make two leaves for each napkin holder. Slightly bend the leaves down the center. Use an 1/8-in. hole punch to create a hole at the top of each leaf. Thread the string through each of the three jingle bells followed by the leaves. Then tie a knot at the base of the string at the back of leaves. Wrap the string around your napkins and tie in place with a bow.

Add Your Personal Touch

The previous menus are sensational, but we all like to add our own touches. To help, the recipes that follow make wonderful substitutions to these dinners. For more grand finales, see the chapters Perfectly Sized Desserts, Sweet Sensations and Cookies with a Classic Twist.

Broccoli and Carrot Cheese Bake

PREP: 25 MIN. **BAKE:** 30 MIN. + STANDING
YIELD: 9 SERVINGS

A creamy sauce flavored with cheese makes vegetables so much more appealing to my crowd. This holiday side dish will please even the pickiest veggie-phobics (kids and men!). It uses vegetables that are available year round, so it works for Easter as well as winter holiday meals.

Trisha Kruse ★ Eagle, Idaho

- 2 cups thinly sliced fresh carrots
- 2 cups fresh broccoli florets
- 3 eggs
- 2 cups 2% milk
- 1/4 cup butter, melted
- 1/2 teaspoon salt
- 1/4 teaspoon ground nutmeg
- 1/4 teaspoon pepper
- 1-1/2 cups (6 ounces) grated Gruyere *or* Swiss cheese, *divided*
- 6 cups cubed egg bread

Place carrots and broccoli in a steamer basket; place in a large saucepan over 1 in. of water. Bring to a boil; cover and steam for 3-4 minutes or until crisp-tender.

In a large bowl, whisk the eggs, milk, butter, salt, nutmeg and pepper. Stir in the vegetables and 1 cup cheese. Gently stir in bread.

Transfer to a greased 11-in. x 7-in. baking dish; sprinkle with remaining cheese. Bake, uncovered, at 325° for 30-35 minutes or until a knife inserted near the center comes out clean. Let stand for 10 minutes before serving.

TO MAKE AHEAD: This recipe can be made a day ahead; cover and refrigerate. Remove from the refrigerator 30 minutes before baking. Bake as directed.

Hazelnut & Honey Roasted Squash

PREP: 15 MIN. **BAKE:** 45 MIN. **YIELD:** 8 SERVINGS

I enjoy both winter squash and nuts so I combined them in this tasty variation on baked acorn squash. I added apples to give it a little extra punch.

Gloria Bradley ★ Naperville, Illinois

- 1/2 cup hazelnuts, toasted
- 1/2 cup butter, cubed
- 2 tablespoons honey
- 1 tablespoon chopped shallot
- 2 medium acorn squash, halved and cut into 1-inch slices
- 1/4 teaspoon salt
- 1/2 cup finely chopped peeled tart apple
- 1 teaspoon lemon juice
- 1/8 teaspoon ground cinnamon

Place the hazelnuts, butter, honey and shallot in a food processor; cover and pulse until nuts are finely chopped.

Place squash in a greased shallow roasting pan; sprinkle with salt. Spread 1/2 cup hazelnut mixture over squash. Bake, uncovered, at 350° for 35 minutes.

In a small bowl, combine apple, lemon juice, cinnamon and remaining hazelnut mixture. Spoon over squash; bake 10-15 minutes longer or until apples and squash are tender.

Company Chicken Madeira

PREP: 35 MIN.   **BAKE:** 15 MIN.   **YIELD:** 6 SERVINGS

The sauce for this chicken is simply sensational! Packed with great herb and veggie flavor, the leeks, fennel and portobello mushrooms make it feel elegant, but it's very easy to make.

Jamie Miller ★ Maple Grove, Minnesota

1	tablespoon minced fresh thyme *or* 1 teaspoon dried thyme
1	tablespoon minced fresh rosemary *or* 1 teaspoon dried rosemary, crushed
1	teaspoon salt
1	teaspoon pepper
1	teaspoon ground coriander
6	boneless skinless chicken breasts (5 ounces *each*)
4	tablespoons butter, *divided*
2	medium leeks (white portion only), halved and thinly sliced
1	fennel bulb, chopped
3/4	pound sliced baby portobello mushrooms
2	tablespoons all-purpose flour
3/4	cup Madeira wine
3/4	cup chicken stock
1/2	cup shredded Parmesan cheese
1/2	cup shredded Gruyere *or* Swiss cheese
2	tablespoons chopped fennel fronds

Combine the thyme, rosemary, salt, pepper and coriander; rub over chicken. In a large skillet over medium-high heat, cook chicken in 2 tablespoons butter for 2 minutes on each side or until browned. Transfer to a greased 13-in. x 9-in. baking dish.

In same skillet, saute the leeks and chopped fennel in remaining butter for 4-6 minutes or until just tender. Add mushrooms; cook 5 minutes longer or until the mushrooms are tender.

Add flour; cook and stir for 1 minute. Gradually add wine and simmer for 2 minutes. Add stock and bring to a boil; cook and stir for 2 minutes or until thickened. Pour over chicken and sprinkle with cheeses.

Bake, uncovered, at 400° for 15-20 minutes or until a thermometer reads 170°. Sprinkle with fennel fronds.

TO MAKE AHEAD: Assemble casserole up to 1 day in advance. Cover and refrigerate. Let stand at room temperature 30 minutes before baking. Bake for 20 to 30 minutes in a preheated oven.

Garlic Orzo Pilaf

PREP/TOTAL TIME: 30 MIN.   **YIELD:** 8 SERVINGS

This is a simple go-to side dish that has lots of taste. I always keep the ingredients on hand, and I find it's even easier than a prepackaged rice side dish because the orzo cooks so quickly.

Dana Cummins ★ Lawrence, Kansas

4	garlic cloves, minced
1/4	to 1/2 teaspoon crushed red pepper flakes
2	tablespoons olive oil
2	cups uncooked orzo pasta
2-1/2	cups chicken stock
1/4	cup grated Parmesan cheese, optional

In a large skillet, saute the garlic and pepper flakes in oil for 1 minute. Add the orzo; saute for 3-5 minutes or until golden brown.

Stir in chicken stock and bring to a boil. Reduce heat; cover and simmer for 15-20 minutes or until pasta is tender. Sprinkle with cheese if desired.

Mixed Mushroom Tartlets

PREP: 40 MIN.   **BAKE:** 15 MIN.   **YIELD:** 8 SERVINGS

I summer in northern Michigan and find the wild morels that grow up there just irresistible. A word of caution...never pick mushrooms if you're not 100% sure they're safe to eat. If morels aren't available, I use whatever mushrooms I find at the supermarket. Crumble goat cheese over the tops of these tarts if you like. Serve as an appetizer or vegetarian entree.

Jennifer Condreay ★ Centennial, Colorado

- 1-1/2 pounds sliced fresh assorted mushrooms
- 1 medium onion, chopped
- 1/2 cup butter
- 3 tablespoons olive oil
- 1/2 cup white wine *or* dry vermouth
- 1 teaspoon minced fresh thyme *or* 1/2 teaspoon dried thyme
- 1 teaspoon salt
- 1 cup heavy whipping cream
- 1 package (17.3 ounces) frozen puff pastry, thawed
- 1 egg yolk
- 1 teaspoon water

In a large skillet, saute mushrooms and onion in butter and oil in batches until tender. Reduce heat to medium. Stir in the wine, thyme and salt. Cook until liquid is reduced by half. Stir in cream. Cook for 10 minutes until thickened. Remove from the heat and set aside.

Unfold one puff pastry sheet. Roll out into a 12-in. x 8-in. rectangle. Cut into eight rectangles. Using a sharp knife, score 1/2 in. from the edges of each pastry (do not cut through).

Transfer to baking sheets. Repeat with remaining sheet of puff pastry. Spoon mushroom mixture into centers. Whisk egg yolk and water; brush over pastry edges.

Bake at 400° for 13-16 minutes or until golden brown.

Editor's Note: For assorted mushrooms, we recommend a mixture of white button, baby portobello, shiitake and oyster mushrooms.

Portuguese Pork Tenderloin

PREP: 20 MIN.   **COOK:** 40 MIN.   **YIELD:** 4 SERVINGS

I won a contest to attend a cooking school in Portugal, where the chef laughed at any ideas regarding light dishes. This is my version of one his recipes; I reduced the olive oil and heavy cream. It reminds me of the flavors of Chef Miguel's roast, but I don't feel guilty about eating it!

Jessie Grearson-Sapat ★ Falmouth, Maine

- 2 large potatoes, peeled and cut into 1-inch cubes
- 3 tablespoons olive oil, *divided*
- 3/4 teaspoon pepper, *divided*
- 1/2 teaspoon salt, *divided*
- 2 cups dry red wine *or* chicken broth
- 1/4 cup tawny port wine *or* grape juice
- 1 cup pitted dried plums
- 2 fresh rosemary sprigs
- 2 pounds pork tenderloin, cut into 1-inch cubes
- 1 cup reduced-sodium chicken broth
- 2 tablespoons reduced-fat cream cheese
- 2 tablespoons heavy whipping cream

Additional fresh rosemary sprigs, optional

Place potatoes in a large bowl; drizzle with 1 tablespoon oil. Sprinkle with 1/2 teaspoon pepper and 1/4 teaspoon salt; toss to coat.

Transfer to a greased 15-in. x 10-in. x 1-in. baking pan. Bake at 400° for 40-45 minutes or until the potatoes are tender, stirring occasionally.

Meanwhile, in a small saucepan, combine the red wine, port wine, plums and rosemary. Bring to a boil; cook until liquid is reduced to about 1 cup, about 25-30 minutes. Remove rosemary and discard. Transfer to a blender; cover and process until smooth. Set aside.

Sprinkle pork with remaining pepper and salt. In a large skillet, brown pork in remaining oil; remove and keep warm.

Add broth, cream cheese, cream and plum mixture to skillet; cook over medium-low heat until blended. Return pork to the pan; cook and stir for 8-10 minutes or until meat is no longer pink. Serve pork and sauce with potatoes. Garnish with additional rosemary if desired.

Bacon-Corn Casserole

PREP: 20 MIN. **BAKE:** 30 MIN. **YIELD:** 8 SERVINGS

I have some family members who rarely eat vegetables. I've tried so many different vegetable recipes over the holidays and have been largely unsuccessful. Then I took an old corn casserole recipe of mother's and jazzed it up. The relatives love it! It's now a holiday must have and it's so easy to do. My rule of thumb; you can't miss with bacon!

Mildred Caruso ★ Brighton, Tennessee

- 2 packages (10 ounces *each*) frozen corn, thawed
- 1 cup heavy whipping cream
- 1/2 cup whole milk
- 2 tablespoons sugar
- 2 tablespoons butter, melted
- 2 green onions, chopped
- 1/4 teaspoon salt
- 1/4 teaspoon pepper
- 1 package (8-1/2 ounces) corn bread/muffin mix
- 3/4 pound bacon strips, cooked and crumbled
- 1/2 cup grated Parmesan cheese, *divided*

Sour cream and additional chopped green onions, optional

In a large bowl, combine the first eight ingredients; stir in the muffin mix and bacon. Fold in 1/4 cup cheese. Transfer to a greased 11-in. x 7-in. baking dish; sprinkle with the remaining cheese.

Bake at 350° for 30-40 minutes or until golden brown. Serve with sour cream and green onions if desired.

Winter Panzanella with Apple Dressing

PREP: 30 MIN. **BAKE:** 30 MIN.
YIELD: 14 SERVINGS (1 CUP EACH)

Panzanella is my favorite salad, and I enjoy it with fresh tomatoes in the summer. Since good tomatoes are hard to find in the winter, I created this version using roasted butternut squash, apple and cranberries.

Julie Merriman ★ Cold Brook, New York

- 1 medium butternut squash, peeled, seeded and cut into cubes
- 2 tablespoons olive oil, *divided*

Dash *each* salt and pepper

- 1 loaf sourdough bread (1 pound), cut into cubes
- 2 tablespoons *each* minced fresh basil, cilantro and mint, *divided*
- 1 cup fresh arugula
- 1 medium apple, thinly sliced
- 1 small red onion, thinly sliced
- 1/2 cup dried cranberries
- 1/2 cup pitted Greek olives, sliced
- 2 tablespoons lime juice
- 1-1/2 teaspoons grated lime peel

APPLE DRESSING:
- 1/4 cup chopped peeled apple
- 2 tablespoons honey, *divided*
- 1 tablespoon plus 1/2 cup olive oil, *divided*
- 1/4 cup white balsamic vinegar
- 1 tablespoon apple brandy *or* apple cider
- 1 tablespoon Dijon mustard
- 1/4 teaspoon salt
- 1/4 teaspoon pepper

Place squash cubes in a 15-in. x 10-in. x 1-in. baking pan. Toss with 1 tablespoon olive oil and sprinkle with salt and pepper. Bake, uncovered, at 400° for 20-25 minutes or until tender and lightly browned, stirring occasionally. Remove from the oven and cool.

In a large bowl, toss bread cubes with 1 tablespoon olive oil and 1 tablespoon each basil, cilantro and mint. Transfer to a baking sheet. Bake at 400° for 10 minutes or until lightly browned, stirring occasionally. Set aside.

Place the cooled squash, arugula, apple slices, onion, cranberries, olives, lime juice and peel, croutons and remaining herbs in a large bowl.

In a small skillet, cook apple in 1 tablespoon each honey and oil over medium heat until apple is softened and caramelized, stirring often. Transfer to a blender.

Add the vinegar, brandy, mustard, salt, pepper and remaining honey. Cover and process until pureed. While processing, gradually add remaining oil in a steady stream. Drizzle over salad; toss to coat.

Spinach Salad with Gorgonzola Pears

PREP: 15 MIN.   **BAKE:** 35 MIN.   **YIELD:** 6 SERVINGS

Juicy pears are stuffed with Gorgonzola cheese, dried cherries and pecans, then served over spicy arugula. Delicious!

Sonya Labbe ★ West Hollywood, California

- 3 medium pears, peeled, halved and cored
- 3 tablespoons lemon juice, *divided*
- 3/4 cup crumbled Gorgonzola cheese
- 1/4 cup dried cherries
- 1/4 cup chopped pecans, toasted
- 1/2 cup apple cider *or* juice
- 1/3 cup packed brown sugar
- 6 cups fresh baby spinach *or* fresh arugula
- 2 tablespoons olive oil
- 1/8 teaspoon salt

Brush pears with 1 tablespoon lemon juice; place cut side up in an ungreased 11-in. x 7-in. baking dish. In a small bowl, combine the cheese, cherries and pecans; spoon into pear cavities. In another bowl, combine cider and brown sugar until sugar is dissolved; pour over pears.

Bake, uncovered, at 375° for 35-45 minutes or until pears are tender, basting occasionally. Set aside pan juices.

Place arugula in a large bowl. Whisk together the oil, salt, remaining lemon juice and 2 tablespoons of reserved pan juices. Drizzle over arugula; toss to coat. Serve with pear halves and remaining pan juices.

Scallops in Shells

PREP: 35 MIN.   **BAKE:** 10 MIN.   **YIELD:** 8 SERVINGS

Just try these buttery scallops in their rich, creamy sauce.

Jane Rossen ★ Binghamton, New York

- 2 cups water
- 16 sea scallops (about 2 pounds)
- 1 teaspoon salt
- 1-1/2 cups thinly sliced fresh mushrooms
- 2 shallots, finely chopped
- 1/4 cup butter, cubed

SAUCE:
- 2 tablespoons butter
- 2 tablespoons all-purpose flour
- 3/4 cup 2% milk
- 2 tablespoons grated Parmesan cheese
- 2 tablespoons sherry
- 1/2 teaspoon salt
- 1/4 teaspoon lemon juice
- 1/4 teaspoon pepper
- 1/8 teaspoon grated lemon peel
- 1/3 cup dry bread crumbs
- 2 tablespoons butter, melted
- 8 food-safe scallop shells

Place water in a saucepan. Bring to a boil. Reduce heat; add scallops and poach, uncovered, for 6 minutes or until firm and opaque. Drain scallops, reserving 1 cup liquid.

Sprinkle the scallops with salt. In a large skillet, saute mushrooms and shallots in butter until tender. Add scallops; cook 2 minutes longer. Remove from the heat; set aside.

For sauce, in a small saucepan, melt butter. Stir in flour until smooth; gradually add milk and reserved poaching liquid. Bring to a boil; cook and stir for 2 minutes or until thickened. Stir in the cheese, sherry, salt, lemon juice, pepper and lemon peel; add to skillet.

Divide scallop mixture among eight scallop shells. Combine bread crumbs and melted butter; sprinkle over tops. Place on an ungreased 15-in. x 10-in. x 1-in. baking pan. Bake at 375° for 8-12 minutes or until crumbs are golden brown.

Holiday
BREADBASKET

Almond Coconut Kringles

PREP: 1 HOUR + CHILLING **BAKE:** 25 MIN. + COOLING
YIELD: 4 KRINGLES (9 SLICES EACH)

My mom was well-known for her delicious kringle that she made from memory. But when she passed away, we didn't have the recipe to carry on this tradition. After searching through her files, we found what we believe was the original, and that's where we began experimenting in the kitchen. The dough remains the same, but I had to adjust the filling ingredients until they finally came out just right. Give this tender, flaky pastry with its almond-and-coconut filling a try, and you'll be as hooked on it as we are!

Deborah Richmond ★ Trabuco Canyon, California

2	cups all-purpose flour
1	cup cold butter, cubed
1	cup (8 ounces) sour cream

FILLING:

1-1/4	cups butter, softened
1	cup packed brown sugar
3	cups sliced almonds, toasted
1-1/2	cups flaked coconut, toasted

GLAZE:

1	cup confectioners' sugar
1	tablespoon butter, softened
1	teaspoon vanilla extract
4	to 6 teaspoons 2% milk

Place flour in a large bowl; cut in butter until crumbly. Stir in sour cream. Wrap in plastic wrap. Refrigerate overnight.

In a small bowl, cream butter and brown sugar until light and fluffy. Stir in almonds and coconut.

Divide dough into four portions. On a lightly floured surface, roll one portion into a 12-in. x 10-in. rectangle. (Keep remaining dough refrigerated until ready to use.) Spread 1 cup filling lengthwise down the center. Fold in sides of pastry to meet in the center; pinch seam to seal. Repeat with remaining dough and filling. Transfer to two ungreased baking sheets. Bake at 375° for 23-27 minutes or until lightly browned.

Remove to wire racks to cool completely. Meanwhile, combine the confectioners' sugar, butter, vanilla and enough milk to achieve desired consistency; drizzle over the pastries.

Chocolate Chip Cranberry Bread

PREP: 20 MIN.　**BAKE:** 1 HOUR + COOLING
YIELD: 1 LOAF (16 SLICES)

This cranberry quick bread has a lovely texture. It became a favorite for fall and winter holidays the very first time I made it. Tart cranberries complement the sweet chocolate perfectly!

Jessica Hornaday ★ Nampa, Idaho

- 2　cups all-purpose flour
- 3/4　cup sugar
- 2　teaspoons baking powder
- 1/2　teaspoon salt
- 1　egg
- 3/4　cup 2% milk
- 6　tablespoons butter, melted
- 1　cup fresh *or* frozen cranberries, halved
- 1　cup miniature semisweet chocolate chips

STREUSEL:
- 1/3　cup packed brown sugar
- 2　tablespoons all-purpose flour
- 1/8　teaspoon ground cinnamon
- 2　tablespoons cold butter

In a large bowl, combine the flour, sugar, baking powder and salt. Whisk the egg, milk and butter; stir into dry ingredients just until moistened. Fold in cranberries and chocolate chips. Transfer to a greased 9-in. x 5-in. loaf pan.

In a small bowl, combine the brown sugar, flour and cinnamon; cut in butter until crumbly. Sprinkle over batter. Bake at 325° for 60-65 minutes or until a toothpick inserted near the center comes out clean.

Cool for 10 minutes before removing from pan to a wire rack to cool completely.

Drizzled Butternut Bread

PREP: 15 MIN.　**BAKE:** 55 MIN. + COOLING
YIELD: 2 LOAVES (12 SLICES EACH)

My two young children love this buttery bread. Squash makes it extra-moist and goes so well with the cinnamon. It's a welcome addition to brunch and dinner tables alike.

Misty Thompson ★ Gaylesville, Alabama

- 1　cup butter, softened
- 1　package (8 ounces) cream cheese, softened
- 2　cups sugar
- 3　eggs
- 2　cups mashed cooked butternut squash
- 1　teaspoon vanilla extract
- 3　cups all-purpose flour
- 1　teaspoon baking powder
- 1　teaspoon ground cinnamon
- 1/2　teaspoon salt
- 1/2　teaspoon baking soda
- 1　cup chopped walnuts

ICING:
- 1　cup confectioners' sugar
- 1/2　teaspoon vanilla extract
- 6　to 8 tablespoons sweetened condensed milk

In a large bowl, cream the butter, cream cheese and sugar until light and fluffy. Add eggs, one at a time, beating well after each addition. Beat in squash and vanilla. Combine the flour, baking powder, cinnamon, salt and baking soda; gradually beat into creamed mixture. Fold in walnuts.

Transfer to two greased 8-in. x 4-in. loaf pans. Bake at 350° for 55-65 minutes or until a toothpick inserted near the center comes out clean. Cool for 10 minutes before removing from pans to wire racks to cool completely.

In a small bowl, combine the confectioners' sugar, vanilla and enough milk to achieve a drizzling consistency. Drizzle over loaves.

Pumpkin Corn Bread

PREP: 15 MIN. **BAKE:** 30 MIN. + COOLING
YIELD: 24 SERVINGS

My corn bread has a subtle pumpkin flavor with hints of cinnamon, nutmeg and clove. It's delightful enough to satisfy my sweet tooth, but it also pairs well with a soup or stew.

Kristin Sanner ★ Chatham, Illinois

- 1-1/2 cups all-purpose flour
- 1 cup cornmeal
- 3/4 cup packed brown sugar
- 2 teaspoons baking powder
- 1-1/2 teaspoons ground cinnamon
- 1/2 teaspoon salt
- 1/2 teaspoon ground nutmeg
- 1/4 teaspoon ground cloves
- 2 eggs
- 1-1/2 cups solid-pack pumpkin
- 1/2 cup 2% milk
- 3 tablespoons butter, melted

In a large bowl, combine the first eight ingredients. In a small bowl, whisk the eggs, pumpkin, milk and butter. Stir into dry ingredients just until moistened. Transfer to a greased 13-in. x 9-in. baking dish.

Bake at 350° for 30-35 minutes or until a toothpick inserted near the center comes out clean. Serve warm.

Pesto Pinwheel Buns

PREP: 30 MIN. + RISING **BAKE:** 25 MIN. **YIELD:** 1 DOZEN

An easy-to-make spinach-basil pesto gives delectable flavor to these tender and delicious rolls.

Taste of Home Test Kitchen

- 1 package (1/4 ounce) active dry yeast
- 3 tablespoons warm water (110° to 115°)
- 1/2 cup warm 2% milk (110° to 115°)
- 2 tablespoons butter, softened
- 1 egg
- 1 tablespoon sugar
- 3/4 teaspoon salt
- 2-1/4 to 2-3/4 cups all-purpose flour

PESTO:
- 1 cup fresh baby spinach
- 1 cup fresh basil leaves
- 2 garlic cloves
- 1/4 cup walnut halves, toasted
- 1/4 cup grated Parmesan cheese
- 1/8 teaspoon pepper
- 1/4 cup olive oil

In a large bowl, dissolve yeast in warm water. Add the milk, butter, egg, sugar, salt and 1-1/2 cups flour. Beat until smooth. Stir in enough of the remaining flour to form a firm dough.

Turn onto a lightly floured surface; knead until smooth and elastic, about 6-8 minutes. Place in a greased bowl, turning once to grease the top. Cover and let rise in a warm place until doubled, about 1 hour.

Meanwhile, place the spinach, basil, garlic, walnuts, cheese and pepper in a food processor; cover and process until blended. While processing, gradually add oil in a steady stream. Set aside.

Punch dough down. Turn onto a lightly floured surface. Roll into a 12-in. x 10-in. rectangle. Spread pesto to within 1/2 in. of edges. Roll up jelly-roll style, starting with a long side; pinch seam to seal. Cut into 12 rolls.

Place rolls cut side up in a greased 13-in. x 9-in. baking pan. Cover and let rise until doubled, about 40 minutes.

Bake at 350° for 25-30 minutes or until golden brown. Remove from pan to a wire rack. Serve warm. Refrigerate any leftovers.

Cranberry-Walnut Toasting Bread

PREP: 30 MIN. + RISING **BAKE:** 45 MIN.
YIELD: 2 LOAVES (12 SLICES EACH)

Looking for a great bread to start your day? My multi-grain loaves are fabulous toasted. They're also good for sandwiches or served warm with dinner.

Tish Stevenson ★ Grand Rapids, Michigan

6	to 6-1/2 cups all-purpose flour
1	cup old-fashioned oats
1/2	cup whole wheat flour
1/3	cup packed brown sugar
2	teaspoons salt
1	package (1/4 ounce) active dry yeast
2-1/2	cups water
2	tablespoons butter
1-1/4	cups dried cranberries *or* cherries
3/4	cup chopped walnuts, toasted

In a large bowl, combine 3 cups all-purpose flour, oats, whole wheat flour, brown sugar, salt and yeast. In a small saucepan, heat water and butter to 120°-130°. Add to dry ingredients; beat just until moistened. Stir in the cranberries, walnuts and enough remaining all-purpose flour to form a soft dough.

Turn onto a floured surface; knead until smooth and elastic, about 6-8 minutes. Place in a greased bowl, turning once to grease the top. Cover and let rise in a warm place until doubled, about 1 hour.

Punch dough down; divide in half. Shape into loaves; place in two greased 9-in. x 5-in. loaf pans. Cover and let rise until doubled, about 45 minutes. Bake at 350° for 45-50 minutes or until golden brown. Remove from pans to wire racks to cool. To serve, cut into thick slices and toast.

Orange-Cumin Focaccia

PREP: 30 MIN. **BAKE:** 20 MIN.
YIELD: 2 LOAVES (8 WEDGES EACH)

My family created this Southwest-inspired bread to go with a themed dinner. But we found that the savory focaccia is really versatile and goes well with many hearty entrees.

Elizabeth Vesich ★ Crown Point, Indiana

1	package (1/4 ounce) active dry yeast
1-1/2	cups warm water (110° to 115°), *divided*
1	cup warm orange juice (110° to 115°)
4	tablespoons olive oil, *divided*
2	tablespoons grated orange peel
3	cups bread flour
1	cup whole wheat flour
3	teaspoons ground cumin
2	teaspoons coarsely ground pepper
1	teaspoon salt

In a large bowl, dissolve yeast in 1/4 cup warm water. Let stand for 5 minutes. Add the orange juice, 3 tablespoons oil, orange peel and remaining water. Combine 2 cups bread flour, whole wheat flour, cumin, pepper and salt; add to the yeast mixture. Beat until smooth. Stir in 3/4 cup bread flour to form a soft dough (dough will be sticky).

Turn out on a floured surface; knead in the rest of bread flour until the dough is smooth and elastic, about 6-8 minutes. Place in a greased bowl, turning once to grease top. Cover and let rise in a warm place for about 1 hour or until doubled.

Punch dough down. Divide in half. Shape each half into a ball, then flatten each into a disk. Cover and let rest for 5 minutes. Grease two baking sheets; sprinkle with whole wheat flour. Shape each portion into a 10-in. circle. Cover and let rise until doubled, about 25 minutes. With fingertips, make several dimples over top of each dough. Brush with remaining oil.

Bake at 375° for 20-25 minutes or until golden brown. Remove to wire racks to cool.

Rustic Country Bread

PREP: 20 MIN. + RISING   **BAKE:** 20 MIN.
YIELD: 1 LOAF (8 WEDGES)

My husband had a favorite sandwich shop that closed. The bread it had used for sandwiches was a sourdough-type with a great texture. After much experimentation, I've finally come close to duplicating the taste and texture he loved!

Debra Keil ★ Owasso, Oklahoma

  1 package (1/4 ounce) active dry yeast
1-1/2 teaspoons sugar
  1 cup warm water (110° to 115°)
  1 teaspoon salt
  1 teaspoon balsamic vinegar
  2 cups all-purpose flour
  1 tablespoon olive oil
Additional water

In a large bowl, dissolve yeast and sugar in warm water. Let stand for 5 minutes. Add the salt, vinegar and 1-1/2 cups flour. Beat until smooth. Stir in enough remaining flour to form a soft dough (dough will be sticky).

Do not knead. Transfer to a greased bowl. Cover and let rise in a warm place until doubled, about 50 minutes.

Stir dough down. Transfer to a greased 9-in. pie plate. Cover and let rise in a warm place until doubled, about 35 minutes. Brush with oil. Bake at 425° for 10 minutes. Reduce heat to 375°; bake 10-15 minutes longer or until golden brown, spritzing twice with additional water.

Sun-Dried Tomato Provolone Bread

PREP: 30 MIN.   **BAKE:** 40 MIN. + COOLING
YIELD: 3 MINI LOAVES (6 SLICES EACH)

This savory quick bread, passed down from my mother, is packed with great flavors. It not only goes well with soups and chowders, but it also makes a delicious accompaniment to beef and chicken entrees.

Marie Rizzio ★ Interlochen, Michigan

1/3 cup oil-packed sun-dried tomatoes
2-1/4 cups all-purpose flour
  2 teaspoons baking powder
  2 teaspoons sugar
1-1/4 teaspoons dried basil
  1 teaspoon salt
1/2 teaspoon baking soda
1/2 teaspoon coarsely ground pepper
  2 eggs
1-1/4 cups buttermilk
  3 tablespoons canola oil
  1 cup (4 ounces) shredded provolone cheese
1/4 cup minced fresh parsley

Drain the tomatoes, reserving 2 tablespoons oil. Chop the tomatoes and set aside.

In a large bowl, combine the flour, baking powder, sugar, basil, salt, baking soda and pepper. In a small bowl, whisk the eggs, buttermilk, oil and reserved sun-dried tomato oil. Stir into dry ingredients just until moistened. Fold in cheese, parsley and sun-dried tomatoes.

Transfer to three greased 5-3/4-in. x 3-in. x 2-in. loaf pans. Bake at 350° for 40-45 minutes or until a toothpick inserted near the center comes out clean. Cool for 10 minutes before removing from pans to wire racks.

Chocolate-Apricot Coffee Cake

PREP: 30 MIN. **BAKE:** 50 MIN. + COOLING
YIELD: 12 SERVINGS

My big sister shared this sensational coffee cake with me. It's the unique combination of flavors in the center swirl that really sets this one above others I've tried. Guests will be surprised and delighted with the apricot-chocolate filling!

Carol Witczak ★ Tinley Park, Illinois

1/3 cup packed brown sugar
1/4 cup chopped walnuts
1/4 cup chopped dried apricots
1/4 cup semisweet chocolate chips
1 tablespoon baking cocoa
1-1/2 teaspoons instant coffee granules
1 teaspoon ground cinnamon
BATTER:
3/4 cup butter, softened
1-1/3 cups sugar
3 eggs
1 teaspoon vanilla extract
2-3/4 cups all-purpose flour
1-1/2 teaspoons baking powder
1-1/2 teaspoons baking soda
3/4 teaspoon salt
2 cups (16 ounces) plain yogurt
1/2 teaspoon confectioners' sugar

In a small bowl, combine the first seven ingredients and set aside.

In a large bowl, cream butter and sugar until light and fluffy. Add eggs, one at a time, beating well after each addition. Beat in vanilla. Combine the flour, baking powder, baking soda and salt; add to the creamed mixture alternately with yogurt, beating well after each addition.

Transfer half of the batter to a greased and floured 10-in. fluted tube pan. Sprinkle filling over batter. Top with remaining batter. Bake at 325° for 50-55 minutes or until a toothpick inserted near the center comes out clean.

Cool for 10 minutes before removing from pan to a wire rack to cool completely. Dust with confectioners' sugar.

Swedish Cream Apple Rings

PREP: 20 MIN. + CHILLING   **BAKE:** 25 MIN. + COOLING
YIELD: 2 RINGS (6 SLICES EACH)

My mother made this classic coffee cake for every important holiday...Christmas, Thanksgiving and Easter. Because she made the dough in advance and let it rise overnight, those mornings weren't so hectic. Now, I carry on the tradition. As I make these, I remember my mom, who was a lot like this recipe—soft and tasteful, but full of surprises!

Heather Hood ★ Hillsboro, Oregon

    1   package (1/4 ounce) active dry yeast
  1/4   cup warm water (110° to 115°)
  3-1/2 cups all-purpose flour
  1/4   cup sugar
  1/2   teaspoon salt
  3/4   cup cold butter, cubed
    1   cup heavy whipping cream (110° to 115°)
  1/4   cup evaporated milk (110° to 115°)
    3   egg yolks

FILLING:
    2   cups finely chopped peeled apples
  1/2   cup raisins
  1/4   cup cinnamon-sugar

GLAZE:
    2   cups confectioners' sugar
    1   teaspoon vanilla extract
    2   to 3 tablespoons 2% milk

In a small bowl, dissolve the yeast in warm water. In a large bowl, combine the flour, sugar and salt. Cut in the butter until crumbly. Add the yeast mixture, cream, milk and egg yolks; stir until mixture forms a soft dough. Cover and refrigerate overnight.

In a small bowl, combine the filling ingredients. Punch down dough; divide in half. On a lightly floured surface, roll out one portion into a 13-in. x 7-in. rectangle. Sprinkle with half of filling.

Roll up jelly-roll style, starting with a long side. Pinch seam to seal. Place seam side down on a greased baking sheet; pinch ends together to form a ring. Repeat with remaining dough and filling. Cover and let rise in a warm place, about 45 minutes.

Bake at 350° for 25-30 minutes or until golden brown. Remove from pans to wire racks to cool. Combine the confectioners' sugar, vanilla and enough milk to achieve a drizzling consistency. Drizzle over warm tea rings.

Cinnamon Yogurt Twists

PREP: 45 MIN. + CHILLING   **BAKE:** 15 MIN.   **YIELD:** 2 DOZEN

I remember the aroma of warm cinnamon twists coming from my mother's kitchen. Now my own family enjoys Mom's recipe. Of course, I've experimented with it and I use yogurt instead of sour cream, which the original recipe called for.

Kristin Hammill ★ New York, New York

    1   package (1/4 ounce) active dry yeast
    1   teaspoon salt
  3-3/4 to 4 cups all-purpose flour
    1   cup butter, cubed
    1   cup plain yogurt
  1/4   cup water
    2   eggs
    1   teaspoon vanilla extract
  3/4   cup sugar
    1   teaspoon ground cinnamon

In a large bowl, combine the yeast, salt and 2-1/2 cups flour. In a small saucepan, heat the butter, yogurt and water to 120°-130°; add to dry ingredients. Beat on medium speed for 2 minutes.

Add the eggs, vanilla and 1/2 cup flour; beat 2 minutes longer. Stir in enough of the remaining flour to form a stiff dough. Do not knead. Cover and refrigerate for 2 hours or overnight.

Combine sugar and cinnamon; set aside. Punch dough down. On a lightly floured surface, roll dough into a 12-in. x 9 in. rectangle. Sprinkle 3 tablespoons cinnamon-sugar over dough; fold into thirds. Give dough a quarter turn and repeat rolling, sugaring and folding three more times.

Roll into a 12-in. x 6-in rectangle. Cut into twenty four 1/2-in.-wide strips; twist. Place on greased baking sheets. Cover and let rise until doubled, about 30 minutes. Bake at 350° for 14-18 minutes or until golden brown. Immediately remove from pans to wire racks to cool.

In a large skillet, saute onion in butter until tender. In bread machine pan, place the water, sour cream, onion mixture, 2 tablespoons sugar, 1-1/2 teaspoons salt, herbs, garlic, flour and yeast in order suggested by manufacturer. Select dough setting (check dough after 5 minutes of mixing; add 1 to 2 tablespoons of water or flour if needed).

When cycle is completed, turn the dough onto a lightly floured surface. Shape into nine balls. Push thumb through centers to form a 1-1/2-in. hole. Place on parchment paper-lined baking sheets. Cover and let rest for 30 minutes, then refrigerate overnight.

Let stand at room temperature for 30 minutes; flatten bagels slightly. In a non-aluminum Dutch oven, bring water to a boil with remaining sugar and salt. Drop bagels, one at a time, into water. Cook for 30 seconds; turn and cook 30 seconds longer. Remove with a slotted spoon; drain well on paper towels.

Sprinkle two ungreased baking sheets with cornmeal; place bagels 2 in. apart on prepared pans. Bake at 425° for 12-15 minutes or until golden brown. Remove to wire racks to cool.

Herbed Onion Bagels

PREP: 30 MIN. + CHILLING   **BAKE:** 15 MIN. + COOLING
YIELD: 9 BAGELS

I created these awesome savory bagels by combining and adapting several other recipes. Spread with cream cheese or onion-and-chive cream cheese for a real treat!

Pam Kaiser ★ Mansfield, Missouri

1/2	cup finely chopped sweet onion
2	tablespoons butter
3/4	cup warm water (70° to 80°)
1/4	cup sour cream
3	tablespoons sugar, *divided*
3-1/2	teaspoons salt, *divided*
1-1/2	teaspoons minced chives
1-1/2	teaspoons dried basil
1-1/2	teaspoons dried parsley flakes
3/4	teaspoon dried oregano
3/4	teaspoon dill weed
3/4	teaspoon dried minced garlic
3	cups bread flour
1	package (1/4 ounce) active dry yeast
3	quarts water
2	tablespoons yellow cornmeal

Making Bagels

1. Shape dough into balls. Push your thumb through the center of the dough, forming a 1-1/2-in. hole. Stretch and shape dough to form an even ring.

2. After bagels have boiled, remove them from water with a slotted spoon. Drain well on paper towels.

Apple Butter Doughnuts

PREP: 45 MIN. + CHILLING   **COOK:** 5 MIN./BATCH
YIELD: 2-1/2 DOZEN

In my family, it's a tradition to make these lovely spiced doughnuts after sledding. The whole family gathers in the kitchen to talk and laugh while we mix these up and fry them. We all think they are the best ever!

Mary June Donovan ★ Clinton, Massachusetts

2	tablespoons butter, softened
1	cup sugar
2	eggs
2	teaspoons vanilla extract
4-1/2	cups all-purpose flour
2	teaspoons baking powder
1	teaspoon baking soda
1	teaspoon salt
1/2	teaspoon ground cinnamon
1/2	teaspoon ground nutmeg
1/2	cup evaporated milk
1	tablespoon lemon juice
1	cup apple butter

Oil for deep-fat frying

BROWNED BUTTER ICING:

1/4	cup butter, cubed
2-1/2	cups confectioners' sugar
1/4	cup evaporated milk
1/2	teaspoon vanilla extract

In a large bowl, beat butter and sugar until crumbly, about 2 minutes. Add eggs, one at a time, beating well after each addition. Beat in vanilla.

Combine the flour, baking powder, baking soda, salt, cinnamon and nutmeg. Combine evaporated milk and lemon juice; let stand 1 minute. Stir in apple butter. Add flour mixture to the creamed mixture alternately with apple butter mixture, beating well after each addition. Cover and refrigerate for at least 2 hours.

Turn onto a lightly floured surface; knead 5-6 times. Roll to 1/4-in. thickness. Cut with a floured 2-1/2-in. doughnut cutter.

In an electric skillet or deep fryer, heat oil to 375°. Fry doughnuts, a few at a time, until golden brown on both sides. Drain on paper towels.

In a small heavy saucepan, cook butter over medium heat until golden brown, about 5 minutes. Pour into a small bowl; beat in the confectioners' sugar, milk and vanilla. Frost doughnuts.

Lemon-Streusel Blueberry Muffins

PREP: 20 MIN. **BAKE:** 25 MIN. **YIELD:** 1 DOZEN

Who doesn't love fresh muffins warm from the oven? My family and friends really enjoy this berry-packed flavor combo with hints of almond and cardamom. And the lemony cinnamon-scented streusel on top is heavenly!

Shirley Riley ★ Water Valley, Mississippi

1/4	cup butter, softened
3/4	cup sugar
1	egg
1	teaspoon vanilla extract
1/2	teaspoon almond extract
1/2	cup 2% milk
2	cups all-purpose flour
2	teaspoons baking powder
1/2	teaspoon salt
1/4	teaspoon ground cardamom
1-1/2	cups fresh *or* frozen unsweetened blueberries

LEMON STREUSEL:

1/2	cup packed brown sugar
1/3	cup all-purpose flour
2	teaspoons grated lemon peel
1/2	teaspoon ground cinnamon
1/4	cup cold butter, cubed

In a small bowl, cream butter and sugar until light and fluffy. Add egg and extracts; beat well. Beat in the milk. Combine the flour, baking powder, salt and cardamom; add to the creamed mixture just until moistened. Fold in the blueberries.

Fill greased or paper-lined muffin cups three-fourths full. In a small bowl, combine brown sugar, flour, lemon peel and cinnamon; cut in butter until crumbly. Sprinkle over the batter. Bake at 375° for 23-27 minutes, or until a toothpick inserted in muffin comes out clean.

Cool for 5 minutes before removing from pan to a wire rack. Serve warm.

Fabric Breadbasket

about 1/2 in. between edges. (Refer to diagram below for placement.) Lay other piece of cloth wrong side down on top of stabilizer pieces and backing cloth. Match all outer edges of the top and bottom cloth pieces.

Use iron with pressing cloth and follow manufacturer's instructions to fuse the layers of square cloth and stabilizer pieces together. There will be four open square shapes at each corner where there is no stabilizer. Use sewable iron-on adhesive tape to tack each piece of ribbon in place at an outer corner of the stabilizer strips. Insert ribbon between loose cloth layers about 2 in. and iron down. (Refer to diagram for placement.)

Pin loose fabric at corners and sew a straight stitch around the outer perimeter of the square about 1/4 in. from the edge. Be careful to sew ribbons in place. Fold all four stiffened sides of the basket up. The loose corner fabric should fold outward, creating a triangle shape at each of the four corners. Tie the two ribbons at each corner in a bow to hold the basket sides in place. Trim ribbons ends to desired length.

Pass your freshly baked breads around the table in a customized fabric breadbasket. It's really simple to make, and you can use different fabrics for fun or elegant entertaining. Don't worry if a little butter or jam gets on the fabric, it can be washed by hand, then laid flat to dry.

For this project you will need 1/4 yd. of 2-sided fusible ultra-firm stabilizer, 1/2 yd. of 100% cotton canvas or duck cloth, sewable iron-on adhesive tape, eight 15-in. lengths of 3/8-in. ribbon, a rotary cutter with cutting mat, an iron with pressing cloth and standard sewing supplies.

Using the rotary cutter and cutting mat, cut two 16-in. square pieces of canvas or duck cloth. Cut one 8-in. square piece and four 2-1/2 x 8-in. strips of stabilizer. Fold over edges of each square cloth 1/2 in. to create a hem and press in place with iron. If desired, create mitered corners by trimming diagonally prior to folding over.

Lay one piece of square cloth right side down. Put square piece of stabilizer centered on cloth. Place one stabilizer strip lengthwise on each side of the center piece leaving

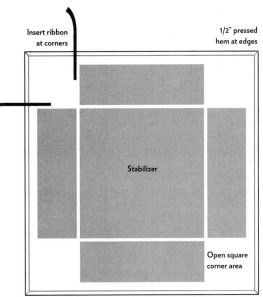

Insert ribbon at corners

1/2" pressed hem at edges

Stabilizer

Open square corner area

PLACEMENT DIAGRAM

Limpa Bread

PREP: 30 MIN. + RISING   **BAKE:** 30 MIN.
YIELD: 2 LOAVES (12 SLICES EACH)

I've entered my bread in several fairs, and it has won every time! Orange and anise give it a subtle but wonderful taste.

Beryl Parrott ★ Franklin, Manitoba

1/2	cup packed light brown sugar
1/4	cup dark molasses
1/4	cup butter, cubed
2	tablespoons grated orange peel
1-1/2	teaspoons salt
1	teaspoon aniseed, lightly crushed
1	cup boiling water
1	cup cold water
2	packages (1/4 ounce *each*) active dry yeast
1/2	cup warm water (110° to 115°)
4-1/2	cups all-purpose flour
3	to 4 cups rye flour
2	tablespoons cornmeal
2	tablespoons butter, melted

In a large bowl, combine the brown sugar, molasses, butter, orange peel, salt, aniseed and boiling water; stir until brown sugar is dissolved and butter is melted. Stir in cold water; let stand until mixture cools to 110° to 115°.

Meanwhile, in a large bowl, dissolve the yeast in warm water. Stir in the molasses mixture; mix well. Add the all-purpose flour and 1 cup rye flour. Beat on medium speed for 3 minutes. Stir in enough remaining rye flour to form a stiff dough.

Turn onto a floured surface; knead until smooth and elastic, about 6-8 minutes. Place in a greased bowl, turning once to grease the top. Cover and let rise in a warm place until doubled, about 1 hour.

Punch dough down. Turn onto a lightly floured surface; divide in half. Shape into two oval loaves. Grease two baking sheets and sprinkle lightly with cornmeal. Place loaves on prepared pans. Cover and let rise until doubled, about 30 minutes.

With a sharp knife, make four shallow slashes across top of each loaf. Bake at 350° for 30-35 minutes or until golden brown. Remove to wire racks; brush with butter.

Pumpkin Date Nut Bread

PREP: 30 MIN.   **BAKE:** 1 HOUR + COOLING
YIELD: 2 LOAVES (16 SLICES EACH)

My family loves this moist and yummy bread! It's packed with nuts and topped with a pretty caramel-colored glaze. The flavors always remind me of autumn.

Wendy Rusch ★ New Richmond, Wisconsin

3-1/2	cups all-purpose flour
3	cups sugar
1-1/2	teaspoons ground cinnamon
1	teaspoon baking soda
1	teaspoon salt
4	eggs
1	can (15 ounces) solid-pack pumpkin
1	cup canola oil
1/3	cup water
1/2	teaspoon vanilla extract
1	package (8 ounces) pitted dates, chopped
1-1/2	cups chopped pecans

CARAMEL GLAZE:

1/4	cup packed brown sugar
1/4	cup sugar
1/4	cup butter, cubed
1/4	cup heavy whipping cream
2/3	cup confectioners' sugar
1	teaspoon vanilla extract

In a large bowl, combine the flour, sugar, cinnamon, baking soda and salt. In a small bowl, whisk the eggs, pumpkin, oil, water and vanilla. Stir into dry ingredients just until moistened. Fold in dates and pecans.

Transfer to two greased 9-in. x 5-in. loaf pans. Bake at 350° for 60-70 minutes or until a toothpick inserted near the center comes out clean. Cool for 10 minutes before removing from pans to wire racks.

For glaze, in a small heavy saucepan, combine the brown sugar, sugar, butter and cream. Cook and stir over low heat until sugar is dissolved.

Increase heat to medium. Do not stir. Cook for 3-6 minutes or until bubbles form in center and syrup turns amber brown. Remove from the heat; transfer to a small bowl. Cool to room temperature. Add confectioners' sugar and vanilla; beat until smooth. Drizzle over loaves.

Peanut Butter Swirls

PREP: 45 MIN. + RISING   **BAKE:** 25 MIN.   **YIELD:** 1 DOZEN

A honey-blond version of the beloved cinnamon bun, these tender peanut butter rolls make a scrumptious breakfast.

Jeanne Holt ★ Mendota Heights, Minnesota

2-3/4 to 3-1/4 cups all-purpose flour
  1/4 cup sugar
    1 package (1/4 ounce) active dry yeast
  3/4 teaspoon salt
    1 cup 2% milk
    6 tablespoons butter, cubed
    1 egg
FILLING:
  1/3 cup sugar
  1/4 cup butter, softened
  1/4 cup plus 2 tablespoons heavy whipping cream, *divided*
    3 tablespoons creamy peanut butter
    2 tablespoons brown sugar
    2 tablespoons honey
  2/3 cup chopped honey-roasted peanuts
  1/2 cup peanut butter chips
    2 cups confectioners' sugar

In a large bowl, combine 1-1/4 cups flour, sugar, yeast and salt. In small saucepan, heat milk and butter to 120°-130°. Add to dry ingredients; beat just until moistened. Add egg; beat until smooth. Stir in enough remaining flour to form a soft dough (dough will be sticky).

Turn onto a floured surface; knead until smooth and elastic, about 6-8 minutes. Place in a greased bowl, turning once to grease the top. Cover and let rise in a warm place until doubled, about 1 hour.

Punch dough down. Turn onto a lightly floured surface. Roll into a 12-in. x 10-in. rectangle. For filling, in a small bowl, combine the sugar, butter, 1/4 cup cream, peanut butter, brown sugar and honey. Stir in peanuts and peanut butter chips. Spread half of filling to within 1/2 in. of edges; reserve remaining filling for topping.

Roll up jelly-roll style, starting with a long side; pinch seam to seal. Cut into 12 slices. Place cut side down in a greased 13-in. x 9-in. baking pan. Cover and let rise in a warm place for 30 minutes.

Bake at 325° for 24-28 minutes or until golden brown. In a small bowl, beat confectioners' sugar, remaining filling and cream; spread over warm rolls. Cool on wire racks.

Chocolate Chip Challah

PREP: 25 MIN. + RISING **BAKE:** 20 MIN. + COOLING
YIELD: 2 LOAVES (12 SLICES EACH)

I'm fond of baking, and since challah is not available where I live, I've created my own version to serve at Christmas and Easter. It's so delicious and not as much work as you might think. This recipe has a subtle chocolate flavor that's accented by melty chocolate chips when served warm. Leftovers are fabulous for French toast or bread pudding.

Lorraine Caland ★ Shuniah, Ontario

1	tablespoon sugar
1	package (1/4 ounce) active dry yeast
1/2	cup warm water (110° to 115°)
1/3	cup canola oil
1/3	cup honey
3	eggs
3	egg yolks
1	teaspoon salt
1	teaspoon vanilla extract
3-1/2	to 4-1/4 cups all-purpose flour
1/2	cup miniature semisweet chocolate chips

GLAZE:

1/4	cup heavy whipping cream
3/4	teaspoon sugar

In a large bowl, dissolve sugar and yeast in warm water; let stand for 5 minutes. Add the oil, honey, eggs, egg yolks, salt and vanilla; mix well.

Add 3 cups flour. Beat on medium speed for 3 minutes or until smooth. Stir in enough remaining flour to form a soft dough (dough will be sticky).

Turn onto a floured surface; knead until smooth and elastic, about 6-8 minutes. Place in a greased bowl, turning once to grease the top. Cover and let rise in a warm place until doubled, about 1 hour.

Punch dough down. Turn onto a lightly floured surface; knead in chocolate chips. Divide dough in half; divide each half into three portions. Shape each piece into a 12-in. rope.

Place three ropes on a greased baking sheet and braid; pinch ends to seal and tuck under. Repeat with remaining dough. Cover and let rise until doubled, about 1 hour.

Combine cream and sugar. Brush some of the mixture over braids. Bake at 350° for 20-25 minutes or until golden brown. Remove to wire racks and brush with remaining cream mixture. Cool.

Orange Scones with Cream Cheese Filling

PREP: 35 MIN. **BAKE:** 15 MIN. **YIELD:** 1 DOZEN

I love making these for company over the holidays. Guests always seem surprised and delighted by the tangy orange-flavored cream cheese filling in these moist scones.

Cara Langer ★ Overland Park, Kansas

FILLING:

6	ounces cream cheese, softened
1/4	cup sugar
1	tablespoon grated orange peel

SCONES:

1-3/4	cups all-purpose flour
3	tablespoons sugar
2	teaspoons baking powder
1/4	teaspoon salt
6	tablespoons cold butter
1/3	cup heavy whipping cream
1	egg
1	tablespoon grated orange peel

TOPPING:

1	egg
1	teaspoon water
2	tablespoons coarse sugar

For filling, in a small bowl, combine all ingredients; set aside.

For scones, in a large bowl, combine the flour, sugar, baking powder and salt. Cut in butter until mixture resembles coarse crumbs. Whisk cream, egg and orange peel; stir into crumb mixture just until moistened. Turn onto a floured surface; knead 10 times.

Divide dough in half. On an ungreased baking sheet, pat each half into a 9-in. circle. On one half of each circle, spread half of the filling to within 1/4 in. of edges. Fold dough over filling; pinch edges to seal.

For topping, beat egg and water; brush over scones. Sprinkle with sugar. Bake at 400° for 13-18 minutes or until golden brown. Cut each into six wedges; serve warm. Refrigerate leftovers.

Seasonal
GET-TOGETHERS

Feliz Navidad

For many people of Hispanic heritage, tamales are the center of special celebrations—especially Christmas! Friends and family come together for tamaladas, party-like gatherings centered around preparing and feasting on these stuffed delicacies cooked in corn husks. There are many traditional tamale fillings, both sweet and savory. Here, we offer chicken and vegetable versions. And to round out your fiesta, consider the Guacamole Shrimp Appetizers, Jalapeno Poppers with Lime Cilantro Dip, Mexican Cheese Spread, Tropical Salad with Pineapple Vinaigrette, Guava Coconut Rum Cocktail and sensational Eggnog Tres Leches Cake. So, spice up your yuletide with these must-try specialties.

Fiesta Tamales

PREP: 1 HOUR + CHILLING   **COOK:** 50 MIN.
YIELD: 2 DOZEN

I love tamales but don't like spending days making them, so I've come up with my own simple yet delicious recipe. When you taste my faster, flavorful tamales, you'll be surprised at just how great they are!

Donna Wilkinson ★ Lakeside, California

DOUGH:

- 4-3/4 cups masa harina
- 2-3/4 cups reduced-sodium chicken broth
- 1-1/4 cups salsa
- 3/4 cup canola oil
- 3/4 cup frozen corn, thawed
- 5 green onions, sliced
- 2 envelopes Goya sazon with coriander and annatto
- 1-1/4 teaspoons salt
- 48 dried corn husks

CHICKEN FILLING:

- 1 small onion, chopped
- 1 tablespoon canola oil
- 1 tablespoon minced chipotle pepper in adobo sauce
- 2 garlic cloves, minced
- 1 teaspoon dried oregano
- 1 teaspoon ground cumin
- 4 cups shredded rotisserie chicken
- 1 can (14-1/2 ounces) reduced-sodium chicken broth

VEGETABLE FILLING:

- 1-1/2 cups sliced ripe olives
- 1-1/2 cups (6 ounces) pepper jack cheese
- 3/4 cup shredded Colby cheese

In a large bowl, combine the masa harina, broth, salsa, oil, corn, onions, sazon seasoning and salt; beat until well blended. Cover and refrigerate overnight.

Place corn husks in a large bowl; cover with cold water and soak for at least 2 hours.

Meanwhile, in a large skillet, saute onion in oil until tender; add the chipotle pepper, garlic, oregano and cumin; saute 1 minute longer. Add chicken and broth. Bring to a boil. Reduce heat; simmer for 15-20 minutes or until liquid is evaporated, stirring occasionally.

For veggie tamales, drain the corn husks and pat dry. Place a corn husk on a work surface with the small end pointing away from you. Place 1/4 cup dough over half of husk closest to you, spreading dough to within 1 in. of edges. Sprinkle olives and cheeses down the center.

Lifting one long side, fold husk over filling so that edges meet, enclosing filling in husk. Fold ends of husk over tamale; tie with corn husk strips. Repeat 11 times. For chicken tamales, use 1/4 cup dough on each corn husk and 1/4 cup chicken mixture. Repeat 11 times, folding and tying each tamale.

Line a large steamer basket with four corn husks. Place basket in a Dutch oven over 1 in. of water; position half of the tamales upright in basket.

Cover tamales with four corn husks. Bring to a boil; cover and steam in batches for 50-60 minutes or until dough peels away from husk, adding hot water to pan as needed and replacing corn husks in pan. Remove husks before eating.

Wrapping Tamales

1. Pat dough to within 1 in. of edges of each corn husk. Top with chicken or olive mixture.

2. Roll corn husk around the filling. Fold top and bottom edges under; tie with kitchen string.

3. Arrange tied tamales in an upright position in a steamer basket.

Guacamole Shrimp Appetizers

PREP: 30 MIN.   **COOK:** 10 MIN. + CHILLING
YIELD: 2 DOZEN

I wanted something other than a cheese-based appetizer, and I found it in this fresh and flavorful snack. Try these tortilla chips topped with a creamy guacamole and zippy shrimp mixture. They're yummy!

Ann Deren-Lewis ★ Bradbury, California

CILANTRO JALAPENO PESTO:
- 2 jalapeno peppers
- 3/4 cup fresh cilantro leaves
- 2 tablespoons pine nuts
- 1 garlic clove, peeled and halved
- 1 tablespoon olive oil

SHRIMP FILLING:
- 12 uncooked medium shrimp, peeled, deveined and cut into 1/2-inch pieces
- 1/4 cup frozen corn, thawed
- 1/4 cup diced sweet red pepper
- 1 tablespoon olive oil

GUACAMOLE:
- 1 medium ripe avocado, peeled and cut in half
- 1/4 cup fresh cilantro leaves
- 2 tablespoons chopped sweet onion
- 2 tablespoons lime juice
- 1 tablespoon sour cream
- 24 nacho tortilla chips *or* tortilla chip scoops

Broil peppers 4 in. from the heat until skins blister, about 5 minutes. With tongs, rotate peppers a quarter turn. Broil and rotate until all sides are blistered and blackened. Immediately place peppers in a small bowl; cover and let stand for 20 minutes.

Peel off and discard charred skin. Remove stems and seeds. Place the roasted jalapenos, cilantro, pine nuts and garlic in a food processor; cover and pulse until chunky. While processing, gradually add oil in a steady stream; set aside.

In a large skillet, saute the shrimp, corn and red pepper in oil for 3-5 minutes or until shrimp turn pink. Remove from the heat; cool for 5 minutes. Add pesto mixture; toss to coat. Cover and refrigerate.

For guacamole, place the avocado, cilantro, onion, lime juice and sour cream in food processor. Cover and pulse until smooth. Cover and chill.

Just before serving, top each tortilla chip with guacamole. Place 2 teaspoons shrimp mixture on each.

Mexican Cheese Spread

PREP: 10 MIN.   **BAKE:** 20 MIN. + COOLING
YIELD: 16-20 SERVINGS

Green taco sauce adds a little punch to this quick, savory appetizer. You can cut it into squares and serve with chips.

Amanda Hosko ★ Aurora, Illinois

- 3 eggs, lightly beaten
- 1 bottle (8 ounces) mild green taco sauce
- 2 cups (8 ounces) shredded cheddar cheese
- 2 cups (8 ounces) shredded Monterey Jack cheese
Tortilla chips

In a large bowl, combine the eggs, taco sauce and cheeses. Pour into a greased 13-in. x 9-in. baking dish. Bake, uncovered, at 350° for 20-25 minutes or until set. Cool for 10 minutes. Cut into triangles. Serve with tortilla chips.

Eggnog Tres Leches Cake

PREP: 40 MIN. + STANDING **BAKE:** 25 MIN. + CHILLING
YIELD: 15 SERVINGS

When the holidays roll around, my family always looks forward to sampling my moist eggnog cake. Its rich seasonal flavor is something to celebrate!

Jan Valdez ★ Chicago, Illinois

1	package (18-1/4 ounces) white cake mix
1-1/3	cups water
2	tablespoons canola oil
3	egg whites
2	cups eggnog
1	can (14 ounces) sweetened condensed milk
1/2	cup 2% milk
1-1/2	cups heavy whipping cream
1/4	cup sugar
1/8	teaspoon ground cinnamon
1/8	teaspoon ground nutmeg

In a large bowl, combine the cake mix, water, oil and egg whites; beat on low speed for 30 seconds. Beat on medium for 2 minutes. Pour into a greased and floured 13-in. x 9-in. baking pan.

Bake at 350° for 25-30 minutes or until a toothpick inserted near the center comes out clean. Cool on a wire rack. Using a skewer, poke holes in cake 1 in. apart.

In a large bowl, combine the eggnog, sweetened condensed milk and 2% milk. Pour a scant 3/4 cup mixture over cake; let stand for 20-30 minutes or until liquid is absorbed. Repeat four times. Cover and refrigerate for 8 hours or overnight.

In a large bowl, beat cream until it begins to thicken. Add sugar; beat until soft peaks form. Spread over cake. Sprinkle with cinnamon and nutmeg. Refrigerate leftovers.

Jalapeno Poppers with Lime Cilantro Dip

PREP: 30 MIN. **BAKE:** 20 MIN.
YIELD: 2 DOZEN (2 CUPS DIP)

Crispy and crunchy with a creamy filling, these little pepper bites always earn rave reviews. They're perfect for any event, from a cocktail soiree to a football-watching party.

Tana Rogers ★ New York, New York

- 12 jalapeno peppers
- 1 package (8 ounces) cream cheese, softened
- 1-1/4 cups (6 ounces) shredded sharp cheddar cheese
- 4 green onions, finely chopped
- 1/3 cup all-purpose flour
- 6 egg whites, lightly beaten
- 1-1/2 cups panko (Japanese) bread crumbs
- 1/2 teaspoon salt
- 1/2 teaspoon pepper

LIME CILANTRO DIP:
- 2 cups (16 ounces) sour cream
- 4 green onions, finely chopped
- 1/4 cup lime juice
- 2 tablespoons minced fresh cilantro
- 1/2 teaspoon garlic salt

Cut jalapenos in half lengthwise and remove seeds. Place jalapenos on an ungreased baking sheet. Broil 4 in. from the heat for 4-6 minutes on each side or until lightly blistered. Cool slightly.

In a small bowl, beat cream cheese and cheddar cheese until blended. Stir in onions. Spoon into pepper halves.

Place the flour, egg whites and bread crumbs in separate shallow bowls. Coat jalapenos with flour, then dip in egg whites and coat with crumbs. Place on a greased baking sheet; sprinkle with salt and pepper. Bake at 350° for 18-20 minutes or until lightly browned.

For dip, in a small bowl, combine all ingredients. Serve with poppers.

Guava Coconut Rum Cocktail

PREP/TOTAL TIME: 5 MIN. **YIELD:** 1 SERVING

My beverage is sensational—a cooling taste of the tropics in a glass! The guava adds a touch of sweetness to the coconut.

Melanie Milhorat ★ New York, New York

Ice cubes
- 2 ounces coconut rum
- 2 ounces guava nectar
- 2 teaspoons lemon juice
- 3 to 4 dashes bitters
- 1 teaspoon simple syrup
- 2 ounces coconut water

GARNISH:
Fresh pineapple wedge

Fill a mixing glass or tumbler three-fourths full with ice. Add rum, guava nectar, lemon juice, bitters and simple syrup; stir until condensation forms on outside of glass. Strain into a chilled cocktail glass. Add ice and top with coconut water. Garnish as desired.

Guava Coconut Punch: Increase the coconut water and guava nectar to 3 ounces each. Eliminate bitters and add 1/8 teaspoon coconut extract.

Tropical Salad with Pineapple Vinaigrette

PREP/TOTAL TIME: 20 MIN. **YIELD:** 4 SERVINGS

The title says it all! Pineapple, macadamia nuts and coconut give this salad a true South-Seas feel. You will love it!

Hazel Hunt ★ Foley, Alabama

- 7 cups torn romaine
- 1 cup chopped fresh pineapple
- 1/2 cup coarsely chopped macadamia nuts, toasted
- 3 green onions, chopped
- 6 bacon strips, cooked and crumbled
- 1/4 cup unsweetened pineapple juice
- 3 tablespoons olive oil
- 2 tablespoons red wine vinegar
- 1 teaspoon honey
- 1/4 teaspoon salt
- 1/8 teaspoon pepper
- 1/4 cup flaked coconut, toasted

In a large salad bowl, toss the romaine, pineapple, macadamia nuts, green onions and bacon.

In a small bowl, whisk the pineapple juice, oil, red wine vinegar, honey, salt and pepper. Pour over salad; toss to coat. Sprinkle with coconut.

New Year's Day Brunch

After staying up late to usher in the New Year, you and your guests will really welcome a leisurely brunch the following morning. Start the new day and year by sipping a cheery Holiday Mimosa and nibbling on Sausage & Cheese Crescents and Winter Fruit Coffee Cake. Follow those treats with one or more of our heartier dishes, such as Baked Banana French Toast, Hash Brown Nests with Portobellos and Eggs, Persimmon Breakfast Parfaits and Smoky Salmon and Goat Cheese Crepes.

Hash Brown Nests with Portobellos and Eggs

PREP: 30 MIN.   **BAKE:** 15 MIN.   **YIELD:** 12 SERVINGS

Hash browns make a fabulous crust for these individual egg quiches. They look like you fussed, but are actually very easy to make. And they've always been a hit at my holiday brunches and other special occasions.

Kate Meyer ★ Brentwood, Tennessee

    3   cups frozen shredded hash brown potatoes, thawed
    3   cups chopped fresh portobello mushrooms
  1/4   cup chopped shallots
    2   tablespoons butter
    1   garlic clove, minced
  1/2   teaspoon salt
  1/4   teaspoon pepper
    2   tablespoons sour cream
    1   tablespoon minced fresh basil
Dash cayenne pepper
    7   eggs, beaten
  1/4   cup shredded Swiss cheese
    2   bacon strips, cooked and crumbled
Additional minced fresh basil, optional

Press 1/4 cup hash browns onto the bottom and up the sides of each of 12 greased muffin cups; set aside.

In a large skillet, saute mushrooms and shallots in butter until tender. Add garlic, salt and pepper; cook 1 minute longer. Remove from the heat; stir in sour cream, basil and cayenne.

Divide eggs among potato-lined muffin cups. Top with mushroom mixture. Sprinkle with cheese and bacon.

Bake at 400° for 15-18 minutes or until eggs are completely set. Garnish with additional basil if desired. Serve warm.

Persimmon Breakfast Parfaits

PREP/TOTAL TIME: 20 MIN.   **YIELD:** 4 SERVINGS

Persimmon season is short compared to apples, oranges or pears. So when they're available, use this delightful fruit in as many ways as possible. Besides adding to breads and salads, punch up your breakfast with this quick yogurt parfait.

Taste of Home Test Kitchen

    2   cups plain yogurt
    1   cup mashed ripe persimmon pulp
    4   teaspoons honey
  1/4   teaspoon ground ginger
  1/4   teaspoon ground cardamom
    1   medium Asian pear, chopped
    2   cups granola
    1   ripe persimmon, peeled and sliced
  1/4   cup pomegranate seeds
  1/4   cup chopped pistachios

Combine the yogurt, persimmon pulp, honey, ginger and cardamom. Spoon 1/4 cup into each of four parfait glasses. Top each with pear and 1/4 cup granola. Layer with 1/4 cup yogurt mixture, persimmon slices and remaining granola. Top with remaining yogurt mixture; sprinkle with pomegranate seeds and pistachios.

New Year's Noisemakers

Make some noise with plastic push-up containers (available at craft or cooking supply stores or online) as the base of these party favors. Use tacky glue to seal bottom of push-up disk to the bottom of container. If desired, spray paint the exterior in your choice of colors and let dry. Cut rectangular strips of patterned paper to fit around the open cylindrical container. Secure paper in place with glue dots or scrapbook adhesive. Embellish top of container with fringe or novelty yarn. Fill with plastic beads and place cap on top. To seal, use tacky glue around cap rim.

Winter Fruit Coffee Cake

PREP: 20 MIN. + STANDING   **BAKE:** 30 MIN. + COOLING
YIELD: 15 SERVINGS

People often say this spice cake with its streusel topping takes them back to their grandmother's kitchen. Filled with apples, pears and raisins, it has a heavenly aroma while baking that will bring your family running for a sample!

Taste of Home Test Kitchen

  1/2 cup golden raisins
  1/4 cup brandy
TOPPING:
    1 cup packed brown sugar
    1 teaspoon ground cinnamon
    2 tablespoons butter, softened
  1/2 cup chopped pecans
CAKE:
  1/2 cup butter, softened
    1 cup packed brown sugar
    2 eggs
    1 teaspoon vanilla extract
    2 cups all-purpose flour
    3 teaspoons baking powder
    1 teaspoon baking soda
  3/4 teaspoon ground cinnamon
  1/4 teaspoon ground nutmeg
  1/8 teaspoon ground cloves
  1/2 teaspoon salt
    1 cup sour cream
  3/4 cup chopped peeled apple
  1/2 cup chopped peeled ripe pear

In a small bowl, soak the raisins in brandy for 1 hour.

In small bowl, combine brown sugar and cinnamon. With clean hands, work butter into sugar mixture until well combined. Add pecans. Refrigerate for 15 minutes.

For cake, in a large bowl, cream butter and sugar until light and fluffy. Beat in eggs and vanilla. Combine the flour, baking powder, baking soda, spices and salt; add to creamed mixture alternately with sour cream. Fold in the apple, pear and raisins (do not drain the raisins). Pour into a greased 13-in. x 9-in. baking dish. Sprinkle with topping.

Bake at 350° for 28-32 minutes or until a toothpick inserted near the center comes out clean. Cool on a wire rack.

Holiday Mimosa

PREP/TOTAL TIME: 5 MIN.   **YIELD:** 1 SERVING

Add a splash of color to your brunch table with a lovely rosy mimosa. It has a refreshing sweet-tart taste.

Jessie Sarrazin ★ Livingston, Montana

    1 tablespoon red coarse sugar
  1/2 ounce raspberry liqueur
    2 ounces ruby red grapefruit juice
    2 ounces Champagne
Grapefruit twist

Sprinkle sugar on a plate. Moisten the rim of a champagne flute with water; hold the glass upside down and dip the rim into sugar.

Pour the raspberry liqueur and grapefruit juice into the glass; top with Champagne. Garnish with a grapefruit twist.

Editor's Note: To make a batch of mimosas (12 servings), slowly pour one bottle (750 ml) chilled Champagne into a pitcher. Stir in 3 cups cranberry juice and 3/4 cup raspberry liqueur.

Salmon and Goat Cheese Crepes

PREP: 1 HOUR + CHILLING   **YIELD:** 10 SERVINGS

Homemade crepes filled with smoked salmon and a fabulous goat-cheese cream will add a real "wow" to any brunch table. Go ahead, impress your guests!

Amy Burton ★ Cary, North Carolina

3	eggs
1-1/4	cups 2% milk
1/2	cup water
1	cup whole wheat pastry flour
1	cup all-purpose flour
3/4	teaspoon salt

FILLING:

12	ounces fresh goat cheese
3/4	cup roasted sweet red peppers
1	tablespoon plus 1-1/2 teaspoons lemon juice
1-1/2	teaspoons smoked paprika
1	garlic clove, peeled and halved
1	pound smoked salmon fillets
2	cups fresh baby spinach
3	tablespoons capers, drained
1	tablespoon snipped fresh dill

Optional garnishes: additional fresh goat cheese, capers and dill

In a large bowl, whisk the eggs, milk and water. Combine the wheat flour, all-purpose flour and salt; add to egg mixture and mix well. Refrigerate for 1 hour.

Meanwhile, in a food processor, combine the goat cheese, red peppers, lemon juice, paprika and garlic; cover and process for 2-3 minutes or until blended. Refrigerate until ready to use.

Heat a lightly greased 8-in. nonstick skillet over medium heat; pour 1/4 cup batter into center of skillet. Lift and tilt pan to coat bottom evenly. Cook until top appears dry; turn and cook 15-20 seconds longer. Remove to a wire rack. Repeat with remaining batter, greasing skillet as needed. When cool, stack crepes with waxed paper or paper towels in between. Spread 2 tablespoons cheese mixture down the center of each crepe. Top each with salmon, spinach, capers and dill; roll up. Garnish with additional cheese, capers and dill if desired.

Sausage Cheese Crescents

PREP: 55 MIN. + RISING **BAKE:** 15 MIN. **YIELD:** 3 DOZEN

My mother says my grandmother made the best-ever butterhorns. I never tasted them, but Mom's were delicious and Grandma, of course, taught her. Through the years, I've had butterhorns filled with everything from fruit to seafood and from meats to raisins!

Paula Marchesi ★ Lenhartsville, Pennsylvania

3-1/4	teaspoons active dry yeast
2	cups warm 2% milk (110° to 115°)
4	eggs
1	cup mashed potato flakes
1	cup butter, softened
1/2	cup sugar
1	teaspoon salt
7	to 8 cups all-purpose flour
12	ounces bulk Italian sausage
3/4	cup shredded cheddar cheese

FINISHING:

1	egg, beaten

In a large bowl, dissolve yeast in milk. Add the eggs, potato flakes, butter, sugar, salt and 4 cups flour. Beat on medium speed for 3 minutes. Stir in enough remaining flour to form a soft dough (dough will be sticky).

Turn onto a floured surface; knead until smooth and elastic, about 6-8 minutes. Place in a greased bowl, turning once to grease top. Cover and let rise in a warm place until doubled, about 1 hour.

In a large skillet, cook sausage over medium heat until no longer pink; drain and set aside to cool.

Punch dough down. Turn onto a lightly floured surface; divide into thirds. Roll each portion into a 12-in. circle; sprinkle with 1 cup sausage and 1/4 cup cheese. Cut each circle into 12 wedges.

Roll up wedges from the wide ends and place point side down 2 in. apart on greased baking sheets. Curve ends to form crescents. Cover and let rise until doubled, about 30 minutes. Brush with egg.

Bake at 375° for 14-18 minutes or until golden brown. Serve warm.

Baked Banana French Toast

PREP: 20 MIN. + CHILLING **BAKE:** 55 MIN. + STANDING
YIELD: 12 SERVINGS

This easy overnight recipe makes a delightful breakfast or brunch entree. The flavor is reminiscent of banana pudding, so I've also served it for dessert.

Nancy Zimmerman ★ Cape May Court House, New Jersey

2	cups sliced ripe bananas
2	tablespoons lemon juice
9	cups cubed French bread
1	package (8 ounces) cream cheese, cubed
9	eggs
4	cups 2% milk
1/2	cup sugar
1/4	cup butter, melted
1/4	cup maple syrup
1/2	teaspoon ground cinnamon

In a small bowl, toss bananas with lemon juice. Place half of bread in a greased 13-in. x 9-in. baking dish; layer with cream cheese, bananas and remaining bread.

In a large bowl, whisk the eggs, milk, sugar, butter, syrup and cinnamon; pour over bread. Cover and refrigerate for 8 hours or overnight.

Remove from the refrigerator 30 minutes before baking. Bake, uncovered, at 350° for 55-65 minutes or until a knife inserted near the center comes out clean. Let stand for 10 minutes before serving.

Cozy Family Christmas Eve

Every family seems to have its own traditions for Christmas Eve. Some may go to midnight services at church, others invite relatives over to open presents, and still others enjoy a quiet, intimate night with just immediate family—the kids trying to be extra-good so Santa will be extra-generous! One tradition that's a favorite in many homes is gathering to read *The Night Before Christmas* after having a delicious meal, such as the Italian-themed menu that follows. The delicacies include: Artichoke and Sun-Dried Tomato Bruschetta, Pasticho, Italian Veggie Salad, Garlic & Herb Parmesan Rolls, Orange Anise Sparklers and our cute Santa & Elf Christmas Cookies.

Santa and Elf Christmas Cookies

PREP: 4-1/2 HOURS + CHILLING
BAKE: 10 MIN./BATCH + STANDING **YIELD:** 3 DOZEN

The kids will be jumping for joy when you bring out a cookie plate filled with Santas and his helper elves. These whimsical treats will be a hit with the adults, too. The butter cookies are easy to shape and a delight to decorate.

Taste of Home Test Kitchen

1	cup butter, softened
1-1/2	cups confectioners' sugar
1	egg
1	teaspoon vanilla extract
1/2	teaspoon almond extract
2-1/2	cups all-purpose flour
1	teaspoon baking soda
1	teaspoon cream of tartar

ROYAL ICING:

1	package (2 pounds) confectioners' sugar
8	teaspoons meringue powder
1/2	teaspoon cream of tartar
1	cup water

Food coloring of your choice
36 miniature marshmallows
Assorted sprinkles and pearl dragees

In a large bowl, cream butter and confectioners' sugar until light and fluffy. Beat in the egg and extracts. Combine the flour, baking soda and cream of tartar; gradually add to creamed mixture and mix well.

Divide dough into thirds. Shape each into a ball, then flatten into a disk. Wrap in plastic wrap and chill in the freezer for 15 minutes or until easy to handle.

For Santas: On a lightly floured surface, roll one portion of dough into a 10-in. circle. Turn a pie plate upside down over circle and cut around the edge with a knife; reserve scraps. Cut into eight wedges.

Place wedges 2 in. apart on ungreased baking sheets. Fold the tip of each wedge down, tucking. a scrap piece of dough (about a 1/2-in. ball) under the upper part of fold.

For elves: Roll another portion of dough into a 10-in. circle. Cut in half; cut one-half into four wedges and the other half into eight wedges. Repeat forming Santas with the large wedges. Transfer small wedges to a baking sheet; fold tips down, forming hats.

Roll remaining portion of dough into a 10-in. circle. Cut into 16 wedges. Transfer to baking sheets; fold tips down.

Bake at 350° for 10-13 minutes or until edges are lightly browned. Cool for 2 minutes. Remove from pans to wire racks to cool completely.

To decorate: In a large bowl, combine confectioners' sugar, meringue powder and cream of tartar; add water.

Beat on low speed just until combined. Beat on high for 4-5 minutes or until stiff peaks form.

Tint icing with colors of your choice. (Keep unused icing covered at all times with a damp cloth. If necessary, beat again on high speed to restore texture.) Working with one cookie at a time, decorate with icing, attach a marshmallow to the tip of hat and finish with sprinkles and dragees as desired. Let stand until set. Store in an airtight container.

Forming Santa's Hat

Roll out the dough according to recipe directions and cut it into wedges. Roll dough scraps into 1/2-in. balls; set aside. Arrange triangles on baking sheet. Fold top point of triangle down 1-1/2 in. over cookie. Slightly flatten a dough ball and place under upper edge of folded hat.

Pasticho (Venezuelan Lasagna)

PREP: 1 HOUR 50 MIN.   **BAKE:** 35 MIN. + STANDING
YIELD: 20 SERVINGS

I knew, since I was a child, that my passion was to cook and to invent new dishes. After sampling this item at a restaurant in Venezuela, I re-created it at home. My father fell in love with the rich, creamy layer and the tomato-meat sauce in my version of a traditional favorite.

Jessica Higgins ★ Oak Park, Illinois

- 1 pound ground beef
- 1 pound ground pork
- 1 large Spanish onion, finely chopped
- 1 celery rib, finely chopped
- 1 small carrot, shredded
- 3 tablespoons olive oil
- 4 garlic cloves, minced
- 2 cans (28 ounces *each*) whole tomatoes with basil, undrained
- 1 can (29 ounces) tomato puree
- 1 bay leaf
- 1 teaspoon salt

MUSHROOM SAUCE:
- 2-1/4 cups sliced baby portobello mushrooms
- 1/3 cup butter, cubed
- 1 tablespoon olive oil
- 6 cups heavy whipping cream
- 1/2 teaspoon salt
- 1/4 teaspoon pepper
- 1-1/4 cups shredded Parmesan cheese

LAYERS:
- 3 packages (9 ounces *each*) no-cook lasagna noodles
- 7 cups (28 ounces) shredded part-skim mozzarella cheese
- 2 cups shredded Parmesan cheese

In a Dutch oven, cook the beef, pork, onion, celery and carrot in oil over medium heat until meat is no longer pink. Add garlic; cook 1 minute longer. Drain. Stir in the tomatoes, tomato puree, bay leaf and salt. Bring to a boil. Reduce heat; simmer, uncovered, for 1 hour.

Meanwhile, in a Dutch oven, saute mushrooms in butter and oil until tender. Add the cream, salt and pepper. Bring to a boil. Stir in Parmesan cheese; cook and stir for 20-25 minutes or until thickened.

Discard bay leaf from meat sauce. Spread 1-1/4 cups meat sauce into a greased 4-qt. baking dish. Top with six noodles. Layer with 1-3/4 cups meat sauce, 1 cup mozzarella cheese, six noodles, 1-1/4 cups mushroom sauce, 1/3 cup Parmesan cheese and 1/2 cup mozzarella cheese. Repeat layers three times. Top with remaining noodles, meat sauce, mushroom sauce, mozzarella cheese and Parmesan cheese (dish will be full).

Cover and bake at 400° for 20 minutes. Uncover; bake 15-20 minutes longer or until golden brown and bubbly. Let stand for 10 minutes before cutting.

Orange Anise Sparkler

PREP: 15 MIN. + STANDING   **YIELD:** 2 QUARTS

A spice-infused simple syrup is the base for this pretty and refreshing orange juice beverage. If the flavor seems too "adult" for the kids, just skip the syrup and mix the orange juice with only club soda.

Taste of Home Test Kitchen

- 1 cup sugar
- 1 cup water
- 4 whole star anise
- 1 cinnamon stick (3 inches)
- 3 cups orange juice, chilled
- 1 bottle (1 liter) club soda, chilled

Orange slices and additional whole star anise

In a small saucepan, combine the sugar, water, star anise and cinnamon. Bring to a boil over medium heat. Cook and stir for 1 minute. Remove from the heat; cover and let stand for 1 hour. Strain mixture, discarding spices. Refrigerate until chilled.

In a large pitcher, combine the orange juice and soda; stir in sugar syrup. Serve in cocktail glasses; garnish with orange slices and star anise.

Italian Veggie Salad

PREP: 30 MIN. + CHILLING   YIELD: 16 SERVINGS

I created this salad when I needed a crowd-pleaser for a community charity drive, and it was a huge success! I've been asked repeatedly for the recipe and now make it for at least six events a year. It keeps very well when refrigerated.

Denise Murphy ★ Waterloo, Iowa

  2 cups fresh baby carrots, quartered lengthwise
1-3/4 cups thinly sliced radishes
  2 celery ribs, sliced
  1 small head cauliflower, broken into florets
  1 bunch broccoli, cut into florets
  6 large fresh mushrooms, thinly sliced
  1 can (2-1/4 ounces) sliced ripe olives, drained
  1 package Italian salad dressing mix
1/3 cup water
1/3 cup white vinegar
1/3 cup olive oil
  1 package (9 ounces) hearts of romaine salad mix
Pepperoncini, optional

In a large bowl, combine the first seven ingredients. In a small bowl, whisk the dressing mix, water, vinegar and oil. Pour over vegetables; toss to coat. Cover and refrigerate for at least 4 hours.

Just before serving, place the romaine in a large serving bowl. Add vegetables; toss to coat. Top with pepperoncini if desired.

Artichoke and Sun-Dried Tomato Bruschetta

PREP/TOTAL TIME: 30 MIN.   YIELD: 3 DOZEN

My family expects me to bring this bruschetta to every gathering! The artichoke and sun-dried tomato combination is a tasty alternative to more traditional versions. I've even tossed the mixture with spaghetti for a fun change of pace!

Terry Skibiski ★ Barrington, Illinois

 36 slices French bread baguette (1/2 inch thick)
  2 tablespoons olive oil
  2 cups marinated quartered artichoke hearts, drained
  1 cup oil-packed sun-dried tomatoes, drained
  1 garlic clove, minced
  1 teaspoon dried oregano
  1 teaspoon dried basil
  1 cup (4 ounces) shredded Italian cheese blend, *divided*

Brush baguette slices with oil. Place bread on ungreased baking sheets. Bake at 400° for 6-8 minutes or until lightly browned. Place the artichokes, tomatoes, garlic, oregano, basil, and 1/2 cup cheese in a food processor; cover and process until coarsely chopped.

Spread 1 heaping tablespoon on each bread slice; sprinkle with remaining cheese. Bake at 400° for 5-10 minutes or until top is bubbly.

TO MAKE AHEAD: Prep baguette slices earlier in the day; store on baking sheets in the refrigerator. Prepare artichoke mixture; cover and refrigerate until ready to assemble. Proceed as directed.

Garlic-Herb Parmesan Rolls

PREP: 20 MIN.   **BAKE:** 20 MIN. + COOLING
YIELD: 16 SERVINGS

Fresh-baked yeast rolls are always a hit at special dinners. To make it easy on the cook, these start in the bread machine. I arrange them in a tree shape for the yuletide season, but they can also be baked in a 13- x 9-inch baking pan.

Lorri Reinhardt ★ Big Bend, Wisconsin

1	cup water (70° to 80°)
2	tablespoons butter, softened
1	egg, lightly beaten
3	tablespoons sugar
2	teaspoons dried minced garlic
1	teaspoon Italian seasoning
1	teaspoon salt
2-1/4	cups bread flour
1	cup whole wheat flour
1	package (1/4 ounce) active dry yeast

TOPPING:

1	tablespoon butter, melted
1	tablespoon grated Parmesan cheese
1	teaspoon Italian seasoning
1/2	teaspoon coarse salt

In bread machine pan, place the first 10 ingredients in order suggested by manufacturer. Select dough setting (check dough after 5 minutes of mixing; add 1 to 2 tablespoons of water or flour if needed).

When cycle is completed, turn dough onto a lightly floured surface; divide into 16 balls. Line a baking sheet with foil and grease the foil. Center one roll near the top of prepared baking sheet. Arrange rolls snugly into four additional rows, adding one more roll for each row, forming a tree shape.

Center remaining ball under tree for trunk.. Cover and let rise until doubled, about 1 hour.

Brush rolls with butter. Combine cheese and Italian seasoning and sprinkle over rolls. Sprinkle with salt. Bake at 350° for 20-25 minutes or until golden brown. Serve warm.

Two TAKES

Beat the kitchen clock this busy holiday season with large-yield recipes that allow you to turn leftovers into two or more spectacular items! Each version will taste like a new freshly made creation, and no one will ever guess that both came from the same time-saving dish!

Petite Pineapple Coconut Cakes

PREP: 25 MIN. + CHILLING   **YIELD:** 9 SERVINGS

Defy wintry weather and transport your guests to the tropics with these change-of-pace single-serving confections. No one will suspect the dessert started with a cake mix!

Taste of Home Test Kitchen

  1 cake layer from Angel Cake Ball Pops
  1 cup plus 3 tablespoons pineapple preserves
  1 teaspoon coconut extract
1-1/2 cups heavy whipping cream
  6 ounces cream cheese, softened
1/3 cup confectioners' sugar
  2 cups large flaked coconut, toasted

Cut cake horizontally into two layers. Place bottom layer on a cutting board. Combine pineapple preserves and extract; set aside 3 tablespoons for frosting. Spread remaining pineapple mixture over cut side of bottom layer. Top with remaining cake layer; cut cake into 9 squares.

In a large bowl, beat cream until stiff peaks form. In another bowl, beat the cream cheese, confectioners' sugar and reserved pineapple mixture; fold in the whipped cream. Spread over the top and sides of each square. Press the coconut into top and sides. Refrigerate for at least 1 hour before serving.

Angel Cake Ball Pops

PREP: 1-1/4 HOURS + FREEZING **BAKE:** 20 MIN. + COOLING
YIELD: 3 DOZEN

Turn cake mix into an adorable treat that will draw smiles of delight from kids and adults alike.

Taste of Home Test Kitchen

- 1 package (18-1/4 ounces) white cake mix
- 1 cup water
- 3 eggs
- 1/3 cup canola oil
- 1 teaspoon vanilla extract
- 1 vanilla bean
- 1/4 cup butter, softened
- 2-1/4 cups plus 2 tablespoons confectioners' sugar, *divided*
- 3 to 4 tablespoons heavy whipping cream

Yellow food coloring

- 1 pound pink candy coating disks
- 2 pounds white candy coating, coarsely chopped

Gold, silver or clear edible glitter

Black and red food-writing pens

- 36 lollipop sticks
- 36 white chocolate-covered miniature pretzels

Styrofoam block

In a large bowl, beat the first five ingredients on low speed for 30 seconds. Beat on medium for 2 minutes. Pour into two greased and floured 9-in. square baking pans.

Bake at 350° for 18-22 minutes or until a toothpick inserted near the center comes out clean. Cool for 10 minutes; remove from pans to wire racks to cool completely.

Split vanilla bean and scrape seeds; set aside. In a large bowl, cream butter until light and fluffy. Beat in 2-1/4 cups confectioners' sugar and vanilla seeds. Add enough cream to achieve desired consistency. Tint 1/3 cup frosting yellow; cover and refrigerate.

Wrap one cake tightly and freeze for up to 1 month for Petite Pineapple Coconut Cakes. Crumble remaining cake layer into a large bowl. Add remaining frosting; mix well.

Shape into thirty-six 1/2-in. and 1-in. balls. Place on waxed paper-lined baking sheets. Freeze until firm.

In a microwave, melt pink candy coating disks; stir until smooth. Dip small balls into coating, allowing excess to drip off. Return to baking sheets. Melt white candy coating. Dip large balls in coating; allow excess to drip off. Sprinkle with glitter. Return to baking sheets. Refrigerate until set.

For each angel, draw face with food-writing pens onto a pink ball. In a bowl, beat yellow frosting and remaining confectioners' sugar until smooth. Pipe onto a pink ball for hair. Dip one end of a lollipop stick into melted coating and insert into a white cake ball, pushing it no more than halfway through. Attach a pink ball with melted candy coating. Using candy coating, attach a pretzel for wings. Insert stick into a Styrofoam block to stand.

Editor's Note: Edible glitter and food-writing pens are available from Wilton Industries. Call 800-794-5866 or visit wilton.com.

1. Dip small balls in melted pink candy coating. Dip large balls in white candy coating and sprinkle with edible glitter. Refrigerate until set.

2. Using food-writing pens, draw faces onto pink balls Pipe yellow frosting on pink ball for hair.

3. Dip one end of a lollipop stick into melted white candy coating and insert no more than halfway into white ball. Attach head and pretzel wings with melted white candy coating. Insert stick into Styrofoam block to allow cake pops to dry, and display.

Cake Mix Extraordinaire

Who knew a simple white cake mix could create two delectable desserts? The cake ball cherubs are as adorable as those from a bakery, and the tropical cake is delish!

Coffee Roast Beef

PREP: 20 MIN. **BAKE:** 2-1/4 HOURS
YIELD: 6 SERVINGS PLUS LEFTOVERS

I used to work in a coffee shop, so the idea of using coffee in this delicious entree just tickles me. It adds such rich flavor.

April Gunterman ★ Centerville, Ohio

- 1 boneless beef chuck roast (5 pounds)
- 2 tablespoons olive oil
- 1 medium onion, chopped
- 1 garlic clove, minced
- 1 teaspoon dried oregano
- 1 teaspoon dried basil
- 1/2 teaspoon pepper
- 3/4 teaspoon salt
- 1 cup strong brewed coffee
- 3/4 cup plus 1/3 cup water, *divided*
- 3/4 cup beef stock
- 3 tablespoons all-purpose flour

In a Dutch oven, brown roast in oil on all sides; set aside. Add onion to pan; saute until tender. Add the garlic and seasonings; cook for 1 minute. Add the coffee, 3/4 cup water and stock; return roast to pan. Bring to a boil. Cover and bake at 325° for 2-1/4 to 2-3/4 hours or until meat is tender.

Remove beef and keep warm. Combine flour and remaining water until smooth. Stir into pan. Bring to a boil; cook and stir for 2 minutes or until thickened.

Shred 2 cups beef for Mini Beef Chimichangas and cube 1-3/4 cups for Spinach Beef Stew. Slice remaining roast and serve with gravy.

Spinach Beef Stew

PREP: 15 MIN. **COOK:** 35 MIN. **YIELD:** 4 SERVINGS

I created this stew by using what I had on hand one night, and it remains a family favorite on cold New England days.

Amy Leary ★ Farmington, Connecticut

- 1 medium onion, chopped
- 1 tablespoon olive oil
- 2 garlic cloves, minced
- 1/3 cup cider vinegar
- 2 tablespoons dry red wine *or* beef broth
- 1 can (29 ounces) tomato sauce
- 1 cup water
- 1/3 cup chopped roasted sweet red peppers
- 3 bay leaves
- 3 tablespoons brown sugar
- 3 teaspoons beef bouillon granules
- 1 teaspoon dried oregano
- 1/2 teaspoon dried basil
- 1/4 teaspoon dried thyme
- 1/4 teaspoon pepper
- 1/3 cup uncooked long grain rice
- 1-3/4 cups leftover cubed cooked Coffee Roast Beef
- 2 cups chopped fresh spinach

In a Dutch oven, saute onion in oil until tender. Add garlic; saute for 1 minute. Stir in vinegar and wine. Bring to a boil; cook until liquid is almost evaporated. Add the tomato sauce, water, peppers, bay leaves, brown sugar, bouillon and seasonings. Bring to a boil. Stir in rice. Reduce the heat; cover and simmer for 15-20 minutes or until rice is tender.

Discard bay leaves. Add beef and spinach; cook and stir until heated through and spinach is wilted.

Mini Beef Chimichangas

PREP: 30 MIN. **COOK:** 5 MIN./BATCH
YIELD: 20 MINI CHIMICHANGAS

Looking to jazz up some leftover roast beef, I came up with these little crispy chimis that my husband absolutely loves!

Danielle Luaders ★ Clever, Missouri

- 2 cups (8 ounces) shredded pepper Jack cheese
- 1 can (15 ounces) black beans, rinsed and drained
- 1 cup (8 ounces) sour cream
- 1 cup (4 ounces) shredded Colby-Monterey Jack cheese
- 1 can (4 ounces) chopped green chilies
- 2 teaspoons ground cumin
- 1 teaspoon salt
- 1/2 teaspoon garlic powder
- 1/2 teaspoon crushed red pepper flakes
- 2 cups shredded cooked Coffee Roast Beef
- 1 package (16 ounces) egg roll wrappers

Oil for deep-fat frying
Guacamole, optional

In a large bowl, combine the first nine ingredients. Stir in cooked beef. Place 1/4 cup filling in the center of one egg roll wrapper. (Keep remaining wrappers covered with a damp paper towel until ready to use.) Fold bottom corner over filling. Fold sides toward center over filling. Moisten remaining corner with water; roll up tightly to seal. Repeat with remaining wrappers and filling.

In an electric skillet or deep fryer, heat oil to 375°. Fry chimichangas in batches for 1-2 minutes on each side or until golden brown. Drain on paper towels. Serve warm with guacamole if desired.

Versatile Roast

The beauty of this comforting roast is that you can turn it into two more unique dinners! Shred 2 cups of the pot roast to make the mini chimis and cube 1-3/4 cups for the satisfying stew.

 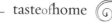

Apple Spice Meatballs

PREP: 50 MIN. **BAKE:** 15 MIN.
YIELD: 6 DOZEN PLUS LEFTOVERS

These little spicy-sweet meatballs are so full of wonderful flavors! They're always a huge hit at parties.

Joyce Conway ★ Westerville, Ohio

1-1/4 cups panko (Japanese) bread crumbs
1 medium onion, finely chopped
1 medium sweet red pepper, finely chopped
1 medium apple, peeled and finely chopped
2 eggs, lightly beaten
1/2 cup canned pumpkin
1/2 cup ketchup
2 teaspoons garlic powder
1 teaspoon salt
1 teaspoon pumpkin pie spice
3/4 teaspoon pepper
1/2 teaspoon crushed red pepper flakes
1 pound ground beef
1 pound bulk hot Italian sausage
SAUCE:
1 can (14 ounces) whole-berry cranberry sauce
1 jar (12 ounces) apple jelly
3/4 cup ketchup
1/2 teaspoon crushed red pepper flakes

In a large bowl, combine the first 12 ingredients. Crumble meats over mixture; mix well. Shape into 1-in. balls.

Place meatballs on greased racks in shallow baking pans. Bake, uncovered, at 375° for 15-20 minutes or until no longer pink. Drain on paper towels.

In a Dutch oven, combine the sauce ingredients. Bring to a boil. Reduce heat; simmer, uncovered, for 10 minutes.

Gently stir in about 6 dozen cooked meatballs and heat through. Save the remaining meatballs for Hungarian Pepper Soup with Romano Crisps or another use.

Hungarian Pepper Soup with Romano Crisps

PREP/TOTAL TIME: 30 MIN. **YIELD:** 8 SERVINGS

This is my delicious version of a classic comfort food from my childhood—stuffed peppers. Cream cheese gives the soup a velvety smoothness.

Moore Dawn ★ Warren, Pennsylvania

1 cup shredded Romano cheese
2 to 3 Hungarian wax *or* banana peppers, seeded and chopped
2 tablespoons butter
2 tablespoons all-purpose flour
2 teaspoons Italian seasoning
1/2 teaspoon salt
1/2 teaspoon pepper
2 cups chicken stock

2 dozen Apple Spice Meatballs
1 can (12 ounces) evaporated milk
1 package (8 ounces) cream cheese, cubed

On a baking sheet, sprinkle 1 tablespoon Romano cheese into a 3-in. circle, repeat 15 times. Bake at 300° for 10-12 minutes or until golden brown.

In a Dutch oven, saute peppers in butter. Stir in flour, Italian seasoning, salt and pepper until blended. Gradually add stock. Bring to a boil; cook and stir for 2 minutes or until thickened. Stir in meatballs, milk and cream cheese; heat through (do not boil). Serve with Romano crisps.

Romano Crisps

1. Cut a piece of parchment paper to fit a baking sheet. On the back side of the paper draw 3-in. circles. Place drawing side down on baking sheet.

2. Sprinkle 1 tablespoon Romano cheese over each circle. Spread out to fill circle. Finish according to recipe directions.

Meatballs on Hand

Bake up a large batch of these meatballs. Cool them, then freeze in a single layer on a waxed paper-lined baking sheet. Once frozen, transfer to a resealable plastic freezer bag. They'll be ready for glazing in Apple Spice Meatballs or to warm you up in the hearty Hungarian Pepper Soup.

Holiday Spice Pancakes

PREP/TOTAL TIME: 30 MIN.   **YIELD:** 8 PANCAKES

With hints of clove, nutmeg, and cinnamon, these pancakes make any breakfast something to celebrate! The perfect blend of flavorings can add spice to your mornings all year long.

Cindy Fuller ★ Forest City, North Carolina

- 1 cup all-purpose flour
- 1/4 cup Mulling Spices
- 1 tablespoon sugar
- 1 tablespoon ground cinnamon
- 1 teaspoon baking powder
- 1/4 teaspoon salt
- 1/8 teaspoon ground nutmeg
- 1 cup 2% milk
- 1 egg
- 2 tablespoons canola oil
- 1 teaspoon vanilla extract

Maple syrup

In a large bowl, combine the flour, Mulling Spices, sugar, cinnamon, baking powder, salt and nutmeg. In a small bowl, whisk the milk, egg, oil and vanilla. Stir into dry ingredients just until moistened.

Pour batter by 1/4 cupfuls onto a greased hot griddle. Turn when bubbles form on top; cook until second side is golden brown. Serve with syrup.

Mulled Wine-Poached Apples

PREP: 20 MIN.   **COOK:** 30 MIN. + CHILLING
YIELD: 6 SERVINGS

No room for a heavy dessert? For a satisfying touch of sweetness at the end of a meal, try these delicious apples. The spices and wine sauce make them something special.

Taste of Home Test Kitchen

- 1 bottle (750 milliliters) merlot
- 1/2 cup Mulling Spices
- 6 medium apples, peeled and cored

In a Dutch oven, bring wine and Mulling Spices to a boil. Reduce heat; carefully add apples. Cover and simmer for 15-20 minutes or just until apples are tender, turning once.

With a slotted spoon, remove apples to a large bowl. Bring wine mixture to a boil; cook, uncovered, until liquid is reduced to about 1/2 cup. Cool. Pour over apples; cover and refrigerate for at least 1 hour before serving.

Mulling Spices

PREP/TOTAL TIME: 10 MIN.   **YIELD:** ABOUT 2 CUPS

My mulling blend is a merry combination of sugar and spice and a nice touch of citrus peel. Use it to flavor pancakes or waffles, wines or cider—and even as a spice blend for poached apples.

Cindy Fuller ★ Forest City, North Carolina

- 2 cups packed brown sugar
- 1 tablespoon ground cinnamon
- 2 teaspoons dried grated lemon peel
- 2 teaspoons dried orange peel
- 1 teaspoon ground nutmeg
- 1/4 teaspoon ground cloves

Place all ingredients in a food processor; cover and process until blended. Store in an airtight container in a cool dry place for up to 1 year.

Mulled Red Wine

PREP/TOTAL TIME: 10 MIN.   **YIELD:** 4 SERVINGS

When there's a nip in the air, come in from the cold and warm up with a relaxing glass of spiced wine.

Taste of Home Test Kitchen

- 1 bottle (750 milliliters) dry red wine
- 1/2 cup Mulling Spices

In a small saucepan, heat wine and Mulling Spices. Strain through a fine mesh strainer. Serve warm.

Mulled Apple Cider: Substitute 3 cups apple cider for the red wine. Decrease Mulling Spices to 1/4 cup.

Winter Flavors

Unlike other homemade mulling spices, there are no whole spices or sticks in this blend. That makes our Mulling Spices great not only for beverages, but also for seasoning pancakes, oatmeal, French toast, baked items and more.

Chocolate-Dipped Apricot Fruitcakes

PREP: 1 HOUR **BAKE:** 45 MIN. + STANDING
YIELD: 4 DOZEN

Here's a hint: Don't call this fruitcake when you serve it. Even people who think they don't like fruitcake will be delighted with these dipped cake squares! The cakes are moist and packed with apricots, dates, raisins, nuts and chocolate.

Jackie Jegla ★ Sanford, Michigan

- 4 cups dried apricots, chopped
- 4 cups coarsely chopped pecans
- 3 cups chopped dates
- 1-1/2 cups golden raisins
- 2 cups all-purpose flour, *divided*
- 1 cup butter, softened
- 1-1/4 cups packed brown sugar
- 5 eggs
- 1/2 cup apricot nectar
- 1/2 cup honey
- 1/4 cup half-and-half cream
- 1 tablespoon lemon juice
- 1 teaspoon baking powder
- 1 teaspoon ground cinnamon
- 1/2 teaspoon salt
- 1/2 teaspoon ground allspice
- 12 ounces white baking chocolate, chopped
- 12 ounces semisweet chocolate, chopped
- Additional melted white and semisweet chocolate and pecan halves, optional

Grease and flour two 13-in. x 9-in. baking pans. Line the bottoms with waxed paper; set aside. Combine the apricots, pecans, dates, raisins and 1/2 cup flour; set aside.

In a large bowl, cream butter and brown sugar until light and fluffy. Add the eggs, one at a time, beating well after each addition. Add the apricot nectar, honey, cream and lemon juice; beat well (mixture will appear curdled).

Combine baking powder, cinnamon, salt, allspice and remaining flour; add to the creamed mixture and mix well. Add apricot mixture and stir well (batter will be very thick).

Pour into prepared pans. Bake at 275° for 45-50 minutes or until a toothpick inserted near the center comes out clean. Cool for 10 minutes before removing from pans to wire racks to cool completely. Set aside one cake for Apricot Fruitcake Trifle. Cut remaining cake into 48 squares.

In a microwave, melt white chocolate; stir until smooth. Dip half of the cake squares into melted white chocolate; allow excess to drip off. Place on waxed paper; let stand until set. Repeat with semisweet chocolate and remaining cake squares.

Garnish with pecans if desired and drizzle with leftover chocolate. Let stand until set. Store in an airtight container.

Apricot Fruitcake Trifle

PREP: 30 MIN. + CHILLING **YIELD:** 12 SERVINGS

A layer of scrumptious, satiny custard plus cake studded with apricots and dates add up to one great seasonal trifle!

Taste of Home Test Kitchen

- 1 Apricot Fruitcake, cubed
- 1/2 cup apricot brandy
- 1/3 cup sugar
- 3 tablespoons all-purpose flour
- 1/4 teaspoon salt
- 2-1/2 cups heavy whipping cream
- 5 egg yolks, beaten
- 3 tablespoons butter, cubed
- 1-1/2 teaspoons vanilla extract
- 3/4 teaspoon ground cinnamon
- 1 cup apricot preserves
- 1/2 cup chopped pecans, toasted

WHIPPED CREAM:
- 2-1/4 cups heavy whipping cream
- 1/4 cup confectioners' sugar
- 1/2 teaspoon vanilla extract
- Additional toasted chopped pecans

Place cake cubes in a large bowl. Drizzle with brandy; toss to coat.

In a small saucepan, combine the sugar, flour and salt. Gradually stir in cream until blended. Bring to a boil; cook and stir for 2 minutes or until thickened and bubbly. Remove from the heat. Stir a small amount of hot mixture into egg yolks. Return all to pan; bring to a gentle boil, stirring constantly. Remove from the heat. Stir in butter, vanilla and cinnamon. Cool completely.

In a small bowl, combine the preserves and pecans; set aside. For whipped cream, in a large bowl, beat cream until soft peaks form. Add confectioners' sugar and vanilla; beat until stiff peaks form.

In a 4-qt. trifle bowl or glass serving bowl, layer a third of the cake cubes, custard, pecan mixture and whipped cream. Repeat twice. Garnish with additional pecans. Cover and refrigerate for at least 1 hour before serving.

Fruity Treats

The unique recipe for Chocolate-Dipped Apricot Fruitcake yields two cakes. Turn one into the bite-sized treats, and use the other for the luscious trifle. With the dried apricot and dates, this recipe does not seem like a traditional fruitcake.

Moroccan Tapenade

PREP/TOTAL TIME: 25 MIN.　**YIELD:** 4 CUPS

The sweet-salty taste of olives paired with figs is an inspired combination! Set out my full-flavored tapenade on your holiday appetizer table and serve with crackers.

Julie Merriman ★ Cold Brook, New York

10	ounces dried figs
3/4	cup tequila
2	cups pimiento-stuffed olives
1	cup pitted Greek olives
1/2	cup pickled hot cherry peppers, seeded and quartered
2	shallots, finely chopped
3	tablespoons fresh lime juice
2	tablespoons olive oil
2	tablespoons minced fresh basil
2	teaspoons ground cumin
2	teaspoons ground coriander
1-1/2	teaspoons grated lime peel

Assorted crackers

Place figs in a food processor; cover and pulse until coarsely chopped. Place in a small bowl; add tequila. Let stand for 10 minutes.

Meanwhile, combine the olives, peppers and shallots in a food processor; cover and pulse until coarsely chopped. Transfer to a large bowl. Stir in the lime juice, olive oil, basil, cumin, coriander and lime peel. Drain figs, pressing to remove liquid. Add figs to the olive mixture. Serve with assorted crackers.

Tapenade-Prosciutto Flatbread Pizza Bites

PREP/TOTAL TIME: 25 MIN.　**YIELD:** 16 WEDGES

I love this flatbread pizza because it combines so many distinctive flavors and textures. You can serve it as an appetizer or even a light lunch.

Julie Merriman ★ Cold Brook, New York

2	tablespoons olive oil
4	whole pita breads
2	packages (4 ounces *each*) herbed fresh goat cheese
4	ounces thinly sliced prosciutto
2	cups Moroccan Tapenade
2	tablespoons thinly sliced fresh basil

Spread oil over both sides of each pita bread. Place on a griddle. Cook over low heat for 2-4 minutes on each side or until golden brown and crispy.

Spread with goat cheese; top with prosciutto. Spread each with 1/2 cup tapenade; sprinkle with basil. Cut into four wedges. Serve immediately.

Tart, Salty Accent

Tapenade is a French invention, but the olive mixture has taken off with hundreds of interpretations. Moroccan Tapenade is great by itself, but it can also be used as a condiment for roasted meats, as a spread for muffalettas and other sandwiches, or as the "sauce" for mini pizzas as shown here.

3   teaspoons grated lemon peel
1/4 teaspoon salt
1/4 teaspoon pepper

Place vegetables and garlic in a large bowl; drizzle with 2 tablespoons oil. Toss well. Place in a single layer in two 15-in. x 10-in. x 1-in. baking pans coated with cooking spray.

Bake, uncovered, at 425° for 20-25 minutes or until tender, stirring occasionally.

Meanwhile, in a small bowl, combine the cheese, basil if desired, parsley, lemon juice, lemon peel, salt, pepper and remaining oil. Transfer vegetables to a large serving bowl. Add Parmesan mixture; toss to coat.

Roasted Vegetable Risotto

PREP: 10 MIN.   **COOK:** 30 MIN.   **YIELD:** 5 SERVINGS

Risotto may seem like an indulgence, but this one is easy to make and the creamy taste is restaurant-quality. The roasted vegetables add color and wonderful flavor to this rich dish.

Erin Breed ★ Cary, North Carolina

3   cups chicken stock
3   garlic cloves, minced
3   tablespoons butter
1   cup uncooked arborio rice
1/4 teaspoon pepper
1/4 cup white wine
2   cups Roasted Green Vegetable Medley
2   tablespoons grated Parmesan cheese

In a large saucepan, heat stock and keep warm. In a large nonstick skillet coated with cooking spray, saute the garlic in butter for 2-3 minutes or until tender. Add the rice and pepper; cook and stir for 2-3 minutes. Reduce heat; stir in wine. Cook and stir until all of the liquid is absorbed.

Add heated broth, 1/2 cup at a time, stirring constantly. Allow the liquid to absorb between additions. Cook just until risotto is creamy and rice is almost tender. (Cooking time is about 20 minutes.) Add the vegetables; cook and stir until heated through. Sprinkle with Parmesan cheese. Serve immediately.

Roasted Green Vegetable Medley

PREP: 20 MIN.   **BAKE:** 20 MIN.   **YIELD:** 13 SERVINGS

I have cooked a lot of things—from family favorites to gourmet, but I'd never roasted vegetables as a side until recently. Now, it's my preferred way to cook them! I've adapted this recipe to use my favorites, but almost any veggie blend can be prepared this way.

Suzan Crouch ★ Grand Prairie, Texas

2   cups fresh broccoli florets
1   pound thin fresh green beans, trimmed and cut into 2-inch pieces
10   small fresh mushrooms, halved
8   fresh Brussels sprouts
2   medium carrots, cut into 1/4-inch slices
1   medium onion, cut into 1/4-inch slices
3   to 5 garlic cloves, peeled and thinly sliced
4   tablespoons olive oil, *divided*
1/2 cup grated Parmesan cheese
3   tablespoons fresh basil leaves, cut into thin strips, optional
2   tablespoons minced fresh parsley
2   tablespoons lemon juice

Vegetable Duo

Don't worry about having leftover roasted veggies. They can be turned into a delicious side with rice and a handful of ingredients...very yummy!

Almost HOMEMADE

Almost Homemade

With the hustle and bustle of the holidays, it can be tough to find time to prepare a meal that truly celebrates the spirit of the season. With the simple sensations found here, however, whipping up an impressive menu is a snap. Each recipe relies on a convenience item that's dressed up with everyday ingredients for a specialty that tastes homemade. Go ahead and serve them all...we'll keep your secret!

Three-Bean Chili with Polenta Crust

PREP: 30 MIN. **BAKE:** 30 MIN. **YIELD:** 6 SERVINGS

Easy to assemble, this zesty one-dish meal is ideal for a busy weeknight. You can dial down the heat a bit by using a Mexican seasoning blend instead of the chili seasoning.

Gilda Lester ★ Millsboro, Delaware

- 1 large onion, chopped
- 1 medium green pepper, chopped
- 2 tablespoons olive oil
- 3 garlic cloves, chopped
- 1 envelope chili seasoning
- 1 tablespoon brown sugar
- 1/4 teaspoon ground allspice
- 1 can (15 ounces) pinto beans, rinsed and drained
- 1 can (15 ounces) black beans, rinsed and drained
- 1 can (15 ounces) white kidney *or* cannellini beans, rinsed and drained
- 1 can (14-1/2 ounces) reduced-sodium chicken broth
- 1 can (10 ounces) diced tomatoes and green chilies, undrained
- 1 tube (1 pound) polenta, cut into thin slices
- 1 cup (4 ounces) shredded pepper jack cheese

In a large skillet, saute onion and pepper in oil until tender. Add garlic, chili seasoning, brown sugar and allspice; cook 1 minute longer. Stir in beans, broth and tomatoes. Bring to a boil. Reduce heat; simmer, uncovered, for 15 minutes.

Transfer to an ungreased 11-in. x 7-in. baking dish (dish will be full). Place dish on a baking sheet. Arrange polenta slices over top; sprinkle with cheese.

Bake, uncovered, at 375° for 30-35 minutes or until bubbly.

Spinach-Stuffed Onions

PREP: 30 MIN. **BAKE:** 50 MIN. **YIELD:** 4 SERVINGS

Take frozen spinach souffle to a new level by stuffing it into onion shells. The onions make a wonderful side for roasts and other meaty entrees.

Kathann Koehler ★ Loveland, Ohio

  4 medium sweet onions
  1 package (12 ounces) frozen spinach souffle, thawed
1/2 cup plus 4 teaspoons shredded Swiss cheese, *divided*
1/4 teaspoon salt
1/8 teaspoon ground nutmeg
  1 tablespoon butter, melted

Peel onions. Cut a 1/2-in. slice from the top of each onion; remove center with a melon baller, leaving 1/2-in. shells. Chop enough of the removed onion to measure 1 tablespoon. (Discard remaining onion or save for another use.)

Place onion shells in a Dutch oven and cover with water. Bring to a boil. Reduce heat; cook, uncovered, for 8-10 minutes or until tender. Drain.

In a small bowl, combine the spinach souffle, 1/2 cup cheese, salt, nutmeg and chopped onion. Brush the onion centers with butter. Fill with spinach mixture. Place on a baking sheet.

Bake, uncovered, at 375° for 45-50 minutes or until souffle is puffed and set. Sprinkle with remaining cheese; bake 5 minutes longer or until cheese is melted.

Banana Cream Cake Trifle

PREP: 30 MIN. + CHILLING **YIELD:** 20 SERVINGS

Whether they're young or young at heart, every guest at your table will love this fun, retro dessert! As an added convenience, you can make it in advance.

Korina Ireland ★ Little Rock, Arkansas

    1 package (15 ounces) cream-filled sponge cakes
    5 large ripe bananas, sliced
  1/2 cup orange juice
    1 package (8 ounces) cream cheese, softened
    2 tablespoons sugar
    1 can (20 ounces) crushed pineapple, undrained
1-1/4 cups cold milk
    1 package (3.4 ounces) instant vanilla pudding mix
    4 cups whipped topping, *divided*
    1 pint fresh strawberries, thinly sliced
Additional sliced bananas and strawberries
Fresh mint, optional

Slice each cake widthwise into eight slices; set aside. Place bananas and orange juice in a bowl; gently stir to coat. In a large bowl, beat cream cheese and sugar until smooth. Add the pineapple, milk and pudding mix; beat on low speed until blended. Fold in 1-1/2 cups whipped topping.

Line bottom and sides of a 4-qt. glass trifle bowl with half of the cake slices. Arrange a third of the banana slices and strawberries against the sides of bowl. Carefully spoon half of the pudding mixture into the bowl. Arrange half of the remaining bananas and strawberries around bowl. Add the remaining cake, bananas, strawberries and pudding in the center of bowl.

Cover and refrigerate for 4 hours or overnight. Before serving, spread with the remaining whipped topping. Garnish with additional bananas, strawberries and mint.

Brie Tartlets with Caramelized Balsamic Onion Marmalade

PREP: 45 MIN. **BAKE:** 10 MIN. **YIELD:** 2-1/2 DOZEN

These elegant, bite-sized tarts combine sweet caramelized onions with creamy Brie to create a simple yet sophisticated appetizer—perfect for your next party.

Erin Chilcoat ★ Smithtown, New York

  4 cups thinly sliced onions
  2 tablespoons butter
1/4 cup packed brown sugar
  1 tablespoon balsamic vinegar
  2 garlic cloves, minced
1/4 teaspoon salt
Dash pepper
  2 packages (1.9 ounces *each*) frozen miniature phyllo tart shells
  1 round (8 ounces) Brie cheese, cut into 30 pieces
Toasted slivered almonds, optional

In a large skillet, saute onions in butter until softened. Add brown sugar, vinegar and garlic. Reduce heat to medium-low; cook, stirring occasionally, for 35-40 minutes or until deep golden brown. Stir in salt and pepper.

Place tart shells on an ungreased baking sheet. Place one piece of cheese in each; top with onion mixture.

Bake at 350° for 8-10 minutes or until lightly browned. Sprinkle with almonds if desired. Serve warm.

TO MAKE AHEAD: The caramelized onion marmalade may be made up to a week in advance. Store covered in the refrigerator.

Wild Rice and Mushroom Soup

PREP: 10 MIN.   **COOK:** 30 MIN.
YIELD: 8 SERVINGS (2 QUARTS)

Frequently requested at family get-togethers, this rich and hearty soup is ready in a flash. Cooking for a vegetarian? Swap in vegetable stock for the beef broth.

Danielle Noble ★ Ft. Thomas, Kentucky

- 1 pound baby portobello mushrooms, chopped
- 2 tablespoons olive oil
- 2 packages (6 ounces *each*) long grain and wild rice mix
- 1 carton (32 ounces) reduced-sodium beef broth
- 1/2 cup water
- 2 cups heavy whipping cream

In a Dutch oven, saute mushrooms in oil until tender. Add the rice, contents of seasoning packet, broth and water. Bring to a boil. Reduce heat; cover and simmer for 25 minutes. Add cream and heat through.

Teriyaki-Portobello Pork Loin

PREP: 25 MIN.   **COOK:** 6 HOURS   **YIELD:** 8 SERVINGS

My family loves my teriyaki pork roast and begs for more! The slow cooker does most of the work, and when I get home from school, the whole house smells wonderful. Since I serve it with instant rice and frozen vegetables, I'm only five minutes from sitting down to a home-cooked meal.

Lori Harris ★ Montgomery City, Missouri

- 1 boneless pork loin roast (3 to 4 pounds)
- 1/2 cup all-purpose flour
- 1 teaspoon Montreal steak seasoning
- 2 tablespoons olive oil, *divided*
- 2 cups sliced baby portobello mushrooms
- 1 medium onion, thinly sliced
- 1 cup water
- 1 cup reduced-sodium teriyaki sauce
- 1 envelope (3/4 ounce) mushroom gravy mix
- 2 tablespoons cornstarch
- 2 tablespoons cold water
  Hot cooked rice

Cut roast in half. In a large resealable plastic bag, combine flour and steak seasoning. Add pork, one portion at a time, and shake to coat.

In a large skillet, brown roast in 1 tablespoon oil on all sides. Transfer meat and drippings to a 4-qt slow cooker. In the same skillet, saute mushrooms and onion in remaining oil until tender; add to slow cooker.

In a small bowl, combine the water, teriyaki sauce and gravy mix; pour over top. Cover and cook on low for 6-8 hours or until pork is tender.

Remove pork to a serving platter and keep warm. Skim fat from cooking juices; transfer to a large saucepan. Bring liquid to a boil. Combine cornstarch and cold water until smooth; gradually stirring into the pan. Bring to a boil; cook and stir for 2 minutes or until thickened. Serve with the pork and rice.

Simple Turtle Cheesecake

PREP/TOTAL TIME: 25 MIN.   **YIELD:** 8 SERVINGS

Need a dessert in minutes? Dress up a store-bought cheesecake with homemade ganache and caramel. It's so simple and yet so special!

Laura McDowell ★ Lake Villa, Illinois

- 1/2 cup semisweet chocolate chips
- 1/2 cup heavy whipping cream, *divided*
- 1 frozen New York-style cheesecake (30 ounces), thawed
- 3 tablespoons chopped pecans, toasted
- 1/4 cup butter, cubed
- 1/2 cup plus 2 tablespoons packed brown sugar
- 1 tablespoon light corn syrup

Place chocolate chips in a small bowl. In a small saucepan, bring 1/4 cup cream just to a boil. Pour over chips; whisk until smooth. Cool slightly, stirring occasionally. Pour over cheesecake. Sprinkle chopped pecans over top. Refrigerate until set.

Melt butter in a small saucepan. Stir in brown sugar and corn syrup. Bring to a boil. Reduce heat; cook until sugar is dissolved, about 1 minute. Stir in the remaining cream and return to a boil. Remove from the heat. Drizzle over top of cheesecake and serve extra sauce on the side.

Supreme Green Vegetable Bake

PREP: 15 MIN.　**BAKE:** 20 MIN.　**YIELD:** 8 SERVINGS

My grandmother passed this recipe down to me. She also offered comments on different ways to prepare it, "so as not to become bored with the same old dish over and over." She was a great inspiration for my love of baking and cooking.

Priscilla Gilbert ★ Indian Harbour Beach, Florida

- 3　eggs, lightly beaten
- 1　can (10-3/4 ounces) condensed cream of mushroom soup, undiluted
- 1/3　cup mayonnaise
- 1-1/2　cups shredded reduced-fat cheddar cheese
- 1　small onion, finely chopped
- 6　cups frozen chopped broccoli, thawed and patted dry
- 1　package (10 ounces) frozen chopped spinach, thawed and squeezed dry
- 1　cup French-fried onions

In a large bowl, combine the first five ingredients. Fold in broccoli and spinach. Transfer to a greased 13-in. x 9-in. baking dish. Sprinkle with French-fried onions.

Bake, uncovered, at 350° for 20-25 minutes or until a thermometer inserted near the center reads 160° and top is lightly browned.

Editor's Note: To change up this vegetable bake, use a different condensed soup like cream of celery or corn, try Swiss, pepper jack or mozzeralla for the cheese and top with buttered bread crumbs, cracker crumbs or crushed cornflakes.

Rosemary Beet Phyllo Bites

PREP/TOTAL TIME: 25 MIN.　**YIELD:** 6 DOZEN

Deep red beets definitely bring a splash of festive color to any appetizer buffet, and the mild rosemary flavor of these appetizers accents the peppery bite of the arugula and the sweet-sour flavor of the pickled vegetables.

Taste of Home Test Kitchen

- 1　jar (16 ounces) pickled whole beets, drained and chopped
- 1　tablespoon olive oil
- 2　teaspoons minced fresh rosemary
- 1　teaspoon grated orange peel
- 2　cups fresh arugula
- 72　frozen miniature phyllo tart shells
- 3/4　cup crumbled feta cheese

Pat beets dry with paper towels; place in a small bowl. Add the olive oil, rosemary and orange peel; toss to combine.

Divide arugula among tart shells; top with beet mixture. Sprinkle with feta cheese.

Avoiding Beet Stains

Beets not only bring a festive red color to foods, but can also cause an unwanted red color to cutting boards, countertops, sinks and hands. Disposable gloves will prevent your hands from acquiring a red stain. Wash off cutting boards, countertops and sinks immediately after use to prevent staining.

Cranberry-Walnut Upside-Down Apple Pie

PREP: 70 MIN. + COOLING **BROIL:** 5 MIN.
YIELD: 8 SERVINGS

No one will ever guess this gooey treat wasn't made from scratch. The foil pie pan makes it easy to transfer the pie to a serving plate for a company-worthy presentation.

Susan Scarborough ★ Fernandina Beach, Florida

- 1 package (37 ounces) frozen apple pie
- 2 tablespoons butter
- 1/2 cup packed brown sugar
- 1/4 cup heavy whipping cream
- 3 tablespoons maple syrup
- 1/3 cup coarsely chopped dried cranberries
- 1/3 cup coarsely chopped walnuts
- 2 teaspoons minced fresh rosemary

Vanilla ice cream

Bake pie according to package directions. Cool on wire rack for 30 minutes or until warm.

Invert pie onto an ovenproof serving plate or foil-lined baking pan. Meanwhile, in a small saucepan, melt butter. Add the brown sugar, cream and syrup; cook and stir until smooth. Stir in the cranberries, walnuts and rosemary; pour over inverted pie.

Broil 6 in. from the heat for 2-4 minutes or until bubbly and walnuts begin to brown. Serve warm with ice cream if desired.

Chicken & Cheese Tortellini Alfredo

PREP: 15 MIN.   **COOK:** 25 MIN.   **YIELD:** 8 SERVINGS

I first tasted the wonderful combination of Alfredo sauce and pesto at a restaurant, and that inspired me to add all kinds of different flavors to Alfredo sauce. The basil pesto is still my favorite, and I've used that combination in this amazing dinner. Let your company be impressed, and don't tell them how easy it was to make!

Kelly Williams ★ Forked River, New Jersey

1/2   pound sliced fresh mushrooms
1   small sweet red pepper, julienned
1   tablespoon olive oil
1   tablespoon butter
1   teaspoon minced garlic
2   packages (9 ounces *each*) refrigerated cheese tortellini
1   jar (15 ounces) Alfredo sauce
1/4   cup prepared pesto
2   packages (10 ounces *each*) ready-to-use grilled chicken breast strips
1   jar (7-1/2 ounces) marinated quartered artichoke hearts, drained and coarsely chopped
1   can (2-1/4 ounces) sliced ripe olives, drained
1   medium tomato, seeded and chopped
Grated Parmesan cheese, optional

In a large skillet, saute the mushrooms and red pepper in oil and butter until tender. Add the garlic; cook 1 minute longer.

Cook the tortellini according to package directions. Meanwhile, in a Dutch oven over medium heat, combine the Alfredo sauce and pesto. Stir in the chicken, artichokes and olives. Cook over medium heat until heated through.

Drain tortellini; add to chicken mixture with tomato. Gently toss to coat. Garnish with the Parmesan cheese if desired.

Doughnut Bread Pudding with Brandy Cream Sauce

PREP: 15 MIN.   **BAKE:** 35 MIN.   **YIELD:** 12 SERVINGS

Here's a fun and super-easy bread pudding for holiday entertaining. It takes just 15 minutes to prep; let it bake while you enjoy dinner. The fail-proof sauce is delightful!

Taste of Home Test Kitchen

12	plain cake doughnuts
1/2	cup chopped pecans
4	eggs
2-1/2	cups 2% milk
2-1/2	cups vanilla ice cream, melted, *divided*
1/4	cup sugar
1	cup dried cranberries
2	tablespoons brandy

Arrange doughnuts in a greased 13-in. x 9-in. baking dish; sprinkle with pecans. Whisk the eggs, milk, 1-1/2 cups ice cream and sugar; pour over the doughnuts. Let stand for 10 minutes or until liquid is absorbed.

Bake, uncovered, at 350° for 30 minutes; sprinkle with cranberries. Bake 10-15 minutes longer or until a knife inserted near the center comes out clean.

Just before serving, combine brandy and remaining ice cream. Serve with warm bread pudding.

Cheddar Hash Brown Casserole

PREP: 10 MIN.   **BAKE:** 45 MIN.   **YIELD:** 12 SERVINGS

My hash brown bake is so popular at family events that I always double the recipe. If you're serving it at brunch, add diced ham for an added boost of protein.

Jann Willard ★ West Salem, Wisconsin

3	cans (10-3/4 ounces *each*) condensed cream of potato soup, undiluted
1	cup (8 ounces) sour cream
1/4	cup chopped onion
1/2	teaspoon garlic salt
1	package (30 ounces) frozen shredded hash brown potatoes, thawed
2	cups (8 ounces) shredded cheddar cheese
1/2	cup grated Parmesan cheese

In a large bowl, combine the soup, sour cream, onion and garlic salt. Stir in potatoes and cheddar cheese. Transfer to a greased 13-in. x 9-in. baking dish. Sprinkle with the Parmesan cheese.

Bake, uncovered, at 350° for 45-50 minutes or until golden brown.

Wine Bottle Candleholders

You can shed a little light on boring holiday centerpieces with this no-fuss idea that takes advantage of items you likely already have on hand.

Gather a few empty wine bottles of varying heights and colors. Soak the bottles in warm sudsy water to remove labels, then wash. Let dry completely. For each bottle, cut the bottom off of a tapered candle until it is your desired height. Trim excess off the perimeter of the candle base until it fits snugly into the bottle top. With a lighter or match, heat the end of the candle until the wax is soft then insert the candle into the bottle top firmly. Light the candle, allowing wax to drip onto the bottle top.

Portobello Gnocchi Salad

PREP/TOTAL TIME: 25 MIN.   **YIELD:** 14 SERVINGS

Pan sauteing the gnocchi eliminates the need to boil it, while creating a wonderfully tasty, crispy coating. The baby bellas lend a rustic earthiness to this Italian-influenced salad.

Fran Fehling ★ Staten Island, New York

- 1 package (16 ounces) potato gnocchi
- 2 tablespoons plus 1/3 cup olive oil, *divided*
- 1/2 pound sliced baby portobello mushrooms
- 3 teaspoons lemon juice
- 3 large plum tomatoes, seeded and chopped
- 1 can (15 ounces) garbanzo beans *or* chickpeas, rinsed and drained
- 1 package (5 ounces) fresh baby arugula *or* fresh baby spinach, coarsely chopped
- 1/2 cup pitted Greek olives, cut in half
- 1/3 cup minced fresh parsley
- 2 tablespoons capers, drained and chopped
- 2 teaspoons grated lemon peel
- 1/2 teaspoon salt
- 1/4 teaspoon coarsely ground pepper
- 1/2 cup crumbled feta cheese
- 1/4 cup chopped walnuts, toasted

In large nonstick skillet over medium-high heat, cook gnocchi in 1 tablespoon oil for 6-8 minutes or until lightly browned, turning once. Remove from the skillet; cool slightly.

In the same skillet, saute mushrooms in 1 tablespoon oil until tender. Place mushrooms and gnocchi in a serving bowl. Add lemon juice and the remaining oil; gently toss to coat.

Add the tomatoes, garbanzo beans, arugula, olives, parsley, capers, lemon peel, salt and pepper; toss to combine. Garnish with cheese and walnuts.

Cranberry-Pistachio Sticky Buns

PREP: 20 MIN. + RISING   **BAKE:** 30 MIN.   **YIELD:** 2 DOZEN

Looking for a fantastic brunch item? Then try these ooey-gooey sticky buns. They use frozen yeast roll dough and couldn't be simpler to make. Let them rise overnight in the refrigerator, then pop them in the oven the next morning.

Athena Russell ★ Florence, South Carolina

- 1 cup chopped pistachios
- 1/2 cup dried cranberries
- 1 teaspoon ground cinnamon
- 24 frozen bread dough dinner rolls, thawed
- 1/2 cup butter, cubed
- 1 cup packed brown sugar
- 1 package (4.6 ounces) cook-and-serve vanilla pudding mix
- 2 tablespoons 2% milk
- 1/2 teaspoon orange extract

Sprinkle the pistachios, cranberries and cinnamon in a greased 13-in. x 9-in. baking dish. Arrange rolls in a single layer on top.

In a small saucepan over low heat, melt butter. Remove from the heat; stir in the brown sugar, pudding mix, milk and extract until smooth. Pour over dough. Cover and refrigerate overnight.

Remove from the refrigerator 30 minutes before baking. Bake at 350° for 30-35 minutes or until golden brown. (Cover loosely with foil if top browns too quickly.) Cool for 1 minute before inverting onto a serving platter.

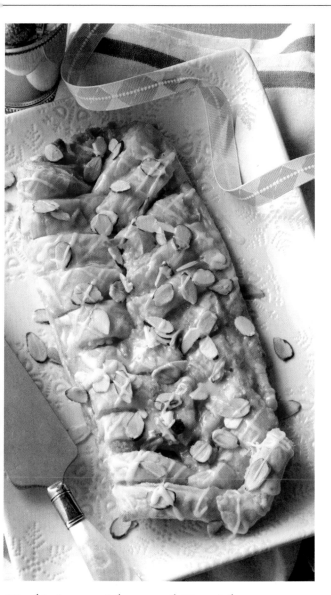

GLAZE:
- 3/4   cup plus 1 tablespoon confectioners' sugar
- 2   tablespoons 2% milk
- 1/2   teaspoon almond extract
- 1/4   cup sliced almonds, toasted

Place the almond paste, butter and sugar in a food processor; cover and pulse until chopped. Add egg and flour; process until smooth.

Unfold puff pastry sheets onto a greased baking sheet. Spread half of the filling mixture down the center third of one pastry sheet. On each side, cut eight strips about 3-1/2 in. into the center. Starting at one end, fold alternating strips at an angle across the filling. Pinch ends to seal. Repeat with remaining pastry and filling. Bake at 375° for 30-35 minutes or until golden brown. Remove to a wire rack.

Combine the confectioners' sugar, milk, and almond extract. Drizzle over braids; sprinkle with almonds. Cut into slices.

Braiding a Filled Bread

Cut strips on each side as recipe directs. Then, starting at one end, fold alternating strips at an angle across the filling. Pinch the ends to seal.

Delicious Almond Braids

PREP: 25 MIN.   **BAKE:** 30 MIN. + COOLING
YIELD: 2 BRAIDS (6 SLICES EACH)

This light, flaky coffeecake is very similar to an almond crescent, and it's so versatile, you could serve it for breakfast, brunch or even dessert. Packaged puff pastry makes it easy, but it tastes like it was prepared at a bakery!

Gina Idone ★ Staten Island, New York

- 1   package (7 ounces) almond paste
- 1/2   cup butter
- 1/2   cup sugar
- 1   egg
- 2   tablespoons all-purpose flour
- 1   package (17.3 ounces) frozen puff pastry, thawed

Buffalo Macaroni and Cheese Bites

PREP: 45 MIN. + CHILLING   **BAKE:** 15 MIN.   **YIELD:** 2 DOZEN

This is one incredible vegetarian buffalo-style appetizer! I give macaroni and cheese a hearty shot of Louisiana-style hot sauce and a savory breading, then bake it and serve with blue cheese dressing. They're guaranteed to disappear.

Ann Donnay ★ Milton, Massachusetts

- 1   package (7-1/4 ounces) macaroni and cheese dinner mix
- 6   cups water
- 2   tablespoons 2% milk
- 1   tablespoon butter
- 1/4 cup Louisiana-style hot sauce
- 1   cup all-purpose flour
- 1   egg, beaten
- 1   can (6 ounces) French-fried onions, crushed
- Blue cheese salad dressing

Set the cheese packet from dinner mix aside. In a large saucepan, bring water to a boil. Add macaroni; cook for 8-10 minutes or until tender. Drain. Stir in the contents of the cheese packet, milk and butter.

Press 2 tablespoonfuls into greased miniature muffin cups. Cover and refrigerate for 3 hours or overnight.

Place the hot sauce, flour, egg and onions in separate shallow bowls. Remove macaroni bites from cups. Dip in the hot sauce and flour, then coat with egg and onions. Place 2 in. apart on a lightly greased baking sheet.

Bake at 400° for 12-15 minutes or until golden brown. Serve with dressing.

Beef Tips with Horseradish Gravy

PREP/TOTAL TIME: 25 MIN. **YIELD:** 4 SERVINGS

No one will ever guess that you spent only 25 minutes making this dinner. The combination of creme fraiche and horseradish gives the purchased beef tips an exceptional flavor. It's definitely special enough for company.

Laura Majchrzak ★ Hunt Valley, Maryland

- 1 package (17 ounces) refrigerated beef tips with gravy
- 1 cup (8 ounces) creme fraiche *or* sour cream
- 2 tablespoons prepared horseradish
- 1/4 teaspoon pepper
- 2 tablespoons minced chives

Hot cooked rice

In a large nonstick skillet, combine the beef tips with gravy, creme fraiche, horseradish and pepper. Cook and stir over medium-low heat until heated through. Sprinkle with chives and serve with rice.

Sun-Dried Tomato Turkey Pinwheels

PREP: 20 MIN. + CHILLING **YIELD:** 40 APPETIZERS

A Mediterranean flair takes simple turkey wraps to new heights in these pretty and so-delicious nibbles.

Taste of Home Test Kitchen

- 2/3 cup sun-dried tomato pesto
- 4 flour tortillas (8 inches)
- 1/2 cup crumbled goat cheese
- 1/3 cup pitted Greek olives, chopped

- 1/4 cup minced fresh basil
- 8 slices deli turkey
- 1 cup fresh baby spinach

Spread pesto over tortillas. Sprinkle each with cheese, olives and basil; layer with turkey and spinach. Roll up tightly and wrap in plastic wrap. Refrigerate for at least 2 hours.

Unwrap and cut each into 10 slices.

Chocolate-Raspberry Angel Food Torte

PREP/TOTAL TIME: 20 MIN. **YIELD:** 12 SERVINGS

Here's a classic angel food cake dressed up in its Christmas best. This no-fuss torte tastes as impressive as it looks.

Lisa Dorsey ★ Pueblo, Colorado

- 1 prepared angel food cake (8 to 10 ounces)
- 1-1/2 cups heavy whipping cream
- 1/4 cup confectioners' sugar
- 1/4 cup baking cocoa
- 1 jar (12 ounces) seedless raspberry jam

Fresh raspberries and mint leaves

Split cake horizontally into four layers. In a large bowl, beat the cream, confectioners' sugar and cocoa until stiff peaks form.

To assemble, place one cake layer on a serving plate; spread with a third of the raspberry jam. Repeat layers twice. Top with remaining cake layer. Spread frosting over top and sides of cake. Chill until serving. Just before serving, garnish with raspberries and mint leaves.

Antipasto Basilico Pizza

PREP/TOTAL TIME: 30 MIN. **YIELD:** 8 SERVINGS

Personalize frozen pizza with your favorite ingredients for a dish that's a snap to make but looks party-special. Cut into small bites to use for appetizers or into wedges for dinner.

Colleen Sturma ★ Milwaukee, Wisconsin

- 1 frozen cheese pizza (12 inches)
- 3 slices deli ham, julienned
- 2 ounces thinly sliced hard salami, julienned
- 1/3 cup chopped roasted sweet red peppers
- 1/3 cup marinated quartered artichoke hearts, drained
- 1/4 cup pitted Greek olives, halved
- 1/4 cup shaved Parmesan cheese
- 1/4 cup minced fresh basil

Place pizza on an ungreased 12-in. pizza pan. Top with ham, salami, peppers, artichoke hearts and olives.

Bake at 450° for 10-12 minutes or until cheese is melted. Sprinkle with Parmesan cheese and basil.

Caramel Apple Crepes

PREP/TOTAL TIME: 25 MIN. **YIELD:** 10 SERVINGS

Start with store-bought crepes, fill them with a rich, cream cheese mixture, then serve with caramelized apples for this mouthwatering dessert or brunch item.

Diane Nemitz ★ Ludington, Michigan

- 1/4 cup butter, cubed
- 1/4 cup packed dark brown sugar
- 2 tablespoons plus 1/4 cup maple syrup, *divided*
- 6 large tart apples, peeled and sliced
- 1 package (8 ounces) cream cheese, softened
- 1/2 teaspoon ground cinnamon
- 12 prepared crepes (9 inches), warmed
  Cinnamon-sugar

In a large skillet over medium heat, melt butter. Add brown sugar and 2 tablespoons syrup; cook and stir over medium heat until sugar is dissolved. Add apples; cook until apples are tender.

In a small bowl, beat the cream cheese, cinnamon and remaining syrup until smooth. Spread over the crepes. Fold crepes into quarters and serve with apple mixture. Sprinkle with cinnamon-sugar.

Artichoke-Spinach Pinwheels

PREP: 20 MIN. + CHILLING **BAKE:** 20 MIN.
YIELD: 2 DOZEN

This is my type of holiday recipe! You can assemble the unbaked pinwheels, freeze, then bake them directly from the freezer whenever you need a treat. Talk about convenience!

Donna Lindecamp ★ Morganton, North Carolina

- 1 can (14 ounces) water-packed artichoke hearts, rinsed, drained and chopped
- 1 package (10 ounces) frozen chopped spinach, thawed and squeezed dry
- 1/2 cup grated Parmesan cheese
- 1/2 cup mayonnaise
- 1/2 teaspoon onion powder
- 1/2 teaspoon garlic powder
- 1/2 teaspoon pepper
- 1 package (17.3 ounces) frozen puff pastry, thawed

In a small bowl, combine the first seven ingredients. Unfold puff pastry. Spread the artichoke mixture over each sheet to within 1/2 in. of edges. Roll up jelly-roll style. Wrap in plastic wrap; freeze for 30 minutes.

Using a serrated knife, cut each roll into 12 slices. Place cut side down on greased baking sheets. Bake at 400° for 18-22 minutes or until golden brown.

TO MAKE AHEAD: Prepare and slice pinwheels as directed. Freeze in a single layer on waxed paper-lined baking sheets. Once frozen, package in freezer bags, separating layers with waxed paper and freeze for up to 1 month. Place frozen pinwheels cut side down on greased baking sheets. Bake at 400° for 20-24 minutes or until golden brown.

Pulled Pork Sandwiches

PREP: 15 MIN.   **COOK:** 7 HOURS   **YIELD:** 6 SERVINGS

Foolproof and wonderfully delicious describes my barbecue pork recipe. Just four ingredients and a slow cooker make a fabulous dish without any effort from you.

Sarah Johnson ★ Chicago, Illinois

- 1   Hormel lemon-garlic pork loin filet (1-1/3 pounds)
- 1   can (12 ounces) Dr. Pepper
- 1   bottle (18 ounces) barbecue sauce
- 6   hamburger buns, split

Place pork in a 3-qt. slow cooker. Pour Dr. Pepper over top. Cover and cook on low for 7-9 hours or until meat is tender.

Remove meat; cool slightly. Discard cooking juices. Shred meat with two forks and return to slow cooker. Stir in barbecue sauce; heat through. Serve on buns.

Bourbon-Glazed Meatballs

PREP: 10 MIN.   **BAKE:** 50 MIN.   **YIELD:** ABOUT 5 DOZEN

A must for any appetizer menu, these mouthwatering meatballs require very little preparation, leaving you plenty of time to finish all those other last-minute party details.

Bob Bratzel ★ Deland, Florida

- 1   package (32 ounces) frozen fully cooked Italian meatballs, thawed
- 1-1/2   cups packed brown sugar
- 1   bottle (12 ounces) chili sauce
- 1/2   cup bourbon
- 1   tablespoon Worcestershire sauce

Place meatballs in a greased 3-qt. baking dish. Combine the remaining ingredients. Pour over meatballs; toss to coat.

Cover and bake at 350° for 50-60 minutes or until heated through.

Cajun Crawfish Sliders

PREP: 25 MIN.   **BAKE:** 10 MIN. + COOLING
YIELD: 4 DOZEN

Add a touch of Southern hospitality to your festivities with our upscale version of a slider. The crawfish gets a touch of spicy goodness from the chipotle mayonnaise and jalapeno.

Taste of Home Test Kitchen

- 1   package (8-1/2 ounces) corn bread/muffin mix
- 1   egg
- 1/3   cup 2% milk
- 3   cups fresh baby spinach, thinly sliced
- 12   ounces frozen cooked crawfish tail meat, thawed and shredded
- 1   cup reduced-fat chipotle mayonnaise
- 48   pickled jalapeno slices

In a large bowl, combine the corn bread mix, egg and milk. Spread into a greased 13-in. x 9-in. baking pan. Bake at 400° for 9-11 minutes or until a toothpick inserted near the center comes out clean. Cool on a wire rack.

Cut corn bread into 1-1/2 in. squares. Top each with spinach, crawfish, mayonnaise and a jalapeno slice.

Editor's Note: 1 cup reduced-fat mayonnaise and 1 tablespoon minced chipotle pepper in adobo sauce may be used for chipotle mayonnaise.

You Say Crawfish, I Say Crayfish

Crawfish, also known as crayfish and crawdads, are a fresh-water crustacean. With their tiny, red claws, they resemble little lobsters.

Perfectly Sized
DESSERTS

Perfectly Sized Desserts

"How big a piece would you like?" is a question heard around dinner tables everywhere when it's time to serve dessert. Now, you can skip the agonizing portion-control issue and dig right into holiday treats with the heavenly creations found here. All the sweets in this chapter yield individual portions, so the size is set! Just put them out and watch everyone's face light up with excitement.

Petite Pear Purses

PREP: 40 MIN. **BAKE:** 15 MIN. **YIELD:** 8 SERVINGS

Little purses shaped from puff pastry make a gorgeous presentation! Each bundle holds a delectable cinnamon-ginger pear filling tucked inside.

Mary Cruz ★ Lancaster, California

- 1/4 cup packed brown sugar
- 2 tablespoons butter
- 2 tablespoons heavy whipping cream
- 1 tablespoon light corn syrup
- 1 cup chopped peeled ripe pear
- 1/2 cup finely chopped dried pineapple
- 1 tablespoon sugar
- 1 teaspoon all-purpose flour
- 1/2 teaspoon ground ginger
- 1/4 teaspoon ground cinnamon
- 1 package (17.3 ounces) frozen puff pastry, thawed
- 1 egg, beaten

In a small heavy saucepan, combine the brown sugar, butter, cream and corn syrup. Cook and stir over medium heat until sugar is dissolved. Bring to a boil. Cook and stir for 1 minute; set aside.

In a large bowl, combine the pear, pineapple, sugar, flour, ginger and cinnamon; stir in caramel mixture.

On a lightly floured surface, unfold puff pastry. Roll each sheet into a 13-in. x 12-in. rectangle. Trim two 1/2-in. strips from a long side of each rectangle. Cut each strip in half widthwise; set aside.

Cut each pastry sheet into four squares; transfer to a parchment paper-lined baking sheet.

Spoon 2 tablespoons pear mixture into the center of each square. Bring two diagonal corners of pastry over filling and pinch together at point. Repeat with remaining two corners; then twist points together to form a purse.

Roll pastry strips into ropes; wrap loosely around the neck of each purse, twisting to secure. Brush with egg. Bake at 400° for 15-18 minutes or until golden brown. Serve warm.

Mocha Mousse with Fresh Raspberries

PREP: 30 MIN. + CHILLING **YIELD:** 6 SERVINGS

Working as a teacher's aide, I don't always have a lot of time to make special treats. I found this recipe which is oh-so simple! It's a favorite cool, refreshing pleasure.

Sandy Zimmerman ★ Pierre, South Dakota

- 4 ounces unsweetened chocolate, chopped
- 1 can (14 ounces) sweetened condensed milk
- 1-1/2 teaspoons vanilla extract
- 1 tablespoon instant coffee granules
- 1 teaspoon hot water
- 2 cups heavy whipping cream
- 2 cups fresh raspberries

In a microwave, melt chocolate; stir until smooth. Transfer to a large bowl; whisk in milk and vanilla. Dissolve coffee granules in hot water. Add to chocolate mixture; beat until smooth. Cover and refrigerate for 15 minutes.

Whip cream until stiff peaks form. Fold 1 cup into chocolate mixture. Set aside the remaining whipped cream and six raspberries.

Spoon 1/4 cup mousse into each of six parfait glasses. Layer each with 2 tablespoons whipped cream, 1/3 cup raspberries and 1/4 cup mousse. Garnish with remaining cream and raspberries. Refrigerate until serving.

Making a Puff Pastry Purse

1. Roll out the dough and cut as recipe directs. Spoon the filling into center of each square. Bring two diagonal corners of pastry over filling and pinch together at point.

2. Repeat with remaining two corners, then twist the points together to form a pouch.

3. Wrap a pastry rope loosely around neck of pouch. Twist to secure. Proceed as recipe directs.

Apple & Cream Meringues

PREP: 30 MIN.   **BAKE:** 50 MIN. + STANDING
YIELD: 8 SERVINGS

An apple pie filling gives my meringues a truly comforting flair. They make an excellent dessert to serve on Christmas as well as Thanksgiving. Whenever I make them, people always ask for seconds…and for the recipe!

Rhonda Braun ★ Land O' Lakes, Florida

- 4 egg whites
- 1 teaspoon vanilla extract
- 1/2 teaspoon cider vinegar
- 1 teaspoon cornstarch
- 1 cup packed brown sugar
- 1-1/4 cups heavy whipping cream
- 1/4 cup confectioners' sugar
- 1 can (21 ounces) apple pie filling

Apple pie spice

Place egg whites in a large bowl; let stand at room temperature for 30 minutes. Using a pencil, draw eight 3-in. circles on a sheet of parchment paper. Place paper, pencil mark down, on a baking sheet; set aside.

Add vanilla and vinegar to egg whites; beat on medium speed until soft peaks form. Beat in cornstarch. Gradually beat in brown sugar, 2 tablespoons at a time, on high until stiff glossy peaks form and sugar is dissolved.

Cut a small hole in the corner of a pastry or plastic bag; insert a #18 star tip. Fill bag with meringue; pipe meringue in a spiral fashion to fill in circles on prepared pan. Pipe twice around the base of each shell in a spiral fashion to make the sides.

Bake at 275° for 50-60 minutes or until set and dry. Turn oven off; leave meringues in oven for 1 hour.

In a large bowl, beat cream until it begins to thicken. Add confectioners' sugar; beat until stiff peaks form. Spoon into meringues. Top with pie filling; sprinkle with pie spice.

TO MAKE AHEAD: Prepare the meringues a few days before. Store in an airtight container.

Tangerine Tuiles with Candied Cranberries

PREP: 2 HOURS + STANDING   **BAKE:** 5 MIN./BATCH
YIELD: 16 SERVINGS

Delicate cookie cups create scrumptious serving bowls for my creamy tangerine mousse. The cranberry syrup makes a colorful and delectable garnish.

Jessie Sarrazin ★ Livingston, Montana

  1 package (12 ounces) fresh cranberries
2-1/2 cups sugar, *divided*
TUILES:
  3 egg whites
3/4 cup confectioners' sugar
1/2 cup all-purpose flour
  6 tablespoons butter, melted
1/2 teaspoon almond extract
1/4 teaspoon salt
TANGERINE CREAM:
  1 carton (8 ounces) mascarpone cheese
1/4 cup honey
  1 tablespoon grated tangerine peel
  2 cups whipped cream
  2 tangerines, peeled, sectioned and chopped

Line a 15-in. x 10-in. x 1-in. baking pan with parchment paper. Place cranberries in pan; sprinkle with 2 cups sugar. Cover and bake at 350° for 1 hour. Cool. Drain, reserving syrup for garnish.

Transfer berries to another parchment paper-lined 15-in. x 10-in. x 1-in. baking pan. Bake at 200° for 1-1/4 to 1-3/4 hours or until almost dry to the touch. Toss with remaining sugar.

Using a pencil, draw four 3-in. circles on a sheet of parchment paper. Place paper, pencil mark down, on a baking sheet; set aside.

In a large bowl, combine the egg whites, confectioners' sugar and flour until blended. Beat in the butter, almond extract and salt.

Spread 1 tablespoon batter over each circle. Bake at 350° for 5-7 minutes or until golden around the edges.

With a spatula, carefully remove cookies and immediately drape over inverted shot glasses or small juice glasses. When cookies are cool, transfer to a wire rack. Repeat with remaining batter, forming 16 tuiles.

In a small bowl, beat the mascarpone, honey and tangerine peel. Fold in whipped cream and tangerines.

To serve, spoon about 3 tablespoons tangerine cream into each cookie. Garnish with candied cranberries and reserved syrup.

TO MAKE AHEAD: Prepare the tuiles a few days before. Store in an airtight container. Candied cranberries can be made two weeks before serving. Store cranberries in a single layer covered lightly with waxed paper. Cover and refrigerate syrup.

Making Tuiles

With a large spatula, remove one tuile from baking sheet and drape over an upside-down shot glass or small juice glass. Working quickly, repeat with remaining tuiles. Tuiles become crisp when cool. To rewarm them, return to the oven for 10 to 30 seconds or until they are warm enough to drape.

Green Tea Cheesecake Tarts

PREP: 20 MIN. + CHILLING   **YIELD:** 6 SERVINGS

We all can use an elegant but easy recipe every once in a while…especially around the busy holiday season. Not only are these cheesecake tartlets super-delicious, but they're also a no-bake treat that makes preparation a snap!

Amy Tong ★ Anaheim, California

    3 to 4 teaspoons matcha (green tea powder)
    4 teaspoons hot water
   12 ounces cream cheese, softened
    1 cup confectioners' sugar
  2/3 cup sour cream
    1 teaspoon vanilla extract
    6 individual graham cracker tart shells
  1/4 cup pistachios, chopped
  1/4 cup pomegranate seeds

In a large bowl, combine the tea powder and water until dissolved. Add cream cheese, confectioners' sugar, sour cream and vanilla. Beat until smooth.

Pipe into tart shells. Sprinkle with pistachios and pomegranate seeds. Refrigerate until serving.

Almond Fudge Cakes

PREP: 1 HOUR   **BAKE:** 20 MIN. + COOLING
YIELD: 10 SERVINGS

I teach in a school with 3 to 4 teachers per grade. I bake this cake in small springform pans so that each group can grab a cake before school and divide it among themselves later. Sometimes I slice the cakes into 3 layers and fill one of them with strawberry preserves or cherry pie filling.

Carleen Johns ★ Brownwood, Missouri

    1 package (18-1/4 ounces) chocolate cake mix
    1 cup (8 ounces) sour cream
  3/4 cup water
  1/2 cup butter, softened
    3 eggs
FILLING:
    1 package (8 ounces) cream cheese, softened
    1 cup confectioners' sugar
  1/2 cup heavy whipping cream, whipped
    1 teaspoon almond extract
GLAZE:
1-1/2 cups confectioners' sugar
    1 cup milk chocolate chips
  1/2 cup butter, cubed
  1/4 cup sweetened condensed milk
    5 teaspoons heavy whipping cream
    1 teaspoon vanilla extract
    1 cup chopped almonds, toasted

In a large bowl, combine the cake mix, sour cream, water, butter and eggs; beat on low speed for 30 seconds. Beat on medium for 2 minutes.

Spoon 1/2 cupfuls into 10 greased 4-in. fluted tube pans. Bake at 350° for 20-25 minutes. Cool for 10 minutes before removing from pans to wire racks to cool completely.

In a small bowl, combine the cream cheese and confectioners' sugar until creamy. Fold in whipped cream and almond extract; set aside.

For glaze, in a large saucepan, combine confectioners' sugar, chocolate chips, butter and milk. Cook and stir over medium heat until smooth. Remove from the heat. Stir in cream and vanilla.

Cut each cake horizontally into two layers. Place each bottom layer on a serving plate; top with 3 tablespoons filling. Replace tops. Spoon glaze over cakes and sprinkle with almonds.

Editor's Note: To bake in 6-oz. ramekins, divide among eight greased ramekins. Bake at 350° for 25-30 minutes or until a toothpick comes out clean.

Baba au Rhum Cakes

PREP: 30 MIN. + CHILLING **BAKE:** 10 MIN. + STANDING
YIELD: 2 DOZEN

This scrumptious treat features fruit-studded yeast breads soaked in a sweet rum glaze. The rum flavor is subtle, so it's as suitable for your holiday brunch buffet as for dessert!

Diane Halferty ★ Tucson, Arizona

     4 cups all-purpose flour
   1/3 cup sugar
     1 package (1/4 ounce) active dry yeast
     1 teaspoon salt
   1/2 cup butter, cubed
   1/2 cup milk
   1/4 cup water
     3 eggs
     1 egg yolk
   1/2 cup dried cranberries
   1/2 cup chopped candied pineapple
   1/4 cup dried currants
RUM SYRUP:
 1-1/4 cups water
   2/3 cup sugar
   1/3 cup spiced rum
    12 red candied cherries, halved

In a large bowl, combine 1 cup flour, sugar, yeast and salt. In a small saucepan, heat the butter, milk and water to 120°-130°. Gradually add to dry ingredients; beat on medium speed for 3 minutes. Add the eggs, egg yolk and 3/4 cup flour; beat on high for 2 minutes.

Stir in the fruit and enough remaining flour to form a soft dough (dough will be sticky). Place in a greased bowl, turning once to grease the top. Cover with plastic wrap and let rise in a warm place until doubled, about 1-1/2 hours.

Stir dough down. Cover the bowl with plastic wrap and refrigerate overnight.

Punch dough down; turn onto a lightly floured surface. Shape dough into 24 balls and place in well-greased muffin cups. Cover and let rise in a warm place until doubled, about 1 hour.

Meanwhile, bring water and sugar to a boil over medium heat. Cook and stir until sugar is dissolved and mixture is syrupy, about 10 minutes. Remove from the heat and cool to room temperature. Stir in rum.

Bake cakes at 375° for 10-14 minutes or until golden brown. Poke holes in cakes with a fork; slowly pour 1 tablespoon rum syrup over each cake. Top each with a cherry half. Let stand for 10 minutes before removing from pans. Serve warm.

Blood Orange Yogurt Tarts

PREP: 30 MIN.   **BAKE:** 15 MIN. + FREEZING + COOLING
YIELD: 6 TARTLETS

Here is one healthy, delicious and beautiful dessert. If you can't find the striking blood oranges, use tangerines, clementines, grapefruits—or a combination of citrus flavors.

Sonya Labbe ★ West Hollywood, California

   1/2 cup chopped walnuts
   1/4 cup sugar
     1 cup all-purpose flour
     6 tablespoons cold unsalted butter, cubed
     2 teaspoons unflavored gelatin
     2 tablespoons cold water
   1/2 cup 2% milk
 1-1/2 cups plain Greek yogurt
   1/3 cup packed brown sugar
     3 medium blood oranges, sectioned

Place walnuts and sugar in a food processor; cover and process until walnuts are finely ground. Add flour; pulse until combined. Add butter; cover and pulse just until mixture forms a ball.

Press onto the bottom and up the sides of six ungreased 4-in. fluted tart pans with removable bottoms. Cover and freeze for 15 minutes.

Bake at 350° for 15 minutes or until golden brown. Cool completely on wire racks.

Meanwhile, in a small bowl, sprinkle gelatin over water; let stand for 1 minute. In a small saucepan, heat milk over medium heat until bubbles form around sides of pan. Add gelatin mixture; stir until gelatin is completely dissolved.

In a small bowl, whisk yogurt and brown sugar until brown sugar is dissolved. Stir in milk mixture. Spoon into cooled crusts. Cover and refrigerate for 2 hours or until set.

Peanut Butter Parfaits

PREP: 40 MIN.   **COOK:** 10 MIN.   **YIELD:** 6 SERVINGS

If you're looking for a super dessert that can be made a day ahead, try these parfaits. The combination of peanut butter and chocolate is sure to be popular with all ages, and the whipped cream topping is delish!

Mary Ann Lee ★ Clifton Park, New York

1-1/2 teaspoons unflavored gelatin
   2 tablespoons cold water
   1 cup 2% milk
 1/4 cup sugar
 1/4 cup creamy peanut butter
   2 tablespoons butter
   2 egg yolks, beaten
   1 teaspoon vanilla extract
   1 cup heavy whipping cream
   3 tablespoons confectioners' sugar
 3/4 cup hot fudge ice cream topping
   3 tablespoons chopped salted peanuts
Chocolate curls

Sprinkle gelatin over cold water; let stand for 1 minute. Microwave on high for 20 seconds. Stir and let stand for 1 minute or until gelatin is completely dissolved.

In a small heavy saucepan, heat the milk, sugar, peanut butter and butter until bubbles form around sides of pan. Whisk a small amount of hot mixture into the egg yolks. Return all to the pan, whisking constantly.

Cook and stir over low heat until mixture is thickened and coats the back of a spoon. Stir in gelatin mixture and vanilla. Quickly transfer to a bowl; place in ice water and stir for 10 minutes or until cold and thickened.

In a large bowl, beat cream until it begins to thicken. Add confectioners' sugar; beat until soft peaks form. Fold half into peanut butter mixture.

Spoon 1 tablespoon ice cream topping into each of six parfait glasses. Top with 1/4 cup peanut butter mixture. Repeat layers. Top with remaining whipped cream; sprinkle with peanuts and chocolate curls. Chill until serving.

Molten Chocolate Cherry Cakes

PREP: 30 MIN.   **BAKE:** 15 MIN.   **YIELD:** 6 SERVINGS

Cinnamon-spiced cherries make my gooey chocolate cakes simply irresistible. Refrigerate any extra sauce and drizzle it over ice cream for a quick treat later in the week.

Ki Russell ★ Greeley, Colorado

   1 package (12 ounces) frozen pitted dark sweet cherries, thawed, undrained
 3/4 cup sugar, *divided*
 1/4 cup cherry brandy
   1 teaspoon ground cinnamon
 3/4 cup butter, cubed
   3 ounces bittersweet chocolate, chopped
   3 ounces semisweet chocolate, chopped
   3 eggs
   6 egg yolks
   6 tablespoons baking cocoa
   2 teaspoons all-purpose flour
Confectioners' sugar

Cut cherries in half; place cherries and their juices in a large saucepan. Add 1/2 cup sugar, cherry brandy and cinnamon. Bring to a boil. Reduce heat; simmer, uncovered, for 5 minutes. Remove from the heat. Using a slotted spoon, remove 1/4 cup cherries; chop and set aside.

In a double boiler or metal bowl over hot water, melt butter and chocolates; stir until smooth. In a bowl, beat eggs, egg yolks and remaining sugar until thick and lemon-colored. Beat in cocoa and flour until well blended. Slowly beat in chocolate mixture. Fold in chopped cherries.

Transfer to six greased 6-oz. ramekins or custard cups. Place ramekins on a baking sheet. Bake at 350° for 15-17 minutes or until a thermometer inserted near the center reads 160° and sides of cakes are set.

Remove from the oven and let stand for 1 minute. Run a knife around edges of ramekins; invert onto dessert plates. Dust with confectioners' sugar. Serve immediately with warm cherry sauce.

Gingerbread Souffles

PREP: 35 MIN. **BAKE:** 20 MIN. **YIELD:** 6 SERVINGS

If you like gingerbread cookies, you'll be thrilled with these golden souffles! The airy dessert has a wonderful ginger flavor that's enhanced with cinnamon, nutmeg and cloves.

Donna Spangler ★ Palmyra, Pennsylvania

7	egg whites
3	tablespoons sugar
1/3	cup butter, cubed
1/3	cup all-purpose flour
1	cup 2% milk
1/2	cup heavy whipping cream
5	egg yolks, beaten
1	cup packed brown sugar
2	tablespoons chopped crystallized ginger
3	teaspoons ground ginger
1	teaspoon ground cinnamon
1/2	teaspoon ground nutmeg
1/4	teaspoon ground cloves

Let egg whites stand at room temperature for 30 minutes. Grease six 6-oz. ramekins or custard cups and lightly sprinkle with sugar; set aside.

In a small saucepan, melt the butter. Stir in the flour until smooth; gradually add the milk and cream. Bring to a boil; cook and stir for 2 minutes or until thickened. Transfer to a large bowl.

Stir a small amount of hot mixture into the egg yolks; return all to the bowl, stirring constantly. Stir in the brown sugar, crystallized ginger and spices until blended; allow to cool slightly.

In a large bowl with clean beaters, beat egg whites until stiff peaks form. With a spatula, stir a fourth of the egg whites into ginger mixture until no white streaks remain. Fold in remaining egg whites until combined. Transfer to prepared dishes.

Bake at 375° for 20-24 minutes or until the top is puffed and center appears set. Serve immediately.

Eggnog Creme Brulee

PREP: 25 MIN. **BAKE:** 35 MIN. + CHILLING
YIELD: 10 SERVINGS

Eggnog, nutmeg and rum give the velvety texture of this brulee its holiday appeal. A crust made of caramelized brown sugar adds the final "yum factor" to this elegant creation.

Taste of Home Test Kitchen

2 cups eggnog
2 cups heavy whipping cream
8 egg yolks
1/3 cup plus 3 tablespoons sugar, *divided*
2 tablespoons spiced rum
1 teaspoon vanilla extract
1/4 teaspoon ground nutmeg
3 tablespoons brown sugar

In a large saucepan, combine the eggnog, cream, egg yolks and 1/3 cup sugar. Cook and stir over medium heat until mixture reaches 160° or is thick enough to coat the back of a metal spoon. Remove from the heat; stir in the rum, vanilla and nutmeg.

Transfer to ten 6-oz. ramekins or custard cups. Place cups in a baking pan; add 1 in. of boiling water to pan. Bake, uncovered, at 325° for 35-40 minutes or until centers are just set (mixture will jiggle). Remove ramekins from water bath; cool for 10 minutes. Cover and refrigerate for at least 4 hours.

In a small bowl, combine the brown sugar and remaining sugar. If using a creme brulee torch, sprinkle custards with sugar mixture. Heat sugar with the torch until caramelized. Serve immediately.

If broiling the custards, place ramekins on a baking sheet; let stand at room temperature for 15 minutes. Sprinkle with sugar mixture. Broil 8 in. from the heat for 4-7 minutes or until sugar is caramelized. Refrigerate for 1-2 hours or until firm.

What's in a Name?

A dessert with a sinfully smooth texture and crunchy topping is an indulgence that most people enjoy. The elegant sounding "Creme Brulee," though, translates from French to English as "burnt cream." Needless to say, that's not a name that jumps off a menu, so "Creme Brulee" became a mainstay.

Spiced Apple Cupcakes

PREP: 25 MIN. **BAKE:** 20 MIN. + COOLING
YIELD: 2 DOZEN

I came up with the combination of cinnamon and cayenne when I was making cinnamon toast one day and accidentally sprinkled cayenne pepper on my toast instead of cinnamon! I decided to just add cinnamon to the cayenne, and I loved it. Since I'm constantly making cupcakes, I thought I'd give my newfound flavor combo a try in that recipe. I loved the end result and hope you do, too. A rich and silky maple frosting makes a great finish for these spicy cakes.

Elisha Ayers ★ Unicoi, Tennessee

1 medium apple, peeled and finely chopped
1/2 teaspoon ground coriander
1/2 cup butter, softened
3/4 cup packed brown sugar
1/2 cup sugar
4 eggs
1 cup unsweetened applesauce
2 cups all-purpose flour
1 teaspoon baking soda
1/2 teaspoon salt
1/2 teaspoon ground cinnamon
1/4 teaspoon ground nutmeg
1/4 teaspoon ground allspice
1/4 teaspoon cayenne pepper

MAPLE CREAM CHEESE FROSTING:

1 package (8 ounces) cream cheese, softened
1/2 cup butter, softened
4 cups confectioners' sugar
2 tablespoons maple syrup
Ground allspice

In a small skillet, saute apple and coriander until tender. Remove from the heat and set aside.

In a large bowl, cream butter and sugars until light and fluffy. Add eggs, one at a time, beating well after each addition. Beat in applesauce (mixture will appear curdled). Combine the flour, baking soda, salt, cinnamon, nutmeg, allspice and cayenne; gradually add to the creamed mixture until combined. Fold in apple mixture. Fill paper-lined muffin cups two-thirds full.

Bake at 350° for 18-22 minutes or until a toothpick inserted near the center comes out clean. Cool for 10 minutes; remove from pans to wire racks to cool completely.

In a small bowl, beat cream cheese and butter until light and fluffy. Add confectioners' sugar and maple syrup; beat until smooth. Pipe frosting onto cupcakes. Sprinkle with allspice. Store in the refrigerator.

Sticky Toffee Pudding

PREP: 40 MIN. **BAKE:** 15 MIN. + COOLING
YIELD: 6 SERVINGS

Wow your guests with their own mini cake desserts. Each moist rich treat is topped with a warm brown-sugar sauce.

Taste of Home Test Kitchen

1	package (8 ounces) pitted dates
1	cup orange juice
1/2	cup butter, softened
1	cup packed brown sugar
3	eggs
2	cups all-purpose flour
1-1/2	teaspoons baking powder
1	teaspoon salt
1	teaspoon ground ginger
1	teaspoon ground cinnamon
1/2	teaspoon baking soda
1	tablespoon grated orange peel
1	teaspoon vanilla extract

TOFFEE SAUCE:

1/2	cup butter, cubed
1	cup packed brown sugar
1	cup heavy whipping cream

Vanilla ice cream or whipped cream

In a small saucepan, combine dates and orange juice. Bring to a boil. Reduce heat; simmer, uncovered, for 5 minutes. Remove from the heat; cool. Pour into a blender; cover and process until smooth.

In a large bowl, cream butter and brown sugar until light and fluffy. Add eggs, one at a time, beating well after each addition. Combine the flour, baking powder, salt, ginger, cinnamon and baking soda; gradually add to creamed mixture. Stir in date mixture, orange peel and vanilla.

Fill six greased 4-in. fluted tube pans two-thirds full. Bake at 375° for 14-18 minutes or until a toothpick inserted near the center comes out clean. Cool for 10 minutes on a wire rack.

Meanwhile, in a small saucepan, melt butter; stir in brown sugar and cream. Bring to a boil over medium heat, stirring constantly. Remove from the heat. To serve, invert puddings onto dessert plates. Serve warm with sauce and ice cream or whipped cream.

Editor's Note: To bake in 10-oz. ramekins, divide among six greased ramekins. Bake at 375° for 22-26 minutes or until a toothpick comes out clean.

A British Classic

Sticky Toffee Pudding is a classic British dessert. The moist, spongy treat can be steamed or baked (our version is baked) and contains dates. The cake-like specialty is topped with a toffee sauce and served with ice cream or custard.

Cookies WITH A CLASSICAL TWIST

Cookies With a Classical Twist

Whether given as hostess gifts, exchanged with friends or simply enjoyed around the tree, Christmas cookies are truly a standby of this magical (and delicious) season. After all, the holidays just wouldn't be the same without platters full of those bite-sized morsels we hold so dear. Looking to add a little flair to your cookie tins this year? Simply consider these sensational treats—each inspired by a classic dessert. Banana Split Cookies and Cashew-Pecan Pie Bars are just some of the impressive sweets found here!

Boston Cream Pie Cookies

PREP: 70 MIN. + CHILLING
BAKE: 10 MIN./BATCH + COOLING   **YIELD:** 4 DOZEN

With a shiny chocolate glaze and luscious vanilla custard, these cute sandwich cookies remind everyone of a Boston staple. What a great way to mix up your cookie platter!

Evangeline Bradford ★ Erlanger, Kentucky

- 6 tablespoons sugar
- 3 tablespoons cornstarch
- 1/4 teaspoon salt
- 1 cup 2% milk
- 6 tablespoons heavy whipping cream
- 1 egg yolk, beaten
- 2 teaspoons vanilla extract

COOKIES:
- 9 tablespoons butter, softened
- 1 cup sugar
- 2 egg yolks
- 1 egg
- 2 teaspoon vanilla extract
- 1/2 teaspoon grated lemon peel
- 1 cup plus 2 tablespoons cake flour
- 1 cup all-purpose flour
- 3/4 teaspoon baking soda
- 1/2 teaspoon salt
- 1/2 cup plus 2 tablespoons buttermilk

GLAZE:

- 2 ounces unsweetened chocolate, chopped
- 4 teaspoons butter
- 1/2 cup whipping cream
- 1 cup confectioners' sugar

In a small heavy saucepan, combine the sugar, cornstarch and salt. Stir in milk and cream until smooth. Cook and stir over medium-high heat until thickened and bubbly. Reduce heat to low; cook and stir 2 minutes longer.

Remove from the heat. Stir a small amount of hot filling into egg yolk; return all to the pan, stirring constantly. Bring to a gentle boil; cook and stir 2 minutes longer. Remove from the heat. Stir in vanilla. Cool for 15 minutes, stirring occasionally. Transfer to a small bowl. Press waxed paper onto surface of custard. Refrigerate for 2-3 hours.

In a large bowl, cream butter and sugar until light and fluffy. Beat in the egg yolks, egg, vanilla and lemon peel. Combine the cake flour, all-purpose flour, baking soda and salt; gradually add to creamed mixture alternately with buttermilk and mix well.

Drop by rounded teaspoonfuls 2 in. apart onto greased baking sheets. Bake at 400° for 5-7 minutes or until firm to the touch. Remove to wire racks to cool completely.

Spread custard over the bottoms of half of the cookies; top with remaining cookies.

For glaze, place chocolate and butter in a small bowl. In a small saucepan, bring cream just to a boil. Pour over chocolate and butter; whisk until smooth. Stir in confectioners' sugar. Spread over cookies; let dry completely. Store in the refrigerator.

TO MAKE AHEAD: Package cookies in an airtight container, separating layers with waxed paper and freeze for up to 1 month. Thaw in a single layer before assembling.

Baklava Rounds

PREP: 40 MIN.   **BAKE:** 20 MIN. + STANDING
YIELD: 32 COOKIES

In need of a sweet treat I could prepare ahead and freeze, I streamlined a recipe I found online. These crispy, flaky little rounds were the result. They were a big hit at an elegant Christmas tea I catered.

Meta West ★ Abilene, Kansas

- 1 cup sugar
- 3/4 cup water
- 10 orange peel strips (1 to 3 inches)

FILLING:

- 1-1/2 cups chopped walnuts
- 1/2 cup slivered almonds
- 1/4 cup sugar
- 1 teaspoon almond extract
- 1/2 teaspoon ground cinnamon
- 1/2 teaspoon ground cloves
- 18 sheets phyllo dough (14-inch x 9-inch sheet size)
- 3/4 cup butter, melted

In a large saucepan, bring the sugar, water and orange peel to a boil. Reduce heat; simmer, uncovered, for 30-35 minutes or until thickened. Strain and discard peel; set aside.

In a food processor, combine the walnuts, almonds, sugar, almond extract, cinnamon and cloves. Cover and process until finely chopped.

Place one sheet of phyllo dough on a work surface; brush with butter. Repeat with two more sheets of phyllo, brushing each with butter. (Keep remaining phyllo covered with plastic wrap and a damp towel to prevent it from drying out.) Sprinkle with 1/3 cup nut mixture. Repeat layers twice.

Roll up jelly-roll style, starting with a long side. Brush roll with butter. Trim edges. Cut into 16 slices, about 3/4 in. each. Place cut side down on a greased 15-in. x 10-in x 1-in. baking pan. Repeat with remaining phyllo, butter and filling.

Bake at 350° for 10 minutes. Gently turn cookies over; bake 10-15 minutes longer or until golden brown. Cool for 5 minutes before removing from pans to wire racks over waxed paper.

Spoon half of the syrup over cookies. Let stand for 15 minutes. Drizzle with remaining syrup. Cool completely.

TO MAKE AHEAD: Prepare as directed. Freeze in a single layer on a waxed paper-lined baking sheet. Once frozen, package in freezer bags, separating layers with waxed paper. Thaw in a single layer before serving.

Strawberry Shortcake Cookies

PREP: 35 MIN. + CHILLING
BAKE: 15 MIN./BATCH + COOLING   **YIELD:** 2 DOZEN

Strawberry shortcake is one of my favorite desserts, so I wanted to capture that wonderful flavor in a cookie. The crispy cookie and sultry frosting offer a delightful burst of flavor you can enjoy any time of year!

Allison Anderson ★ Avondale, Arizona

　2　cups all-purpose flour
1/2　cup sugar
Dash salt
2/3　cup cold butter
　2　tablespoons water
　1　teaspoon vanilla extract
FROSTING:
1/2　cup butter, softened
3/4　cup fresh strawberries, sliced
　2　tablespoons 2% milk
　5　cups confectioners' sugar
Additional sliced fresh strawberries, optional

In a large bowl, combine the flour, sugar and salt. Cut in butter until mixture resembles coarse crumbs. Combine water and vanilla; stir into crumb mixture just until moistened. Cover and refrigerate for 1-2 hours or until firm.

On a lightly floured surface, roll out to 1/4-in. thickness; cut with a floured 3-in. round cookie cutter. Place 1 in. apart on greased baking sheets.

Bake at 325° for 15-18 minutes or until lightly browned. Cool for 2 minutes before removing to wire racks to cool completely.

In a large bowl, beat the butter, strawberries and milk until combined. Gradually add confectioners' sugar; beat until blended. Spread over cookies; garnish with additional sliced strawberries if desired.

Sacher Torte Brownies

PREP: 45 MIN. + FREEZING   **BAKE:** 20 MIN. + COOLING
YIELD: 4 DOZEN

Elevate your brownies to a new level with this sinfully delicious idea. Dried apricots and apricot preserves complement the dense chocolate brownies oh-so well.

Pat Schmeling ★ Germantown, Wisconsin

　12　dried apricots
　10　ounces bittersweet chocolate, coarsely chopped, *divided*
3/4　cup butter, cubed
　3　eggs
1-1/2　cups sugar
1-1/2　teaspoons vanilla extract
1-1/2　cups all-purpose flour
1/4　teaspoon baking soda
1/4　teaspoon salt
　1　cup apricot preserves
GLAZE:
　6　ounces bittersweet chocolate, coarsely chopped
1/4　cup heavy whipping cream
　2　tablespoons butter

Cut apricots into quarters. In a microwave, melt 1 ounce chocolate; stir until smooth. Dip one end of apricots in chocolate; allow excess to drip off. Place on waxed paper; let stand until set.

Line a greased 15-in. x 10-in. x 1-in. baking pan with waxed paper and grease the paper; set aside. In a microwave, melt butter and remaining chocolate; stir until smooth. Cool slightly.

In a large bowl, beat eggs and sugar. Stir in vanilla and chocolate mixture. Combine the flour, baking soda and salt; gradually add to chocolate mixture.

Transfer to prepared pan. Bake at 325° for 15-20 minutes or until a toothpick inserted near the center comes out clean (do not overbake). Cool for 10 minutes before removing from pan to a wire rack to cool completely.

Place preserves in a food processor; cover and process until smooth. Cut brownie into four 7-1/2-in. x 5-in. rectangles. Spread preserves over two rectangles; top with remaining rectangles. Cover and freeze for 20 minutes. Cut each rectangle into 12 squares; cut each square diagonally into two triangles.

For glaze, in a microwave-safe bowl, combine the chocolate, cream and butter. Microwave at 50% power for 1-2 minutes or until smooth, stirring twice. Cool slightly, stirring occasionally. Drizzle over brownies. Top each with an apricot piece.

Classic Cherry Pie Cookies

PREP: 1-1/2 HRS. + CHILLING
BAKE: 10 MIN./BATCH + COOLING   **YIELD:** 5 DOZEN

These "mini pies" promise to steal the show on any cookie tray! Buttercream frosting is piped over cherry preserves for a sweet lattice "crust" that's sure to garner lots of smiles.

Lorri Reinhardt ★ Big Bend, Wisconsin

1/2	cup butter, softened
1	cup sugar
1	egg
1/2	teaspoon vanilla extract
1-3/4	cups all-purpose flour
1/2	teaspoon baking soda
1/4	teaspoon salt

FROSTING:

2/3	cup butter, softened
5	cups confectioners' sugar
1-1/4	teaspoons vanilla extract
5	to 10 teaspoons 2% milk
3/4	teaspoon baking cocoa
2	drops yellow food coloring
1	jar (12 ounces) cherry preserves

In a large bowl, cream butter and sugar until light and fluffy. Beat in egg and vanilla. Combine the flour, baking soda and salt; gradually add to creamed mixture and mix well. On a lightly floured surface, shape dough into two 6-in. rolls; wrap each in plastic wrap. Refrigerate for 1 hour or until firm.

Unwrap and cut into 3/8-in. slices. Place 2 in. apart on greased baking sheets. Bake at 375° for 8-10 minutes or until lightly browned. Remove to wire racks to cool completely.

For frosting, in a large bowl, cream butter until light and fluffy. Beat in the confectioners' sugar, vanilla and enough milk to achieve piping consistency. Tint frosting with cocoa and food coloring. Cut a small hole in the corner of a pastry or plastic bag; fill with frosting.

Spread preserves over cookies to within 1/4 in. of edges. Pipe lines across the top of each cookie, forming a lattice. Pipe a fluted edge around the tops of cookies.

BLUEBERRY PIE COOKIES: Substitute blueberry jam for the cherry preserves.

Piping the Lattice "Crust" for Classic Cherry Pie Cookies

1. With pastry or plastic bag, pipe five evenly spaced lines lengthwise across the top of the cookies, then pipe five more lines widthwise across cookies. Lines should be about 1/2 inch apart.

2. Pipe frosting around the top edge of cookie in a small zig-zag pattern to make a fluted edge.

Raspberry Cheesecake Bars

PREP: 30 MIN. **BAKE:** 35 MIN. + CHILLING
YIELD: 2 DOZEN

My family's love of raspberries and cheesecake makes this a perfect recipe for us. Serve small squares alongside cookies or slice into larger pieces for an incredible dessert.

Jill Cox ★ Lincoln, Nebraska

- 1 cup all-purpose flour
- 1 cup finely chopped pecans
- 1/3 cup packed brown sugar
- 1/4 teaspoon ground cinnamon
- 1/4 teaspoon salt
- 1/3 cup cold butter
- 1 jar (12 ounces) seedless raspberry jam, *divided*
- 2 packages (8 ounces *each*) cream cheese, softened
- 3/4 cup sugar
- 1/2 teaspoon grated lemon peel
- 1/2 teaspoon vanilla extract
- 3 eggs, lightly beaten

TOPPING:

- 1-1/2 cups (12 ounces) sour cream
- 3 tablespoons sugar
- 1 teaspoon vanilla extract

In a small bowl, combine the flour, pecans, brown sugar, cinnamon and salt. Cut in butter until crumbly. Press onto the bottom of a greased 13-in. x 9-in. baking dish. Bake at 350° for 10-12 minutes or until lightly browned. Cool on a wire rack for 5 minutes.

Set aside 3 tablespoons jam; spread remaining jam over crust. In a large bowl, beat cream cheese and sugar until smooth. Beat in lemon peel and vanilla. Add eggs; beat on low speed just until combined. Spoon over jam; spread evenly. Bake for 20-25 minutes or until filling is almost set.

In another bowl, combine the sour cream, sugar and vanilla; spread over cheesecake. Warm remaining jam and swirl over top. Bake 5-7 minutes longer or just until set.

Cool on a wire rack for 1 hour. Refrigerate for at least 2 hours. Cut into bars.

Caramel Apple Cookies

PREP: 40 MIN.   **BAKE:** 10 MIN./BATCH + STANDING
YIELD: 4 DOZEN

I love dressing up my little chocolate chip cookies to resemble miniature caramel apples. Dip the caramel-covered sweets in the chopped nuts, sprinkles or mini chips of your choice. They're a darling addition to any party or potluck!

Tammy Daniels ★ Batavia, Ohio

- 1/2 cup butter, softened
- 1/4 cup confectioners' sugar
- 1/4 cup packed brown sugar
- 1/4 teaspoon salt
- 1 egg
- 1/2 teaspoon vanilla extract
- 2 cups all-purpose flour
- 1/2 cup miniature semisweet chocolate chips
- 48 round toothpicks
- 1 package (11 ounces) Kraft caramel bits
- 2 tablespoons water
- 1 cup finely chopped pecans

In a large bowl, cream the butter, sugars and salt until light and fluffy. Beat in egg and vanilla. Gradually add flour to creamed mixture and mix well. Stir in chips.

Shape into 1-in. balls; place 2 in. apart on greased baking sheets. Bake at 350° for 10-12 minutes or until set. Immediately insert a round toothpick in center of each cookie. Remove to wire racks to cool completely.

In a small saucepan, combine caramels and water. Cook and stir over medium-low heat until smooth. Holding a cookie by the toothpick, dip the bottom two-thirds of cookie in caramel mixture, turning to coat. Allow excess to drip off. Immediately dip the bottom and sides in pecans.

Place on waxed paper. Repeat with remaining cookies, caramel mixture and pecans. Let stand until set.

Lemon Meringue Pie Cookies

PREP: 25 MIN. + CHILLING   **BAKE:** 25 MIN. + STANDING
YIELD: 5 DOZEN

Here's a way to have the refreshing flavor of lemon meringue pie in a handheld cookie. An easy homemade lemon curd is spooned onto each heavenly meringue cookie. Every bite is truly a melt-in-your-mouth delight.

Taste of Home Test Kitchen

- 3 egg whites
- 1/2 teaspoon vanilla extract
- 1/4 teaspoon cream of tartar
- 3/4 cup sugar

LEMON CURD:

- 4 eggs
- 1-1/3 cups sugar
- 1/3 cup lemon juice
- 4 teaspoons grated lemon peel
- 3 tablespoons butter

Place egg whites in a large bowl; let stand at room temperature for 30 minutes. Add vanilla and cream of tartar; beat on medium speed until soft peaks form. Gradually beat in sugar, 1 tablespoon at a time, on high until stiff peaks form.

Cut a small hole in the corner of a pastry or plastic bag; insert a #24 star tip. Fill bag with meringue. Pipe 1-in. circles 2 in. apart onto parchment paper-lined baking sheets. Pipe once around the base of each shell for sides.

Bake at 300° for 25 minutes or until set and dry. Turn oven off; leave meringues in oven for 1 hour.

Meanwhile, in a small heavy saucepan over medium heat, whisk the eggs, sugar, lemon juice and peel until blended. Add butter; cook, whisking constantly, until mixture is thickened and coats the back of a metal spoon. Transfer mixture to a small bowl; cool for 10 minutes. Cover and refrigerate until chilled.

Just before serving, spoon lemon curd into the center of cookies. Refrigerate leftovers.

TO MAKE AHEAD: Prepare the meringues a few days before. Store in an airtight container. Lemon curd can be made the day before serving. Cover and refrigerate.

Magical Meringue

When making meringue cookies, test for stiff egg white peaks by tilting the mixing bowl, making sure the whites do not slide around. The egg whites should stand straight in peaks. Sugar is dissolved when the mixture feels silky smooth between your fingers.

Blue Ribbon Carrot Cake Cookies

PREP: 50 MIN.   **BAKE:** 10 MIN./BATCH + COOLING
YIELD: 4 DOZEN

I just love carrot cake, so I created these cookies to enjoy that flavor without needing a fork. I entered my recipe in the Los Angeles County Fair in 2007, and not only did I win first place, but my treats were also named Best of Division!

Marina Castle ★ La Crescenta, California

- 1   cup butter, softened
- 1   cup packed brown sugar
- 3/4   cup sugar
- 2   eggs
- 1-1/2   teaspoons vanilla extract
- 1/2   teaspoon rum extract
- 3   cups all-purpose flour
- 1/2   cup old-fashioned oats
- 1-1/2   teaspoons ground cinnamon
- 3/4   teaspoon salt
- 3/4   teaspoon baking soda
- 1/2   teaspoon ground ginger
- 1/2   teaspoon ground nutmeg
- 1   cup chopped walnuts, toasted
- 3/4   cup shredded carrots
- 3/4   cup raisins

FILLING:
- 1   package (8 ounces) cream cheese, softened
- 1/2   cup butter, softened
- 1-1/4   cups confectioners' sugar
- 1   teaspoon vanilla extract
- 1/2   cup chopped walnuts, toasted
- 2   tablespoons crushed pineapple

Additional confectioners' sugar

In a large bowl, cream butter and sugars until light and fluffy. Beat in the eggs and extracts. Combine the flour, oats, cinnamon, salt, baking soda, ginger and nutmeg; gradually add to creamed mixture and mix well. Stir in the walnuts, carrots and raisins.

Drop by rounded teaspoonfuls 2 in. apart onto greased baking sheets. Flatten with a glass dipped in sugar. Bake at 350° for 9-11 minutes or until lightly browned. Remove to wire racks to cool completely.

In a small bowl, beat the cream cheese, butter, confectioners' sugar and vanilla until light and fluffy. Stir in walnuts and pineapple. Spread over the bottoms of half of the cookies; top with remaining cookies. Sprinkle both sides with additional confectioners' sugar. Store in the refrigerator.

TO MAKE AHEAD: Package cookies in an airtight container, separating layers with waxed paper and freeze for up to 1 month. Thaw in a single layer before filling.

Tiramisu Nanaimo Bars

PREP: 30 MIN. + CHILLING   **YIELD:** 2-1/2 DOZEN

I love tiramisu, and after tasting Nanaimo bars at a local bakery, I decided to combine the two desserts into one. More convenient to eat than traditional tiramisu, these bars are bound to be a hit with everyone on your Christmas list.

Susan Riley ★ Allen, Texas

1/2	cup butter, softened
1/3	cup baking cocoa
1/4	cup sugar
2	teaspoons instant coffee granules
1	egg, lightly beaten
1-1/2	cups graham cracker crumbs
1	cup finely chopped flaked coconut
1/2	cup chopped pecans

FILLING:

1/2	cup butter, softened
2	tablespoons heavy whipping cream
1	tablespoon rum
1	teaspoon vanilla extract
2	cups confectioners' sugar

GLAZE:

2/3	cup semisweet chocolate chips
2	tablespoons butter

Baking cocoa

In large heavy saucepan, combine the butter, cocoa, sugar and coffee. Cook and stir over medium-low heat until melted. Whisk a small amount of hot mixture into egg. Return all to the pan, whisking constantly. Cook and stir over medium-low heat until mixture reaches 160°. Remove from the heat.

Stir in the cracker crumbs, coconut and pecans. Press into a foil-lined 8-in. square baking pan. Refrigerate for 30 minutes or until set.

For filling, in a large bowl, beat the butter, whipping cream, rum and vanilla until blended. Gradually beat in confectioners' sugar until smooth; spread over crust.

In a microwave, melt chocolate chips and butter; stir until smooth. Spread over top. Refrigerate until set. Cut into bars and dust with cocoa.

Nanaimo Bars

Nanaimo bars, a classic Canadian pastry, are named for Nanaimo, British Columbia. The no-bake bar has three layers. A chocolate base is made of graham crackers, butter, coconut, nuts and cocoa powder. The creamy middle layer uses custard powder in Canada or pudding mix in the US, confectioners' sugar, butter and milk or cream to create a buttercream. Then the bar is topped with dark chocolate. These chilled treats are rich and heavenly, with many variations. Ingredients can vary from recipe to recipe.

Apple Crisp Crescents

PREP: 30 MIN. + CHILLING **BAKE:** 20 MIN./BATCH
YIELD: 3 DOZEN

Talk about comfort and joy! It just wouldn't be Christmas without these tender pastries filled with cinnamony apples.

Betty Lawton ★ Pennington, New Jersey

  2 cups all-purpose flour
1/8 teaspoon salt
  1 cup cold butter
  1 egg, *separated*
2/3 cup sour cream
1/2 teaspoon vanilla extract
  1 cup finely chopped peeled tart apple
1/3 cup finely chopped walnuts
1/4 cup raisins, chopped
2/3 cup sugar
  1 teaspoon ground cinnamon

In a large bowl, combine flour and salt; cut in butter until mixture resembles coarse crumbs. In a small bowl, whisk the egg yolk, sour cream and vanilla; add to crumb mixture and mix well. Cover and refrigerate for 4 hours or overnight.

Divide dough into thirds. On a lightly floured surface, roll each portion into a 10-in. circle. Combine the apple, walnuts, raisins, sugar and cinnamon; sprinkle 1/2 cup over each circle. Cut each circle into 12 wedges.

Roll up each wedge from the wide end and place point side down 1 in. apart on greased baking sheets. Curve ends to form crescents. Whisk egg white until foamy; brush over crescents.

Bake at 350° for 18-20 minutes or until lightly browned. Remove to wire racks to cool. Store in an airtight container.

Black Forest Thumbprint Cookies

PREP: 25 MIN.+ CHILLING **BAKE:** 10 MIN./BATCH
YIELD: 5 DOZEN

My treat is special because I captured the flavors of two classic desserts—Black Forest Cake and cherries jubilee. The fudgy chocolate cookie is filled with a no-cook cherry mixture; chopped almonds complement the amaretto flavor in the filling. Best of all, these eye-catching bites are perfect for dressing up your holiday cookie trays.

Barbara Estabrook ★ Rhinelander, Wisconsin

    1 cup butter, softened
1-1/3 cups sugar
    2 egg yolks
 1/4 cup 2% milk
    1 teaspoon almond extract
    2 cups all-purpose flour
 2/3 cup baking cocoa
 1/2 teaspoon salt
FILLING:
1/2 cup dried cherries
1/2 cup cherry spreadable fruit
  2 teaspoons amaretto
  1 teaspoon grated lemon peel
  2 egg whites, lightly beaten
1-1/4 cups chopped almonds

In a large bowl, cream butter and sugar until light and fluffy. Beat in the egg yolks, milk and extract. Combine the flour, cocoa and salt; gradually add to creamed mixture and mix well. Cover and refrigerate for 1 hour.

In a food processor, combine the cherries, spreadable fruit, amaretto and lemon peel. Cover and pulse until chopped; set aside. Place egg whites and almonds in separate shallow bowls. Roll dough into 1-in. balls. Coat in egg whites, then roll in almonds.

Place 1 in. apart on ungreased baking sheets. Using the end of a wooden spoon handle, make an indentation in the center of each cookie. Fill with cherry mixture. Bake at 350° for 10-12 minutes or until set. Remove to wire racks to cool. Store in an airtight container.

Root Beer Float Cookies

PREP: 45 MIN. **BAKE:** 10 MIN./BATCH + COOLING
YIELD: 2-1/2 DOZEN

A hint of old-fashioned root beer flavors these chewy-soft and delectable cookies. They're great with ice cream!

Jim Gordon ★ Beecher, Illinois

1/2	cup butter, softened
1	cup packed brown sugar
1	egg
1	teaspoon root beer concentrate
1-3/4	cups all-purpose flour
1/2	teaspoon salt
1/2	teaspoon baking soda

FILLING:

1/4	cup butter, softened
1-1/3	cups confectioners' sugar
1	teaspoon water
1	teaspoon root beer concentrate

In a large bowl, cream butter and brown sugar until light and fluffy. Beat in egg and root beer concentrate. Combine the flour, salt and baking soda; gradually add to creamed mixture and mix well.

Shape dough into 3/4-in. balls. Place 2 in. apart on ungreased baking sheets. Bake at 375° for 6-8 minutes or until lightly browned. Remove to wire racks to cool completely.

In a small bowl, beat the filling ingredients until smooth. Spread on the bottoms of half of the cookies; top with remaining cookies.

TO MAKE AHEAD: Package cookies in an airtight container, separating layers with waxed paper and freeze for up to 1 month. Thaw in a single layer before filling.

Yule Log Cookies

PREP: 2 HOURS + CHILLING
BAKE: 10 MIN./BATCH + STANDING   **YIELD:** 4 DOZEN

These adorable little yule logs will look fantastic on any cookie tray. The chewy snacks are coated with chocolate and sprinkled with ground pistachios. The miniature mushrooms come together easily with marshmallows and baking cocoa.

Taste of Home Test Kitchen

2/3	cup pistachios
2	tablespoons sugar
4	cups semisweet chocolate chips, *divided*
1/2	cup butter, softened
1-1/2	cups packed brown sugar
2	eggs
1/4	cup whole milk
1	teaspoon almond extract
3-1/4	cups all-purpose flour
2	tablespoons baking cocoa
2	teaspoons baking powder
3/4	teaspoon salt
1	egg white, lightly beaten
2	tablespoons shortening

Ground pistachios
MUSHROOMS:
Miniature marshmallows
Baking cocoa

Place the pistachios and sugar in a food processor; cover and process until ground. Set aside. In a microwave, melt 1 cup chocolate chips; stir until smooth.

In a large bowl, cream butter and brown sugar until light and fluffy. Beat in the eggs, melted chocolate, milk and almond extract. Combine the flour, cocoa, baking powder and salt; gradually add to creamed mixture and mix well. Stir in pistachio mixture.

Divide dough into eight portions. Wrap in plastic wrap and refrigerate for 3 hours or until firm.

Shape each portion into an 18-in. rope; cut each into six logs. Place 2 in. apart on greased baking sheets. Cut the ends of each log at an angle. Using a small amount of egg white, attach removed pieces to each log, forming branches.

Bake at 350° for 10-12 minutes or until set. Remove to wire racks.

In a microwave, melt remaining chocolate chips and shortening; stir until smooth. Working in batches, dip cookies in chocolate, allowing excess to drip off. With the tines of a fork, make strokes in the chocolate to resemble bark. Dust with ground pistachios.

For mushrooms, pinch half of each marshmallow to form a stem; flatten the other half for cap of mushroom. Dust tops of mushrooms with cocoa. Attach to cookies with a small amount of melted chocolate.

Let stand until set. Store in an airtight container.

1. Roll one portion of the dough into an 18-in. rope, using a large cutting board. Apply even pressure as you roll.

2. Cut rope into 3-in. logs. Cut the ends of each log on the diagonal. Attach the dough scraps on top of the log with a little beaten egg white to make stumps. Bake as directed.

3. While cookies are baking, make marshmallow mushrooms. Pinch half of each marshmallow to form the stem, then flatten the other half on counter for cap. Repeat making as many as desired. Dust each with cocoa.

4. Place cookies on a wire rack covered with waxed paper. Brush cool cookies with melted chocolate. Allow to partially set. Draw fork tines down the length of the cookie to create bark. Using a toothpick, make swirls on ends and stumps. Sprinkle logs with ground pistachios for moss. Attach mushrooms to logs before chocolate is completely set.

Cashew-Pecan Pie Bars

PREP: 40 MIN. **BAKE:** 25 MIN. + COOLING
YIELD: 2 DOZEN

You've got to try these! Bars with a buttery shortbread crust and a rich maple-flavored topping just loaded with pecans and cashews. A little piece is all you'll need.

Karen Haen ★ Sturgeon Bay, Wisconsin

2	cups all-purpose flour
1/4	cup sugar
1/2	teaspoon salt
1/2	teaspoon baking powder
1	cup cold butter, cubed

TOPPING:

1	cup packed brown sugar
1	cup maple syrup
3/4	cup butter, cubed
1-1/2	cups coarsely chopped cashews
1-1/2	cups coarsely chopped pecans
3	tablespoons heavy whipping cream

Line a 13-in. x 9-in. baking pan with foil; grease the foil and set aside.

In a large bowl, combine the flour, sugar, salt and baking powder. Cut in butter until mixture resembles coarse crumbs. Press into prepared pan. Bake at 350° for 25-30 minutes or until golden brown.

Meanwhile, in a large saucepan, combine the brown sugar, syrup and butter. Bring to a boil over medium heat; cook and stir for 3 minutes. Remove from the heat; stir in the cashews, pecans and cream.

Pour over crust. Bake 25-30 minutes longer or until filling is set. Cool on a wire rack. Using foil, lift bars out of pan. Discard foil; cut into bars.

Banana Split Cookies

PREP: 40 MIN.   **BAKE:** 10 MIN./BATCH + COOLING
YIELD: 5 DOZEN

We garnished a banana-shaped cookie with homemade frosting, a chocolate drizzle, nuts and cherries. It truly looks like a bite-size banana split. Yum!

Taste of Home Test Kitchen

- 1/2   cup butter, softened
- 6   tablespoons sugar
- 6   tablespoons packed brown sugar
- 1   egg
- 1   medium ripe banana, mashed
- 1/4   cup sour cream
- 1/2   teaspoon vanilla extract
- 1-1/4   cups all-purpose flour
- 1/2   teaspoon baking soda
- 1/4   teaspoon salt
- 1   cup (6 ounces) semisweet chocolate chips
- 6   tablespoons chopped walnuts
- 1/4   cup dried cherries, chopped

BUTTERCREAM FROSTING:
- 1/3   cup butter, softened
- 3   cups confectioners' sugar
- 1   teaspoon vanilla extract
- 3   to 4 tablespoons 2% milk

GLAZE:
- 1/3   cup butter, cubed
- 2   ounces unsweetened chocolate
- 2   cups confectioners' sugar
- 1-1/2   teaspoons vanilla extract
- 3   to 6 tablespoons hot water
- 10   red candied cherries, chopped
- 2   tablespoons chopped walnuts

In a large bowl, cream butter and sugars until light and fluffy. Beat in the egg, banana, sour cream and vanilla. Combine the flour, baking soda and salt; gradually add to creamed mixture and mix well. Fold in the chocolate chips, walnuts and dried cherries.

Place dough in a heavy-duty resealable plastic bag; cut a 3/4-in. hole in one corner of bag. Pipe 2-in. strips about 2-in. apart onto greased baking sheets. Bake at 375° for 6-8 minutes or until lightly browned. Remove to wire racks.

In a large bowl, cream butter until light and fluffy. Beat in the confectioners' sugar, vanilla and enough milk to achieve desired consistency. Pipe three mounds over each cookie.

For glaze, in a small saucepan, combine butter and chocolate. Cook and stir over low heat until smooth. Remove from the heat. Stir in the confectioners' sugar, vanilla and enough water to achieve a drizzling consistency. Drizzle over tops; sprinkle with candied cherries and walnuts.

Sweet
SENSATIONS

Lemon Jelly Candies

PREP: 25 MIN. **COOK:** 10 MIN. + CHILLING
YIELD: ABOUT 1-1/2 POUNDS

Dress up your holiday cookie trays with these tart and pretty candies guaranteed to add a little sparkle to any assortment.

Taste of Home Test Kitchen

2	envelopes unflavored gelatin
1-1/4	cups water, *divided*
2-1/4	cups sugar, *divided*
2	packages (3 ounces *each*) lemon gelatin
1/2	cup lemon juice
1	teaspoon grated lemon peel
1/4	cup clear edible glitter

Line an 8-inch square pan with foil and spray foil with cooking spray; set aside.

In a small bowl, sprinkle unflavored gelatin over 1/3 cup water; set aside.

In a small saucepan, combine 2 cups sugar and remaining water. Bring to a boil over medium heat. Cook and stir until the sugar dissolves. Cook, without stirring, until candy thermometer reads 260° (hard-ball stage). Remove from the heat.

Stir lemon gelatin and unflavored gelatin mixture into hot syrup; stir until gelatin dissolves. Stir in lemon juice and peel. Pour into prepared pan. Cover and refrigerate overnight or until candy is set.

Combine edible glitter and remaining sugar; spread half of mixture over a 14-in. x 12-in. piece of parchment paper. Invert candy onto the parchment paper. Cut candy into triangles and coat with the remaining glitter mixture. Store the candy in an airtight container at room temperature for up to 1 week.

Gold Nugget Carrot Cake

PREP: 25 MIN. **BAKE:** 25 MIN. + COOLING
YIELD: 16 SERVINGS

Old-fashioned and heavenly, my moist, spicy carrot cake is likely to bring back sweet memories of holidays past.

Barbara Estabrook ★ Rhinelander, Wisconsin

1-1/2	cups sugar
1	cup plus 2 tablespoons canola oil
3	eggs
1/2	cup orange marmalade
1-1/2	teaspoons almond extract
2-1/4	cups all-purpose flour
2	teaspoons baking powder
2	teaspoons ground cinnamon
1	teaspoon salt
1/4	teaspoon baking soda
1/4	teaspoon ground nutmeg
2	cups shredded carrots
4	ounces white baking chocolate, finely chopped
3/4	cup chopped almonds
1/3	cup finely chopped crystallized ginger

FROSTING:

2	packages (one 8 ounces, one 3 ounces) cream cheese, softened
1/4	cup butter, softened
1-3/4	cups confectioners' sugar
3	tablespoons orange marmalade
1/2	teaspoon ground cinnamon
1/4	cup finely chopped crystallized ginger

Line two 9-in. round baking pans with waxed paper; grease and flour the pans and paper. Set aside.

In a large bowl, beat the first five ingredients until well blended. Combine the flour, baking powder, cinnamon, salt, baking soda and nutmeg; gradually beat into sugar mixture until blended. Stir in the carrots, chocolate, almonds and ginger. Transfer to prepared pans.

Bake at 350° for 25-30 minutes or until a toothpick inserted near the center comes out clean. Cool for 10 minutes; remove from pans to wire racks to cool completely.

For frosting, in a large bowl, beat cream cheese and butter until fluffy. Add the confectioners' sugar, marmalade and cinnamon; beat until smooth. Stir in ginger.

Place one cake layer on a serving plate; spread with 1 cup frosting. Top with remaining cake layer. Frost top and sides of cake. Store in the refrigerator.

Chocolate-Orange Cream Puffs

PREP: 35 MIN.   **BAKE:** 20 MIN. + COOLING
YIELD: 2 DOZEN

*Here's a triple treat for chocolate lovers…chocolate cream
puffs with a rich, satiny-smooth chocolate-orange filling and
a topping of homemade chocolate syrup. Yum!*

Agnes Ward ★ Stratford, Ontario

    1   cup water
  1/2   cup butter, cubed
    1   ounce semisweet chocolate, chopped
  1/4   teaspoon salt
    1   cup all-purpose flour
    4   eggs

CHOCOLATE ORANGE FILLING:
    2   cups (12 ounces) semisweet chocolate chips
  2/3   cup reduced-fat evaporated milk
    2   tablespoons orange marmalade
    2   tablespoons orange liqueur
    4   cups whipped topping

CHOCOLATE SYRUP:
  1/2   cup sugar
  1/4   cup baking cocoa

    1   tablespoon cornstarch
Dash salt
    1   cup water
    1   teaspoon vanilla extract

In a large saucepan, bring the water, butter, chocolate and
salt to a boil. Add flour all at once and stir until a smooth
ball forms. Remove from the heat; let stand for 5 minutes.
Add eggs, one at a time, beating well after each addition.
Continue beating until mixture is smooth and shiny.

Drop by tablespoonfuls 2 in. apart onto greased baking
sheets. Bake at 400° for 20-25 minutes or until set. Pierce
side of each puff with tip of knife. Remove to wire racks;
cool. Split puffs open; remove tops and set aside. Discard
soft dough from inside.

For filling, in a small saucepan, combine the chocolate
chips, milk and marmalade. Cook and stir until chips are
melted. Cool to room temperature. Stir in orange liqueur;
fold in whipped topping. Refrigerate until ready to use.

For syrup, in a small saucepan, combine the sugar, cocoa,
cornstarch and salt. Stir in water until blended. Bring to a
boil; cook and stir for 2 minutes or until thickened. Remove
from the heat; stir in vanilla. Cool to room temperature.

Just before serving, fill cream puffs with filling; drizzle
with chocolate syrup.

Toffee Bar Brownie Torte

PREP: 45 MIN. **BAKE:** 25 MIN. + COOLING
YIELD: 16 SERVINGS

*Heads will turn when you serve this showstopping cake!
The mild espresso frosting is a perfect partner for the rich,
bittersweet brownie layers.*

Megan Byers ★ Wichita, Kansas

2	cups butter, cubed
16	ounces bittersweet chocolate, chopped
3	cups sugar
8	eggs, lightly beaten
2	teaspoons vanilla extract
2-1/2	cups all-purpose flour
1/2	teaspoon salt

FILLING AND FROSTING:

1/4	cup instant espresso powder
4	teaspoons boiling water
3	cups heavy whipping cream
1	cup confectioners' sugar, *divided*
3	teaspoons vanilla extract, *divided*
2	cartons (8 ounces *each*) mascarpone cheese
1/8	teaspoon salt
1	package (8 ounces) toffee bits

Grease three 9-in. round baking pans and line with
parchment paper; set aside. In a large saucepan, melt butter
and chocolate over low heat, stirring often. Remove from
the heat; cool.

In a large bowl, whisk sugar, eggs, vanilla and chocolate
mixture until smooth. Stir in flour and salt until blended.
Pour into prepared pans.

Bake at 350° for 24-28 minutes or until a toothpick
inserted near the center comes out clean. Cool for
10 minutes before removing from pans to wire racks to
cool completely.

In a small bowl, dissolve espresso powder in boiling
water. In a large bowl, beat cream until soft peaks form.
Add 1/3 cup confectioners' sugar, 1 teaspoon vanilla and
2 tablespoons espresso liquid; beat until stiff peaks form.
Reserve 1 cup for filling; refrigerate remaining mixture
for frosting.

In another large bowl, combine the cheese, salt, and
remaining confectioners' sugar, vanilla and espresso liquid;
beat on medium speed for 2 minutes or until fluffy. Fold in
reserved whipped cream mixture.

Place one brownie layer on a serving plate; spread with
half of the filling. Repeat layers. Top with third brownie
layer; frost top and sides of torte with chilled whipped
cream mixture. Sprinkle toffee bits over top and sides of
torte. Store in the refrigerator.

TO MAKE AHEAD: Brownie layers can be made a day in advance. Store
each layer in a resealable plastic bag at room temperature.

Cherry-Walnut Cake Roll

PREP: 45 MIN.   **BAKE:** 10 MIN. + COOLING
YIELD: 12 SERVINGS

Fit for any festive occasion, this fruity, old-world cake roll tastes every bit as scrumptious as it looks!

Taste of Home Test Kitchen

- 1/2 cup dried cherries
- 1/4 cup cherry brandy
- 4   eggs, *separated*
- 2   tablespoons plus 1/3 cup sugar, *divided*
- 2   tablespoons canola oil
- 1   teaspoon vanilla extract
- 1/2 teaspoon lemon extract
- 1/2 cup all-purpose flour
- 1/4 cup ground walnuts
- 1   teaspoon ground cinnamon
- 3/4 teaspoon baking powder

FILLING/FROSTING:
- 2   packages (one 8 ounces, one 3 ounces) cream cheese, softened
- 1   cup confectioners' sugar
- 1   cup heavy whipping cream, whipped

Melted semisweet chocolate, optional

Combine cherries and cherry brandy; cover and let stand overnight.

Place egg whites in a small bowl; let stand at room temperature for 30 minutes. Line a greased 15-in. x 10-in. x 1-in. baking pan with waxed paper; grease the paper and set aside.

In a large bowl, beat egg yolks until slightly thickened. Gradually add 2 tablespoons sugar, beating on high speed until thick and lemon-colored, about 5 minutes. Beat in the oil, vanilla and lemon extract.

With clean beaters, beat egg whites on medium speed until soft peaks form. Gradually beat in remaining sugar, 1 tablespoon at a time, on high until stiff peaks form; fold into yolk mixture. Combine the flour, walnuts, cinnamon and baking powder; gradually fold into egg mixture. Spread into prepared pan.

Bake at 375° for 10-12 minutes or until cake springs back when lightly touched. Cool for 2 minutes. Invert onto a kitchen towel dusted with confectioners' sugar. Gently peel off waxed paper. Roll up cake in the towel jelly-roll style, starting with a short side. Cool completely on a wire rack.

In a large bowl, beat cream cheese until smooth. Beat in confectioners' sugar. Fold in whipped cream. Unroll cake; spread with 1-1/4 cups filling to within 1/2 in. of edges.

Drain cherries and pat dry with paper towels. Arrange cherries over filling. Starting at the short side, roll up cake; place seam side down on a serving platter. Frost cake with remaining filling. Drizzle with melted chocolate if desired. Cover and refrigerate until serving.

Chocolate Mascarpone Truffles

PREP: 50 MIN. + CHILLING   **YIELD:** ABOUT 4 DOZEN

These luscious, satiny truffles are so versatile...omit the pistachios and try all three of the variations listed below.

Diane Fuqua ★ Baltimore, Maryland

12	ounces semisweet chocolate, chopped, *divided*
4	ounces dark chocolate, chopped
1/2	cup heavy whipping cream
1/2	cup mascarpone cheese
1-3/4	cups pistachios, chopped

In a small heavy saucepan, combine 4 ounces semisweet chocolate, the dark chocolate, cream and cheese. Cook and stir over low heat until smooth. Transfer to a small bowl; cover and refrigerate for 3 hours or until firm enough to shape. Shape into 1-in. balls and place on waxed paper-lined baking sheets. Chill for 1-2 hours or until firm.

In a microwave, melt remaining semisweet chocolate; stir until smooth. Dip balls in chocolate; allow excess to drip off. Roll in pistachios. Place on waxed paper; let stand until set. Store in the refrigerator.

Tropical Truffles: Stir 1/2 cup chopped dried bananas, 3 tablespoons dark rum and 1/4 teaspoon ground ginger into melted chocolate mixture. Chill and shape as directed; roll truffles in chopped toasted coconut.

Cherry Truffles: Place 3/4 cup chopped dried tart cherries in a small bowl. Cover with 3 tablespoons cherry brandy; let stand for 30 minutes. Drain cherries, reserving 1 tablespoon brandy; stir cherries and reserved brandy into melted chocolate mixture. Chill and shape as directed; roll truffles in chopped sliced toasted almonds.

Hazelnut Truffles: Stir 3 tablespoons hazelnut liqueur into melted chocolate mixture. Chill and shape as directed; roll truffles in chopped toasted hazelnuts.

Chocolate-Coffee Bean
Ice Cream Cake

PREP: 15 MIN. + FREEZING   **YIELD:** 12 SERVINGS

At our school, we celebrate faculty birthdays. I needed a quick treat that would appeal to everyone. This frosty and impressive dessert not only fit my needs, but it was a huge hit with all!

Karen Beck ★ Alexandria, Pennsylvania

- 1-3/4 cups chocolate wafer crumbs (about 28 wafers)
- 1/4 cup butter, melted
- 2 quarts coffee ice cream, softened
- 1/3 cup chocolate-covered coffee beans, finely chopped
- 2-1/4 cups heavy whipping cream
- 1 cup plus 2 tablespoons confectioners' sugar
- 1/2 cup plus 1 tablespoon baking cocoa
- 1/2 teaspoon vanilla extract

Chocolate curls and additional chocolate-covered coffee beans

In a small bowl, combine wafer crumbs and butter; press onto the bottom and up the sides of a greased 9-in. springform pan. Freeze for 10 minutes.

In a large bowl, combine ice cream and coffee beans; spoon over the crust. Cover and freeze for 2 hours or until firm.

In a large bowl, beat cream until it begins to thicken. Add confectioners' sugar, cocoa and vanilla; beat until stiff peaks form. Spread over ice cream. (Pan will be full.)

Cover and freeze for 4 hours or overnight. Remove from the freezer 10 minutes before serving. Garnish with chocolate curls and coffee beans.

Blood-Orange
Pomegranate Sorbet

PREP: 20 MIN. + FREEZING   **YIELD:** 3-1/2 CUPS

Here's the perfect dessert for busy holiday hostesses. It's easy, refreshing, lovely and can be made ahead for convenience. Best of all? It will melt any and all resistance to dessert!

Taste of Home Test Kitchen

- 8 medium blood oranges
- 1 cup sugar
- 1 cup pomegranate juice
- 2 tablespoons orange liqueur

Blood orange slices and pomegranate seeds

Grate 1 tablespoon orange peel; set aside. Squeeze juice from all of the oranges. Strain and discard pulp. In a small saucepan, combine the sugar, orange juice and peel. Cook and stir over medium heat until sugar is dissolved. Set aside to cool.

In a large bowl, combine the orange juice mixture, pomegranate juice and orange liqueur. Fill cylinder of ice cream freezer two-thirds full; freeze according to manufacturer's directions.

Transfer to a freezer container; freeze for 4 hours or until firm. Spoon into dessert dishes. Garnish with orange slices and pomegranate seeds.

Grasshopper Baked Alaska

PREP: 45 MIN. + FREEZING   **BAKE:** 5 MIN.
YIELD: 12 SERVINGS

Can you believe it? This stunning dessert is completely make-ahead, including the meringue. All you need to do is bake it for a few minutes in the oven before serving.

Taste of Home Test Kitchen

- 1/2 cup butter, cubed
- 2 ounces unsweetened chocolate, chopped
- 1 cup sugar
- 1 teaspoon vanilla extract
- 2 eggs
- 3/4 cup all-purpose flour
- 1/2 teaspoon baking powder
- 1/2 teaspoon salt
- 2 quarts vanilla ice cream, softened
- 1 package (4.67 ounces) mint Andes candies, chopped
- 2 tablespoons creme de menthe
- 1 tablespoon creme de cacao

Green food coloring, optional

MERINGUE:
- 8 egg whites
- 1 cup sugar
- 1 teaspoon cream of tartar

In a microwave-safe bowl, melt butter and chocolate; stir until smooth. Stir in sugar. Beat in vanilla and eggs, one at a time, beating well after each addition. Combine the flour, baking powder and salt; stir into chocolate mixture.

Transfer to a greased 8-in. round baking pan. Bake at 350° for 30-35 minutes or until a toothpick inserted near the center comes out with moist crumbs (do not overbake). Cool for 10 minutes before removing from pan to a wire rack to cool completely.

Meanwhile, in a large bowl, combine the ice cream, Andes candies, liqueurs and, if desired, food coloring. Transfer to an 8-in. round bowl (1-1/2 qts.) lined with plastic wrap; freeze until set.

In a large heavy saucepan, combine the egg whites, sugar and cream of tartar. With a hand mixer, beat on low speed for 1 minute. Continue beating over low heat until egg mixture reaches 160°, about 8 minutes. Transfer to a bowl; beat until stiff glossy peaks form and sugar is dissolved.

Place brownie on an ungreased foil-lined baking sheet; top with inverted ice cream mold. Remove plastic wrap. Immediately spread meringue over ice cream, sealing to edges of brownie. Freeze until ready to serve, up to 24 hours.

Bake at 400° for 2-5 minutes or until meringue is lightly browned. Transfer to a serving plate; serve immediately.

Apple Butter Bread Pudding

PREP: 20 MIN. + STANDING   **BAKE:** 50 MIN.
YIELD: 12 SERVINGS

This is one of my mother's best recipes! I'm sure your family will be as crazy about it as ours has always been. We like to serve this for dessert or as a very special breakfast treat.

Jerri Gradert ★ Lincoln, Nebraska

- 1/3 cup raisins
- 1 cup apple butter
- 6 croissants, split

CUSTARD:
- 8 eggs
- 3 cups 2% milk
- 1-1/2 cups sugar
- 2 teaspoons vanilla extract
- 1/4 teaspoon salt

STREUSEL:
- 1/2 cup all-purpose flour
- 1/2 cup packed brown sugar
- 1/4 teaspoon salt
- 1/4 cup cold butter

Place raisins in a small bowl. Cover with boiling water; let stand for 5 minutes. Drain and set aside.

Combine apple butter and raisins. Spread over croissant bottoms; replace tops. Cut each croissant into three pieces; place in a greased 13-in. x 9-in. baking dish.

In a large bowl, combine the eggs, milk, sugar, vanilla and salt. Pour over croissants; let stand for 30 minutes or until bread is softened.

In a small bowl, combine the flour, brown sugar and salt. Cut in butter until mixture resembles coarse crumbs. Sprinkle over top.

Bake, uncovered, at 350° for 50-60 minutes or until a knife inserted near the center comes out clean. Serve warm. Refrigerate leftovers.

Orange-Swirled Cheesecake Dessert

PREP: 55 MIN.   **BAKE:** 30 MIN. + CHILLING
YIELD: 16 SERVINGS

Swirls of homemade orange curd drift through these delectable white chocolate cheesecake bars. The delicate flavor always reminds me of a childhood treat...Orange Creamsicles!

Margee Berry ★ White Salmon, Washington

- 6 ounces shortbread cookies (about 23)
- 1/3 cup slivered almonds
- 1/4 cup butter, melted
- 6 tablespoons plus 3/4 cup sugar, *divided*
- 1 tablespoon cornstarch
- 1/4 cup orange juice
- 2 tablespoons plus 1-1/2 teaspoons cold water
- 2 teaspoons finely grated orange peel
- 1 egg yolk
- 3 ounces white baking chocolate, chopped
- 3 tablespoons heavy whipping cream
- 2 packages (8 ounces *each*) cream cheese, softened
- 2 tablespoons all-purpose flour
- 3 eggs, lightly beaten
- 1/4 cup sour cream

Place cookies and almonds in a food processor; cover and process until fine crumbs form. Stir in butter. Press into an ungreased 9-in. square baking pan. Bake at 325° for 15 minutes or until set. Cool on a wire rack.

Meanwhile, in a small saucepan, combine 6 tablespoons sugar and cornstarch. Stir in the orange juice, water and orange peel until blended. Cook and stir for 2 minutes or until thickened. Whisk a small amount of the hot mixture into the egg yolk. Return all to the pan. Reduce the heat. Cook, whisking continuously, for 1 minute. Set aside to cool completely.

Place baking chocolate in a small bowl. In a small saucepan, bring cream just to a boil. Pour over chocolate; whisk until smooth. Cool.

In a large bowl, beat cream cheese and remaining sugar until smooth. Beat in flour. Add eggs; beat on low speed just until combined. Beat in the sour cream and white chocolate mixture just until combined.

Place 1/4 cup cream cheese mixture in a small bowl; stir in orange mixture until well blended.

Pour plain cream cheese mixture over crust. Drop orange batter by tablespoonfuls randomly over top. Cut through batter with a knife to swirl.

Bake at 325° for 30-35 minutes or until filling is set. Cool on a wire rack for 1 hour. Refrigerate for at least 2 hours. Cut into squares. Store in the refrigerator.

Chocolate-Raspberry Polka Dot Cake

PREP: 1 HOUR + CHILLING
BAKE: 20 MIN. + COOLING **YIELD:** 16 SERVINGS

Tender chocolate cake layers are spread with a delightful raspberry whipped cream and silky ganache. The entire cake is draped in a rich chocolate glaze, then decorated with polka dots for a whimsical touch. What's not to love?

Rebekah Radewahn ★ Wauwatosa, Wisconsin

- 3/4 cup baking cocoa
- 3/4 cup boiling water
- 3/4 cup unsalted butter, softened
- 1-1/2 cups sugar
- 1-1/2 cups packed brown sugar
- 3 eggs
- 3 teaspoons vanilla extract
- 3/4 cup buttermilk
- 3/4 cup water
- 3 cups cake flour
- 1 teaspoon baking powder
- 1/2 teaspoon baking soda
- 1/4 teaspoon plus 1/8 teaspoon salt

GANACHE:
- 4 ounces semisweet chocolate, chopped
- 1 cup heavy whipping cream
- 1 teaspoon raspberry extract

RASPBERRY CREAM:
- 1 package (10 ounces) frozen sweetened raspberries, thawed
- 1-1/2 cups heavy whipping cream, whipped

GLAZE:
- 1 pound semisweet chocolate, chopped
- 1-1/2 cups unsalted butter, cubed
- 2 tablespoons corn syrup
- 2 teaspoons raspberry extract

GARNISH:
- 2 ounces white candy coating, melted
- 1 ounce dark chocolate candy coating, melted

Blue food coloring, optional

Line three 9-in. round baking pans with waxed paper; grease and flour the pans and paper. Set aside.

Dissolve cocoa in boiling water; cool. In a bowl, cream the butter and sugars until light and fluffy. Add eggs, one at a time, beating well after each addition. Beat in cocoa mixture and vanilla. In a bowl, combine buttermilk and water; set aside. Combine the flour, baking powder, baking soda and salt; add to the creamed mixture alternately with buttermilk mixture, beating well after each addition.

Transfer to prepared pans. Bake at 350° for 20-25 minutes or until a toothpick inserted near the center comes out clean. Cool for 10 minutes before removing from pans to wire racks to cool completely.

For ganache, place chocolate in a small bowl. In a small saucepan, bring cream just to a boil. Pour over chocolate; whisk until smooth. Stir in extract. Refrigerate until chilled. In a small bowl, beat chocolate mixture until soft peaks form, about 15 seconds.

For raspberry cream, place raspberries in a food processor, cover and process until blended. Strain raspberries, reserving juice. Discard seeds. Gently fold juice into whipped cream.

Cut each cake horizontally into two layers. Place one cake layer on a serving plate; spread with 1 cup raspberry cream. Top with another cake layer; spread with half of the ganache. Repeat raspberry and ganache layers. Top with another cake layer; spread with remaining raspberry cream. Top with remaining cake layer. Refrigerate for 1 hour or until set.

For glaze, in a microwave, melt the chocolate, butter and corn syrup; stir until smooth. Stir in extract. Cool slightly, stirring occasionally. Pour over cake.

For garnish, in a microwave, melt candy coating in separate bowls; stir until smooth. Tint half of the white coating using blue coloring if desired. Pipe or spoon melted coating onto waxed paper in different sized circles; let stand until set. Press circles onto cake. If desired, stack circles on top of each other, using melted coating to hold them in place. Refrigerate cake until serving.

TO MAKE AHEAD: Cake can be made 1 day ahead.

Nut Fruit Bark

PREP: 15 MIN. + CHILLING **YIELD:** 1-1/2 POUNDS

Here's a sophisticated version of fruit bark. Espresso powder gives a rich mocha flavor to the dark chocolate. If you're a fan of sweet-salty treats, be sure to use the sea salt.

Tom Faglon ★ Somerset, New Jersey

- 1 pound dark chocolate, coarsely chopped
- 1 teaspoon instant espresso powder
- 1/2 cup dried cherries *or* blueberries, *divided*
- 1/2 cup macadamia nuts, chopped and *divided*
- 1/2 cup chopped cashews, *divided*
- 1/2 teaspoon coarse sea salt, optional

Line the bottom and sides of a 15-in. x 10-in. x 1-in. baking pan with parchment paper; grease the paper and set aside.

In a double boiler or metal bowl over hot water, melt chocolate; stir until smooth. Stir in espresso powder and half of the cherries and nuts. Spread into prepared pan; top with remaining cherries and nuts (pan will not be full). Sprinkle with sea salt if desired. Refrigerate for 15 minutes or until firm.

Break into pieces. Store in an airtight container.

Hazelnut Mocha Eclairs

PREP: 40 MIN. **BAKE:** 25 MIN. + COOLING
YIELD: 14 SERVINGS

Just looking at these chocolaty eclairs can make your mouth water. They make a special ending to any meal or a wonderful treat with an afternoon cup of coffee.

Carol Witczak ★ Tinley Park, Illinois

- 1/2 cup water
- 1/2 cup 2% milk
- 1/2 cup butter, cubed
- 1 tablespoon sugar
- 1/4 teaspoon salt
- 1 cup all-purpose flour
- 4 eggs

FILLING:
- 1 tablespoon instant coffee granules
- 1 tablespoon boiling water
- 2 cups heavy whipping cream
- 1/4 cup confectioners' sugar
- 1/2 cup chopped hazelnuts, *divided*

TOPPING:
- 1/2 cup milk chocolate chips, melted

In a large saucepan, bring the water, milk, butter, sugar and salt to a boil. Add flour all at once and stir until a smooth ball forms. Remove from the heat; let stand for 5 minutes. Add eggs, one at a time, beating well after each addition. Continue beating until mixture is smooth and shiny.

Place a large round tip in a disposable pastry bag or heavy duty resealable plastic bag and cut a small hole in one corner of the bag. Transfer dough to prepared bag. Pipe 3-in. strips about 3 in. apart on greased baking sheets. Bake at 400° for 10 minutes. Reduce heat to 350°; bake 15-20 minutes longer or until golden brown. Pierce the side of each eclair with the tip of a knife. Remove to wire racks; cool. Split eclairs open; remove tops and set aside. Discard soft dough from inside.

For filling, dissolve coffee granules in boiling water; cool. In a small bowl, beat cream and confectioners' sugar until stiff peaks form. Fold in coffee mixture and 1/4 cup hazelnuts. Refrigerate.

Fill the eclairs just before serving; replace tops. Spread with melted chocolate. Sprinkle with remaining hazelnuts. Refrigerate leftovers.

Piping Eclairs

Place a large round tip (about 3/4 in. in diameter) in disposable pastry bag or heavy-duty resealable plastic bag. Cut a small hole in the corner of bag. Fill bag with dough. Pipe 3-in.-long strips on a greased baking sheet, leaving 3 in. of space between each strip.

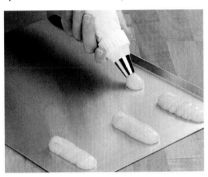

White Chocolate-Raspberry Mousse Cheesecake

PREP: 50 MIN. **BAKE:** 50 MIN. + CHILLING
YIELD: 16 SERVINGS

Ideal for Christmas dinner dessert, a New Year's celebration or even a holiday tea party, one thing's for sure...the blend of flavors in this creamy cheesecake is simply heavenly!

Crystal Morris ★ Alliance, Ohio

- 2 cups graham cracker crumbs
- 1/2 cup butter, melted
- 1/3 cup sugar

FILLING:
- 2 cups white baking chips, *divided*
- 3 packages (8 ounces *each*) cream cheese, softened
- 3/4 cup sugar
- 1/3 cup sour cream
- 1 tablespoon all-purpose flour
- 1 teaspoon vanilla extract
- 3 eggs, lightly beaten

MOUSSE:
- 1 envelope unflavored gelatin
- 3 tablespoons cold water
- 1 tablespoon lemon juice
- 1 package (12 ounces) frozen unsweetened raspberries, thawed
- 1/2 cup sugar
- 1 egg plus 1 egg yolk, beaten
- 1/4 cup raspberry liqueur

- 1-1/2 cups heavy whipping cream, whipped
Fresh raspberries, optional

Place a greased 10-in. springform pan on a double thickness of heavy-duty foil (about 18 in. square). Securely wrap foil around pan.

In a small bowl, combine the cracker crumbs, butter and sugar. Press onto the bottom of prepared pan.

In a microwave, melt 1 cup white chips; stir until smooth. Set aside to cool. In a bowl, beat cream cheese and sugar until smooth. Beat in the sour cream, flour and vanilla. Beat in melted chips. Add eggs; beat on low speed just until combined. Fold in remaining chips. Pour into crust.

Place springform pan in a large baking pan; add 1 in. of hot water to larger pan. Bake at 325° for 50-60 minutes or until center is just set and top appears dull. Remove springform pan from water bath. Cool on a wire rack for 10 minutes. Carefully run a knife around edge of pan to loosen; cool 1 hour longer.

Meanwhile, in a small bowl, sprinkle gelatin over cold water and lemon juice; let stand for 1 minute. Place raspberries in a food processor; cover and process until smooth. Strain; discard seeds.

In a heavy saucepan, heat sugar and 1/2 cup raspberry puree until bubbles form around sides of pan. Whisk a small amount of hot mixture into egg mixture. Return all to the pan, whisking constantly. Cook and stir over low heat until mixture reaches 160°. Remove from the heat.

Whisk a small amount of hot liquid into gelatin mixture; stir until gelatin is completely dissolved. Stir in liqueur and remaining hot raspberry mixture. Stir in remaining raspberry puree. Cover and refrigerate for 30 minutes. Fold in whipped cream. Spread over cheesecake.

Refrigerate overnight. Remove sides of pan. Garnish with fresh raspberries if desired.

Cherry-Nut White Fudge

PREP: 30 MIN.   **COOK:** 30 MIN. + CHILLING
YIELD: 2 POUNDS

Ring in Christmas with a fudge that's studded with all the colors of the season! Flecked with red and green candied cherries and chunks of pecans, it makes a great gift, too.

Flo Burtnett ★ Gage, Oklahoma

  2 teaspoons plus 1/4 cup butter, *divided*
  2 cups sugar
  1 cup half-and-half cream
1/4 cup light corn syrup
1/2 teaspoon salt
  1 cup miniature marshmallows
  1 teaspoon vanilla extract
1/2 cup pecan halves
1/3 cup red candied cherries
1/3 cup green candied cherries

Line an 8-in. square dish with foil and grease the foil with 2 teaspoons butter; set aside.

In a large heavy saucepan, combine the sugar, cream, corn syrup, salt and remaining butter. Bring to a boil over medium heat, stirring until sugar is dissolved. Cook over medium-low heat, without stirring until a candy thermometer reads 240° (soft-ball stage). Remove from the heat; stir in marshmallows and vanilla.

With a wooden spoon, beat until mixture begins to lose its gloss, about 10 minutes. Fold in pecans and candied cherries. Pour into prepared pan. Refrigerate for 2 hours or until firm.

Using foil, lift the fudge out of the pan. Discard foil; cut fudge into 1-in. squares. Store in an airtight container in the refrigerator.

Eggnog Tiramisu Trifle

PREP: 1-1/2 HOURS   **COOK:** 30 MIN. + CHILLING
YIELD: 21 SERVINGS

Rich and absolutely fabulous—my family's five-star dessert is laced with holiday spirits and is almost too pretty to eat. You and your guests will relish every luscious bite!

Tonya Burkhard ★ Davis, Illinois

12	egg yolks
1-2/3	cups sugar, *divided*
2-3/4	cups water, *divided*
1/4	cup dark rum
1/4	cup brandy
1/2	teaspoon ground nutmeg
4	cartons (8 ounces *each*) mascarpone cheese
2	cups heavy whipping cream
2	teaspoons vanilla extract
1	cup (6 ounces) semisweet chocolate chips
1	cup coffee liqueur
1/3	cup instant espresso powder
70	crisp ladyfinger cookies

In a double boiler or metal bowl over simmering water, constantly whisk the egg yolks, 1-1/3 cups sugar, 1/4 cup water, rum, brandy and nutmeg until mixture reaches 160° or is thick enough to coat the back of a spoon, about 25 minutes. Remove from the heat; gradually whisk in cheese.

In a large bowl, beat cream until it begins to thicken. Add the vanilla; beat until stiff peaks form. Fold into mascarpone mixture.

Place chocolate chips in a food processor; cover and process until finely chopped.

In a small saucepan, bring remaining water to a boil. Stir in the coffee liqueur, espresso powder and remaining sugar until sugar is completely dissolved. Dip 14 ladyfingers into mixture; arrange in a single layer in a 5-qt. glass bowl. Spread 2 cups mascarpone mixture over the ladyfingers. Sprinkle with 3 tablespoons chocolate. Repeat layers four times. Cover and refrigerate overnight.

Plum Pudding

PREP: 35 MIN. **COOK:** 2 HOURS
YIELD: 8 SERVINGS (1/2 CUP SAUCE)

An adaptation of the traditional holiday staple, my spiced plum pudding stays true to those time-honored flavors.

Deb Thompson ★ Lincoln, Nebraska

1/2	cup butter, softened
1/2	cup sugar
2	eggs
1/2	cup 2% milk
1/2	cup molasses
1-1/2	cups all-purpose flour
1-1/2	teaspoons baking powder
1/2	teaspoon baking soda
1/2	teaspoon ground cinnamon
1/8	teaspoon ground cloves
1/8	teaspoon ground nutmeg
1	medium apple, peeled and chopped
1	cup raisins
1/2	cup chopped maraschino cherries
1/2	cup chopped dates

SAUCE:

1/3	cup sugar
3/4	teaspoon cornstarch
1/2	cup boiling water
1/2	teaspoon butter
1/4	teaspoon ground nutmeg

In a bowl, cream butter and sugar until light and fluffy. Beat in the eggs, milk and molasses. Combine the flour, baking powder, baking soda and spices; gradually add to creamed mixture. Stir in the apple, raisins, cherries and dates.

Pour into a well-greased 6-cup pudding mold or metal gelatin mold. Cover with foil. Place on a rack in a deep stockpot. Add 1 in. of boiling water to pot; cover and boil gently for 2 to 2-1/2 hours or until a toothpick inserted near the center comes out clean, replacing water as needed. Let stand for 5 minutes before unmolding.

For sauce, in a saucepan, combine sugar and cornstarch. Stir in water until smooth. Bring to a boil over medium heat; cook and stir for 1-2 minutes or until thickened. Remove from the heat. Stir in butter and nutmeg. Unmold pudding onto a serving plate; cut into wedges. Serve warm with sauce.

Steamed Puddings

You do not need to run out and buy special equipment to steam a pudding on the range top. A stockpot and small metal cooling rack will do the trick. Place the rack in the stockpot and add the amount of water the recipe directs. Place the prepared pudding mold on the rack and steam for time given in the recipe.

Cherry Pecan Upside-Down Cake

PREP: 25 MIN. **BAKE:** 40 MIN. + COOLING
YIELD: 8 SERVINGS

Cherries give a terrific twist to classic pineapple upside-down cake. The crowning touch on each piece is the creamy topping.

Eleanor Froehlich ★ Rochester, Michigan

- 1/4 cup butter, melted
- 3/4 cup packed brown sugar
- 2 cans (15 ounces *each*) pitted dark sweet cherries, drained
- 1/2 cup chopped pecans

CAKE:
- 1/2 cup butter, softened
- 1 cup plus 2 tablespoons sugar
- 3 eggs
- 1/2 teaspoon vanilla extract
- 1-1/2 cups cake flour
- 1 teaspoon baking powder
- 1/4 teaspoon salt
- 1/2 cup buttermilk

TOPPING:
- 1/2 cup heavy whipping cream
- 1/2 cup mascarpone cheese
- 2 tablespoons confectioners' sugar
- 1/8 teaspoon almond extract
- 1/8 teaspoon vanilla extract

Pour butter into an ungreased 9-in. round baking pan; sprinkle with brown sugar. Arrange cherries in a single layer over brown sugar; top with pecans.

In a large bowl, cream butter and sugar until light and fluffy. Add eggs, one at a time, beating well after each addition. Beat in vanilla. Combine the flour, baking powder and salt; add to the creamed mixture alternately with buttermilk, beating well after each addition.

Spoon over pecan layer. Bake at 350° for 40-45 minutes or until a toothpick inserted near the center comes out clean. Cool for 10 minutes before inverting onto a serving plate.

For topping, in a large bowl, beat cream and cheese until it begins to thicken. Gradually add confectioners' sugar and extracts; beat until stiff peaks form. Serve with cake.

Sour Cream Pumpkin Cake

PREP: 30 MIN.   **BAKE:** 50 MIN. + COOLING
YIELD: 12 SERVINGS

The nicely spiced streusel in the center of this cake is a marvelous surprise and complements the cinnamony pumpkin flavor. It's lovely for dessert or breakfast.

Elaine Holmberg ★ Norfolk, Nebraska

2/3	cup packed brown sugar
1-1/4	teaspoons ground cinnamon
1/4	teaspoon ground allspice
2-1/2	teaspoons cold butter

BATTER:

1	cup butter, softened
2	cups sugar
4	eggs
1	cup (8 ounces) sour cream
1	cup canned pumpkin
2	teaspoons vanilla extract
3	cups all-purpose flour
3	teaspoons ground cinnamon
2	teaspoons baking soda
1	teaspoon salt

GLAZE:

1-1/2	cups confectioners' sugar
2	tablespoons orange juice

In a small bowl, combine the brown sugar, cinnamon and allspice. Cut in butter until crumbly; set aside.

In a large bowl, cream butter and sugar until light and fluffy. Add eggs, one at a time, beating well after each addition. Beat in the sour cream, pumpkin and vanilla. Combine the flour, cinnamon, baking soda and salt; gradually add to creamed mixture.

Pour half of the batter into a greased 10-in. fluted tube pan. Sprinkle with reserved crumb mixture; top with remaining batter. Bake at 350° for 50-55 minutes or until a toothpick inserted near the center comes out clean.

Cool for 10 minutes before removing from pan to a wire rack to cool completely. Combine glaze ingredients; drizzle over cooled cake.

Fresh Pear Ginger Crisp

PREP: 15 MIN. + CHILLING **BAKE:** 35 MIN.
YIELD: 9 SERVINGS

Gingersnaps lend a nice crunch to my homey, heartwarming classic featuring the season's juiciest fruit—pears!

Linda Robertson ★ Cozad, Nebraska

1   cup crushed gingersnap cookies (about 20 cookies)
1/2 cup old-fashioned oats
1/2 cup packed brown sugar
1/4 teaspoon ground ginger
1/4 teaspoon ground cloves
1/8 teaspoon salt
1/3 cup butter, softened
7   medium pears (about 2-1/2 pounds), peeled and thinly sliced
2   tablespoons all-purpose flour
Vanilla ice cream, optional

In a small bowl, combine the first six ingredients. With clean hands, work butter into oat mixture until well combined. Refrigerate for 15 minutes.

Place pears in a small bowl; add flour and toss to coat. Transfer to a greased 8-in. square baking dish; sprinkle with oat mixture.

Bake, uncovered, at 350° for 35-40 minutes or until topping is golden brown and fruit is tender. Serve warm with ice cream if desired.

Caramel Cookie Candy

PREP: 45 MIN.　**COOK:** 30 MIN. + CHILLING
YIELD: 4 DOZEN

Our homemade candy bars combine a smooth, silky caramel and a delicate vanilla cookie. When you set a plate of these chewy treats out, we guarantee they won't last long.

Taste of Home Test Kitchen

2	teaspoons plus 2/3 cup butter, softened, *divided*
3/4	cup confectioners' sugar
1	egg
1-1/2	teaspoons vanilla extract
2	cups all-purpose flour
1/2	teaspoon baking powder
1/2	teaspoon salt

CARAMEL LAYER:

1	cup sugar
1	cup corn syrup
1	cup butter, cubed
1	can (14 ounces) sweetened condensed milk
1	teaspoon vanilla extract
2-1/2	pounds dark chocolate candy coating

Line a 13-in. x 9-in. pan with foil and grease the foil with 2 teaspoons butter; set aside.

In a large bowl, cream confectioners' sugar and the remaining butter until light and fluffy. Beat in egg and vanilla. Combine flour, baking powder and salt; gradually add to the creamed mixture and mix well. Press dough into prepared pan. Bake at 375° for 16-20 minutes or until lightly browned. Cool on a wire rack.

For caramel, combine the sugar, corn syrup and butter in a large saucepan. Bring to a boil over medium heat, stirring constantly. Boil gently for 4 minutes without stirring. Remove from the heat; gradually stir in milk.

Reduce heat to medium-low and cook until a candy thermometer reads 238° (soft-ball stage), stirring constantly. Remove from the heat; stir in the vanilla. Pour over the prepared crust. Refrigerate for 2 hours or until caramel is set.

Using foil, lift candy out of pan. Gently peel off foil; cut into 3-1/4-in. x 3/4-in. bars. In a microwave, melt candy coating; stir until smooth. Dip bars in chocolate; allow excess to drip off. Place on a waxed paper-lined sheet; refrigerate until set. If desired, drizzle leftover candy coating over bars. Store in an airtight container.

White Chocolate-Cranberry-Pecan Tart

PREP: 25 MIN　**BAKE:** 40 MIN. + COOLING
YIELD: 16 SERVINGS

The first time I tasted my friend's dessert was at a Christmas party she was hosting. I got a copy of the recipe and now it's a yuletide tradition for my family. The white chips, cranberries and orange peel take pecan pie to scrumptious new heights!

Karen Moore ★ Jacksonville, Florida

Pastry for single-crust pie (9 inches)

1	cup fresh *or* frozen cranberries
1	cup pecan halves
1	cup white baking chips
3	eggs
3/4	cup packed brown sugar
3/4	cup light corn syrup
2	tablespoons all-purpose flour
1	teaspoon grated orange peel

Whipped cream, optional

Roll out pastry to fit an 11-in. tart pan with removable bottom; trim edges. Sprinkle with the cranberries, pecans and chips. In a small bowl, whisk the eggs, brown sugar, corn syrup, flour and orange peel; pour over chips.

Bake at 350° for 40-45 minutes or until a knife inserted near the center comes out clean. Cool on a wire rack. Serve with whipped cream if desired.

Golden Harvest Apple Pie

PREP: 30 MIN.   **BAKE:** 55 MIN. + COOLING
YIELD: 8 SERVINGS

You'll think Grandma was baking in the kitchen when you take your first bite of this old-fashioned pie. The golden, tender crust holds a mouthwatering apple filling with just a hint of orange.

Drew Menne ★ Vineyard Haven, Massachusetts

2 cups all-purpose flour
1 teaspoon salt
3/4 cup shortening
5 tablespoons cold water
FILLING:
2 tablespoons all-purpose flour
1/2 cup sugar
1 teaspoon ground cinnamon
1 teaspoon ground nutmeg

6 cups thinly sliced peeled tart apples
3 tablespoons orange marmalade
2 tablespoons butter
1 tablespoon milk

In a large bowl, combine the flour and salt; cut in the shortening until crumbly. Gradually add water, tossing with a fork until dough forms a ball. Divide dough in half so that one portion is slightly larger than the other. Roll out larger portion to fit a 9-in. pie plate. Transfer pastry to pie plate. Trim pastry even with edge.

Sprinkle flour over the pastry. Combine the sugar, cinnamon and nutmeg; layer into pastry alternately with apples. Dot with marmalade and butter.

Roll out remaining pastry to fit top of pie. Place over filling. Trim, seal and flute edges. Cut slits in pastry. Brush with milk.

Bake at 425° for 15 minutes. Reduce heat to 375°; bake 40-50 minutes longer or until crust is golden brown and filling is bubbly. Cool completely on a wire rack.

Novel
GIFTS

Novel Gifts

Good books and tasty treats are always welcomed gifts during the holiday—so much so, that we paired them together throughout this colorful section. Each story was the inspiration for a delicious counterpart that's perfect for gift giving. What a "novel" idea!

Chocolate-Dipped Lavender Pine Nut Brittle

PREP: 15 MIN.   **COOK:** 25 MIN.   **YIELD:** 3 POUNDS

Take your friends on a trip to the south of France with your uniquely flavored brittle and the novel "Chocolat" by Joanne Harris. What's not to love about a gift that combines a lush story and luscious mouthwatering treats?

Taste of Home Test Kitchen

1   tablespoon butter, melted
3   cups sugar
1   cup light corn syrup
1/2   cup water
4-1/2   cups pine nuts
1/4   cup butter, softened
2   teaspoons baking soda
2   teaspoons vanilla extract
1   teaspoon dried lavender flowers
1/2   teaspoon salt
1   pound dark chocolate candy coating, coarsely chopped

Grease two 15-in. x 10-in. x 1-in. pans with melted butter; set aside.

In a large saucepan, combine the sugar, corn syrup and water. Cook, without stirring, over medium heat until a candy thermometer reads 230° (thread stage). Carefully add pine nuts; cook and stir constantly until mixture reaches 300° (hard-crack stage).

Remove from the heat; stir in the softened butter, baking soda, vanilla, lavender and salt. Immediately pour into prepared pans. Spread to 1/4-in. thickness. Cool before breaking into pieces.

In a microwave, melt chocolate coating; stir until smooth. Dip each candy piece halfway into the melted chocolate; allow excess to drip off. Place on waxed paper and let stand until set. Store in an airtight container.

Editor's Note: We recommend that you test your candy thermometer before each use by bringing water to a boil; the thermometer should read 212°. Adjust your recipe temperature up or down based on your test.

Mother of Pearl Bookmark

Make a lovely personalized gift in no time at all. Any avid reader will appreciate these simple but sophisticated bookmarks. Give them with books, as stocking stuffers or use for party favors.

Purchase a 1-1/2-in. or larger bead or pendant, 5 matching smaller beads and 2 matching 1/2-in. pendants. You'll also need a 36-in. length of 3/8-in. ribbon, 5 eye pins, 2 small jump rings, 2 fold-over cord ends, chain and a round-nose pliers and wire cutters.

Fold the ribbon in half and push the folded end through the hole on the large bead or pendant. Once a small loop forms pull the ribbon ends through to secure in place.

Attach your fold-over cord ends with the holes facing away from the ribbon ends. Use the round-nose pliers to turn down the edges of the fold-over cord ends. To make more secure, use a dot of tacky glue on each ribbon end prior to folding edges over. Let dry.

String a single bead centered onto each eye pin. Fold wire over the bead at each end making right angles. Use the round-nose pliers to make small loops at each bead end. To make loops, start about 1/4-in. away from the bead end, with palm upward, roll your wrist inward toward the bead. Trim excess wire at base of loop. Repeat for all beads.

Make 2 strands of beads, one with two beads and one with three beads. Use pliers to slightly open the loops on each bead end and insert into a loop on another bead end, then close loops. Repeat to join beads into two separate strands. Attach one strand to each of the fold-over cords in the same manner. At the end of each beaded strand, attach a 1/2-in. pendant using a small jump ring.

Italian Herb Dipping Blend

PREP/TOTAL TIME: 25 MIN.   **YIELD:** 4 SERVINGS PER BATCH

"Bread Alone," by Judith Hendricks, makes the perfect gift match with this herb-flecked dipping oil...and a crusty loaf.

Cynthia Greenfeather ★ Nowata, Oklahoma

- 2/3 cup dried basil
- 2/3 cup dried parsley flakes
- 6 tablespoons dried rosemary, crushed
- 2 tablespoons dried minced garlic
- 2 tablespoons dried marjoram
- 2 tablespoons dried oregano
- 4 teaspoons sugar
- 2 teaspoons salt
- 2 teaspoons coarsely ground pepper
- 1 teaspoon crushed red pepper flakes

ADDITIONAL INGREDIENTS (for *each* batch):
- 1/2 cup olive oil

Italian *or* French bread

Combine the first 10 ingredients. Transfer to small spice jars. Store in a cool dry place for up to 1 year. Shake before using. Yield: 16 batches (2 cups mix).

To prepare dipping blend: In a small skillet, heat 2 tablespoons seasoning mix with olive oil just until heated through. Serve with bread.

Pop 'n' Rock Popcorn

PREP/TOTAL TIME: 15 MIN.   **YIELD:** 8 CUPS

Each bite of this crackly, sweet snack mix tickles your tongue. It's the ideal antidote for Dr. Seuss' sour main character in his seasonal tale, "How the Grinch Stole Christmas!"

Melanie Sandoval ★ East Hartford, Connecticut

- 1 package (3.3 ounces) natural microwave popcorn
- 1 cup white baking chips
- 2 envelopes watermelon Pop Rocks candy
- 2 envelopes strawberry Pop Rocks candy

Microwave popcorn according to package directions. Place in a large bowl.

In a microwave, melt baking chips; stir until smooth. Pour a third over popcorn; gently toss to combine. Add the remaining melted chips; toss to coat.

Divide coated popcorn between two bowls. Sprinkle one with watermelon candy and the other with strawberry candy. Stir candy into popcorn mixture. Immediately spread each onto parchment paper; let stand until set. Break into pieces. Store in separate airtight containers.

Gingerbread Babies

PREP: 2 HOURS + CHILLING
BAKE: 10 MIN./PER BATCH + STANDING
YIELD: ABOUT 2-1/2 DOZEN

Preschoolers and their parents will be enthralled with the antics of "Gingerbread Baby" by Jan Brett. This story is a twist on the classic tale of the gingerbread boy—with a baby getting into much mischief. You'll love munching on these homemade cookies as you read and snuggle together.

Taste of Home Test Kitchen

- 3/4 cup butter, softened
- 1 cup packed brown sugar
- 1 egg
- 3/4 cup molasses
- 4 cups all-purpose flour
- 2 tablespoons baking cocoa
- 2 teaspoons ground ginger
- 1-1/2 teaspoons baking soda
- 1-1/2 teaspoons ground cinnamon
- 3/4 teaspoon ground cloves
- 1/2 teaspoon ground cardamom
- 1/2 teaspoon ground nutmeg
- 1/4 teaspoon salt

ICING:
- 2 cups confectioners' sugar
- 2 tablespoons plus 2 teaspoons water
- 4-1/2 teaspoons meringue powder
- 1/4 teaspoon cream of tartar

Red paste food coloring

In a large bowl, cream butter and brown sugar until light and fluffy. Beat in egg and molasses. Combine the flour, cocoa, ginger, baking soda, cinnamon, cloves, cardamom, nutmeg and salt; gradually add to creamed mixture and mix well. Cover and refrigerate for 2 hours or until easy to handle.

On a lightly floured surface, roll dough to 3/8-in. thickness. Cut with a floured 4-in. gingerbread man cookie cutter. Place 2 in. apart on ungreased baking sheets; reroll scraps.

Bake at 350° for 8-10 minutes or until edges are firm. Remove to wire racks to cool.

In a large bowl, combine the confectioners' sugar, water, meringue powder and cream of tartar; beat on low speed just until combined. Beat on high for 4-5 minutes or until stiff peaks form. Tint desired amount of icing red. (Keep unused icing covered at all times with a damp cloth.)

Using pastry bags and small round tips, decorate cookies as desired. Let dry at room temperature for several hours or until firm. Store in an airtight container.

Red Lentil Soup Mix

PREP: 25 MIN.   **COOK:** 45 MIN.   **YIELD:** 4 CUPS PER BATCH

Heroine Marjan of "Pomegranate Soup," by Marsha Mehran, wins over the townspeople of a rural Irish community with her Red Lentil Soup. Treat yourself or a friend to a steaming bowlful of your own recipe—and a copy of Marjan's saga!

Taste of Home Test Kitchen

- 1/4 cup dried minced onion
- 2 tablespoons dried parsley flakes
- 2 teaspoons ground allspice
- 2 teaspoons ground cumin
- 2 teaspoons ground turmeric
- 1-1/2 teaspoons salt
- 1 teaspoon garlic powder
- 1 teaspoon ground cardamom
- 1 teaspoon ground cinnamon
- 1 teaspoon pepper
- 1/2 teaspoon ground cloves
- 2 pounds dried red lentils

ADDITIONAL INGREDIENTS (for *each* batch):
- 1 medium carrot, finely chopped
- 1 celery rib, finely chopped
- 1 tablespoon olive oil
- 2 cans (14-1/2 ounces *each*) vegetable broth

In a small bowl, combine the first 11 ingredients. Place 2/3 cup lentils in each of four 12-ounce jelly jars or cellophane gift bags. Evenly divide onion mixture among jars and top with another scant 2/3 cup lentils. Store in a cool dry place for up to 6 months. Yield: 4 batches.

To prepare one batch of soup: In a large saucepan, saute carrot and celery in oil until tender. Add soup mix and broth. Bring to a boil. Reduce heat; cover and simmer for 25-30 minutes or until lentils are tender.

Herbed Cheese Crackers

PREP: 25 MIN. + CHILLING   **BAKE:** 15 MIN./BATCH
YIELD: ABOUT 3 DOZEN

Cuddle with your kids while reading Nicholas Edwards' tale, "Santa Paws." And enjoy some yummy, bone-shaped crackers, the perfect treat to go with this book about a homeless puppy spreading the true meaning of Christmas in a small town!

Taste of Home Test Kitchen

- 2 cups (8 ounces) shredded cheddar cheese
- 1 cup all-purpose flour
- 1 teaspoon garlic powder
- 1 teaspoon dill weed
- 1 teaspoon dried oregano
- 1/2 teaspoon salt
- 1/4 cup butter, cubed
- 2 tablespoons water

Place the first six ingredients in a food processor; cover and pulse to blend. Add butter; cover and pulse until mixture resembles coarse crumbs. While processing, gradually add water just until moist crumbs form.

Shape dough into a disk; wrap in plastic wrap and refrigerate for 30 minutes or until easy to handle.

On a lightly floured surface, roll dough to 1/8-in. thickness. Cut with a floured 2-in. cookie cutter. Place 1 in. apart on parchment paper-lined baking sheets.

Bake at 350° for 12-15 minutes or until edges are lightly browned (crackers should be crisp). Remove to wire racks to cool completely. Store in an airtight container.

Holiday Reindeer Cookies

PREP: 45 MIN. + STANDING   **YIELD:** 32 COOKIES

Gather the kids around the tree on Christmas Eve to feast on these adorable reindeer cookies during a retelling of that family favorite by Clement Clarke Moore, "Twas the Night Before Christmas." If you listen closely, you just might hear the sound of reindeer hooves on the roof!

Taste of Home Test Kitchen

1-1/2	pounds dark chocolate candy coating, chopped
1	package (16 ounces) Nutter Butter cookies
32	miniature marshmallows, cut in half widthwise

Black decorating gel

32	red-hot candies
64	miniature pretzels

In a microwave, melt candy coating; stir until smooth. Dip one cookie in chocolate; allow excess to drip off. Place on waxed paper.

Attach two marshmallow halves onto cookie for eyes; add decorating gel for pupils. Add a red-hot for nose. Attach two pretzels for antlers. Repeat. Let stand until set.

Homemade Limoncello

PREP: 40 MIN. + STANDING   **YIELD:** 1-1/2 QUARTS

In Jenny Nelson's tale, "Georgia's Kitchen," a professional chef hones her culinary skills in the Italian countryside. Pair her book with a bottle of your Homemade Limoncello, guaranteed to rival store-bought versions. The after-dinner liqueur is considered the national drink of Italy, and it's sure to be a hit with your friends and family!

Taste of Home Test Kitchen

10	medium lemons
1	bottle (750 milliliters) vodka
3	cups water
1-1/2	cups sugar

Using a vegetable peeler, peel rind from lemons (save lemons for another use). With a sharp knife, scrape pith from peels and discard. Place lemon peels and vodka in a large glass or plastic container. Cover and let stand at room temperature for at least 2 weeks, stirring once a week.

In a large saucepan, bring water and sugar to a boil. Reduce heat; simmer, uncovered, for 10 minutes. Cool completely.

Strain vodka mixture, discarding lemon peels. Return mixture to container; stir in sugar mixture. Pour into glass bottles; seal tightly. Let stand for 2 weeks. Serve chilled.

Sugar Plum Kringles

PREP: 1 HOUR + CHILLING **BAKE:** 20 MIN.
YIELD: 4 PASTRIES (6 SLICES EACH)

*Couple Charles Dickens' holiday classic, "A Christmas Carol,"
with homemade kringle from your kitchen for neighbors and
friends. This recipe makes four kringles, so you'll have one to
keep and three to give away. Even Scrooge would approve!*

Taste of Home Test Kitchen

2	cups all-purpose flour
1	cup cold butter
1	cup (8 ounces) sour cream
3/4	cup plum jam, *divided*
4	teaspoons grated orange peel
8	teaspoons finely chopped walnuts *or* pecans, *divided*
1-1/4	cups confectioners' sugar
2	tablespoons 2% milk
4	teaspoons sugar
1/2	teaspoon ground cinnamon

Place flour in a large bowl; cut in butter until crumbly. Stir
in sour cream. Wrap in plastic wrap. Refrigerate for 1 to
1-1/2 hours or until easy to handle.

Divide dough into four portions. On a lightly floured
surface, roll one portion into a 12-in. x 6-in. rectangle.
(Keep remaining dough refrigerated until ready to use.)
Spread 3 tablespoons jam lengthwise down the center. Fold
in sides of pastry to meet in the center; pinch seam to seal.
Sprinkle with 1 teaspoon each nuts and orange peel. Repeat.
Place on two ungreased baking sheets.

Bake at 375° for 18-22 minutes or until lightly browned.
In a small bowl, combine confectioners' sugar and milk;
drizzle over warm pastries. Combine the sugar, cinnamon
and remaining nuts; sprinkle over warm pastries.

Almond Ginger Cookies

PREP: 35 MIN. **BAKE:** 10 MIN./BATCH **YIELD:** 3-1/2 DOZEN

*Think outside the box this season and wrap up a memorable
tale of young love between a Chinese boy and Japanese girl in
the 1940s, along with these nutty traditional Chinese cookies.
Jamie Ford's "Hotel on the Corner of Bitter and Sweet," is a
gift as delicious as the homemade treats!*

Shirley Warren ★ Thiensville, Wisconsin

1	cup shortening
1/4	cup packed brown sugar
1/2	cup plus 3 tablespoons sugar, *divided*
1	egg
1	teaspoon almond extract
2	cups all-purpose flour
1-1/2	teaspoons baking powder
1/4	teaspoon salt
1/3	cup crystallized ginger, finely chopped
2	tablespoons sliced almonds

In a large bowl, cream the shortening, brown sugar and
1/2 cup sugar until light and fluffy. Beat in egg and extract.
Combine the flour, baking powder and salt; gradually add
to creamed mixture and mix well. Stir in ginger.

Shape into 1-in. balls. Roll in the remaining sugar. Place
2 in. apart on ungreased baking sheets. Flatten with the
bottom of a glass. Press an almond slice into the center of
each cookie.

Bake at 350° for 9-11 minutes or until edges are lightly
browned. Cool for 2 minutes before removing to wire racks.
Store in an airtight container.

Hazelnut Macarons

PREP: 30 MIN. **BAKE:** 10 MIN./BATCH **YIELD:** 5 DOZEN

Written with her grandnephew, "My Life in France" is the touching memoir of Julia Child's life and adventures with French cuisine. Any Francophile on your gift list would love a copy, along with these crisp, chewy French-style macarons!

Taste of Home Test Kitchen

  6 egg whites
1-1/2 cups hazelnuts
2-1/2 cups confectioners' sugar
Dash salt
  1/2 cup superfine sugar
ESPRESSO FILLING:
  1 cup sugar
  6 tablespoons water
  6 egg yolks
  4 teaspoons instant espresso powder
  1 teaspoon vanilla extract
1-1/2 cups butter, softened
  6 tablespoons confectioners' sugar

Place egg whites in a small bowl; let stand at room temperature for 30 minutes.

Place hazelnuts in a 15-in. x 10-in. x 1-in. baking pan. Bake at 350° for 7-10 minutes or until lightly toasted and fragrant. Transfer to a clean kitchen towel; cool. Rub briskly with a towel to remove the skins.

Place confectioners' sugar and hazelnuts in a food processor. Cover and process until hazelnuts are ground.

Add salt to egg whites; beat on medium speed until soft peaks form. Gradually add superfine sugar, 1 tablespoon at a time, beating on high until stiff peaks form. Fold in hazelnut mixture.

Place mixture in a heavy-duty resealable plastic bag; cut a small hole in a corner of bag. Pipe 1-in.-diameter cookies 2 in. apart onto parchment paper-lined baking sheets. Bake at 350° for 9-12 minutes or until lightly browned and firm to the touch. Cool completely on pans on wire racks.

For filling, in a heavy saucepan, bring sugar and water to a boil; cook over medium-high heat until sugar is dissolved. Remove from the heat. Add a small amount of hot mixture to egg yolks; return all to the pan, stirring constantly. Cook 2-3 minutes longer or until mixture thickens, stirring constantly. Remove from the heat; stir in espresso powder and vanilla. Cool to room temperature.

In a stand mixer with the whisk attachment, cream butter until fluffy, about 3 minutes. Gradually beat in cooked sugar mixture. Beat in confectioners' sugar until fluffy. Refrigerate until filling reaches spreading consistency, about 10 minutes.

Spread on the bottoms of half of the cookies; top with remaining cookies. Store in the refrigerator.

Herbed Nut Mix

PREP/TOTAL TIME: 20 MIN. **YIELD:** 2 CUPS

Crack open a package of this slightly sweet, herb-scented nut mix to pass around while your family becomes engrossed and enchanted with a reading of the magical dream of Marie in E.T.A. Hoffman's "Nutcracker."

Sonya Labbe ★ West Hollywood, California

  1 cup salted cashews
  1/2 cup pecan halves
  1/2 cup whole almonds
  1 tablespoon butter
  1 tablespoon brown sugar
1-1/2 teaspoons minced fresh rosemary
1-1/2 teaspoons minced fresh thyme

Spread the cashews, pecans and almonds into an ungreased 15-in. x 10-in. x 1-in. baking pan. Bake at 350° for 8-10 minutes or until toasted, stirring occasionally.

In a large saucepan, combine butter and brown sugar. Cook and stir until sugar is dissolved. Remove from the heat; stir in rosemary and thyme. Add nuts and toss to coat.

Spread on waxed paper to cool. Store in an airtight container in the refrigerator.

TO MAKE AHEAD: May be frozen for up to 3 months.

Dulce de Leche Hot Chocolate Pods

PREP: 20 MIN. + CHILLING   **COOK:** 5 MIN.
YIELD: 14 PODS - 2 SERVINGS PER POD

Drop one of these chocolate pods into some steaming milk for two cups of no-fuss hot chocolate in moments! A box of them wrapped up with Laura Esquivel's novel, "Like Water for Chocolate," is a wonderful, relaxing gift for any busy hostess.

Taste of Home Test Kitchen

  24   ounces 53% cacao dark baking chocolate *or* semisweet
         chocolate, chopped
    1   can (13.4 ounces) dulce de leche
  1/2 cup heavy whipping cream
Gold colored sugar and pearl dust, optional
ADDITIONAL INGREDIENT (for *each* pod):
  1-1/2 cups whole milk

Place chocolate in a large bowl. In a small saucepan, bring dulce de leche and cream just to a boil, stirring constantly. Pour over chocolate; whisk until smooth.

Spoon 1/4 cup chocolate mixture into 14 paper-lined muffin cups; sprinkle with gold sugar if desired. Refrigerate for 8 hours or until firm.

Brush with gold dust if desired. Store in an airtight container in the refrigerator for up to 3 weeks.

To prepare hot chocolate: Bring 1-1/2 cups milk just to a boil; add one pod. Whisk until dissolved.

Editor's Notes: This recipe was tested with Nestle's dulce de leche. Look for it in the international foods section. Pearl dust is available from Wilton Industries. Call 800-794-5866 or visit wilton.com.

Homemade Fettuccine

PREP: 1-1/4 HOURS + STANDING   **YIELD:** 1-1/4 POUNDS

Elizabeth Gilbert's desire for self-enlightenment takes her through Italy, India and Indonesia in "Eat, Pray, Love." A copy of her bestselling book, along with this fresh fettuccine, makes a delicious present—and read—for a special friend!

Taste of Home Test Kitchen

3-1/2 to 4 cups semolina flour
   1 teaspoon salt
   1 cup warm water

Combine 3-1/2 cups flour and salt in a large bowl. Make a well in the center. Pour water into well and stir together, forming a ball.

Turn onto a floured surface; knead until smooth and elastic, about 8-10 minutes, adding remaining flour if necessary to keep dough from sticking to surface and hands (dough will be stiff). Shape into a rectangle; cover and let rest for 30 minutes.

Divide dough into fourths. On a floured surface, roll each portion into a 16-in. x 8-in. rectangle. Dust dough with flour to prevent sticking while rolling. Cut into 1/8-in. slices. Separate noodles onto clean towels; let dry overnight (let dry in the shape the noodles will be stored in). Package dry pasta.

To cook fettuccine: Fill a Dutch oven three-fourths full with water. Bring to a boil. Add noodles; cook, uncovered, for 8-10 minutes or until tender. Drain.

Editor's Note: For a simple fresh tomato sauce, toss cooked pasta with 1 pound chopped plum tomatoes, 1/3 cup pesto, 1/4 teaspoon salt and 1/4 teaspoon ppepper. Sprinkle with Parmesan cheese.

Fruit and Nut Granola

PREP: 20 MIN. **BAKE:** 30 MIN. **YIELD:** 8 CUPS

Snack on some good-for-you granola loaded with nuts, grains and fruit, while you read about one woman's quest to cook healthier and redefine her life after divorce. "Good Enough to Eat," by Stacey Ballis, is warm, funny and includes recipes!

Jess Apfe ★ Berkeley, California

4	cups old-fashioned oats
1	cup Wheaties
3/4	cup slivered almonds
1/2	cup sunflower kernels
1/2	cup salted cashews
1/3	cup chopped pecans
1/4	cup chopped hazelnuts
1/2	cup packed brown sugar
1/2	cup orange juice
1/3	cup honey
1/4	cup canola oil
1	teaspoon vanilla extract
3/4	cup chopped dried apricots
1/3	cup dried cranberries
1/3	cup raisins

In a large bowl, combine the first seven ingredients. In a small saucepan, combine the brown sugar, orange juice, honey and oil. Cook and stir over medium heat until brown sugar is dissolved. Remove from the heat; stir in vanilla. Pour over oat mixture and stir to coat.

Transfer to two greased and foil-lined 15-in. x 10-in. x 1-in. baking pans. Bake at 325° for 30-35 minutes or until crisp, stirring every 10 minutes. Cool completely on a wire rack. Stir in dried fruits. Store in an airtight container.

Holiday Cranberry Jelly

PREP: 25 MIN. **PROCESS:** 10 MIN. **YIELD:** 8 HALF-PINTS

Louisa May Alcott begins her account of the four March sisters during the Christmas season. Now you can spread some holiday cheer with this rosy pink cranberry jelly and a copy of "Little Women."

Nancy Davis ★ Tualatin, Oregon

4	cups cranberry juice
6-1/2	cups sugar
2	pouches (3 ounces *each*) liquid fruit pectin

In a Dutch oven, combine cranberry juice and sugar. Bring to a full rolling boil over high heat, stirring constantly. Stir in pectin. Boil for 1 minute, stirring constantly.

Remove from the heat; skim off foam. Carefully ladle hot liquid into hot half-pint jars, leaving 1/4-in. headspace. Remove air bubbles; wipe rims and adjust lids. Process for 10 minutes in a boiling-water canner.

Swirled Peppermint Marshmallows

PREP: 55 MIN. + STANDING **YIELD:** 1-1/2 POUNDS

The fluffy, airy texture of these homemade marshmallows is as magical as the glistening snowflakes falling throughout Chris Van Allsburg's children's classic, "The Polar Express."

Taste of Home Test Kitchen

2	teaspoons butter
3	envelopes unflavored gelatin
1	cup cold water, *divided*
2	cups sugar
1	cup light corn syrup
1/4	teaspoon salt
3/4	teaspoon peppermint extract
10	to 12 drops food coloring
1/4	cup confectioners' sugar
1/4	cup finely ground peppermint candies

Line a 13-in. x 9-in. pan with foil and grease the foil with butter; set aside.

In a large metal bowl, sprinkle gelatin over 1/2 cup water; set aside. In a large heavy saucepan, combine the sugar, corn syrup, salt and remaining water. Bring to a boil, stirring occasionally. Cook, without stirring, until a candy thermometer reads 240° (soft-ball stage).

Remove from the heat and gradually add to gelatin. Beat on high speed until mixture is thick and the volume is doubled, about 15 minutes. Beat in extract. Spread into prepared pan. Quickly drop food coloring over candy; cut through candy with a knife to swirl. Cover and let stand at room temperature for 6 hours or overnight.

Combine confectioners' sugar and peppermint candies. Using foil, lift marshmallows out of pan. With a knife or pizza cutter coated with cooking spray, cut into 1-in. squares; toss in confectioners' sugar mixture. Store in an airtight container in a cool dry place.

Red Velvet Pancakes

PREP: 30 MIN.   **COOK:** 15 MIN./BATCH
YIELD: 16 PANCAKES PER BATCH

Who doesn't love red velvet cake? These pancakes are my breakfast variation! Why not make it a Christmas tradition to enjoy a special pancake breakfast while reading the enchanting fables in "Letters from Father Christmas," penned by J.R.R. Tolkien for his children.

Sue Brown ★ West Bend, Wisconsin

10	cups all-purpose flour
1-1/4	cups sugar
2/3	cup baking cocoa
6	teaspoons baking soda
4	teaspoons baking powder
5	teaspoons salt

ADDITIONAL INGREDIENTS (for *each* batch):

2	cups buttermilk
2	eggs
2	tablespoons red food coloring

Butter and maple syrup

In a large bowl, combine the first six ingredients. Place 2 cups in each of five resealable plastic bags or containers. Store in a cool dry place for up to 6 months. Yield: 5 batches (10 cups mix).

Pour batter by 1/4 cupfuls onto a greased hot griddle; turn when bubbles form on top. Cook until the second side is golden brown. Serve with butter and syrup.

To prepare pancakes: Pour mix into a large bowl. In a small bowl, whisk the buttermilk, eggs and food coloring. Stir into dry ingredients just until moistened.

Deck
THE HALLS

Tree Trimming 101

A beautifully decorated Christmas tree always adds to the magic of the holidays.

Many families have particular expectations or traditions when it comes to "putting up" the tree. For some, it's the date the tree is decorated that's special. For others it could be as simple as the hanging of Grandma's homemade ornaments. Many families host tree-trimming parties, while others enjoy the time spent just with intimate family.

Regardless of how you dress the tree, here are some easy ideas to help you spruce up your evergreen like a pro.

Once the tree is set in the desired location, add the lights. Instead of wrapping them around your tree, string them around the branches, starting at the trunk and working out toward the room. Plan on a strand of 100 lights for every foot of tree.

After the lights are set, string the garlands. Use less garland near the top and add more as you work your way down. Thin garlands look best when draped from branch to branch, while thick garlands are more appealing wrapped loosely around the tree. For every foot of tree, you'll need about two strands of garlands.

Garlands or ribbon can also be arranged like streamers from the top of the tree to the lower branches. Be sure to maintain even spaces between vertical rows of garland.

When hanging ornaments, the general rule is to hang larger ornaments near the bottom of the tree and smaller ones on top. To add depth, place some near the trunk, others closer to the tips of the branches. Use about 40 ornaments for every foot of tree. Using the same hangers for all the ornaments creates a clean look, but for a touch of class, tie ornaments onto the tree with ribbon.

Complete your decorating with your favorite tree topper, then stand back and look for "holes." Adjust the lights, garland and/or ornaments as needed.

Finally, it's time for the tree skirt. Instead of relying on a purchased skirt, try using a few yards of fabric wound around the tree's base or create your own family heirloom by crafting the Felt Tree Skirt found on page 180.

Dismantling the Tree

When it's time to pack up your treasures, remove the items from the tree in reverse order. If needed, wash or dry-clean the tree skirt before storing. Package ornaments carefully, and avoid storing them in areas of extreme heat or cold. Wind garlands around cardboard or into a loose ball and secure with rubber bands or twist ties. Check the light strands before storing. Toss out any

with frayed wires or cracked sockets. Avoid the frustration of untangling the lights next year, by using a purchased light reel or by wrapping the lights around sturdy cardboard cut into a square. Make sure you can easily access the plug when you wind the light strands around the cardboard. That way it will be simple to do the light check before stringing the lights next year.

Lighting Up the Holidays

Christmas lights come in an array of styles and shapes. With sets available in multicolors, single colors, blinking varieties, chasing lights and more, it's easy to feel overwhelmed in the trim-a-tree area of your local department store.

The most popular type of holiday light is the miniature bulb, as it offers bright sparkles of light on nearly any tree. Rice lights are smaller and give tiny pinpoints of light, making them ideal for table-top trees and decorations. "Globe" and "teardrop" lights describe the shape of bulbs that are larger than the miniature lights and work best on tall or wide trees.

When it comes to outdoor lighting, consider C7 and C9 bulbs because they illuminate large areas. Net lights are convenient to drape over bushes or wrap around tree trunks, and rope lights making stringing outdoor lights easy.

LED Versus Incandescent Lights

The biggest differences between LED and incandescent lights are cost and safety. LED lights cost more than incandescent, but use significantly less energy. LED lights don't produce heat, resist breakage and last longer than incandescent bulbs. Also, LED lights now come in a variety of colors and designs. There are even solar-powered LED strands. Keep these factors in mind when purchasing outdoor lights.

Dimensional Ornaments

CRAFT LEVEL: BEGINNER

FINISHED SIZE: Circle ornament measures about 4-1/2 in. across. Tree measures about 5-1/4 in. tall x 4-1/2 in. wide. Star measures about 5 in. across.

Here's an easy and enjoyable way to design a theme tree…or simply construct a few trims to fill out your tree. The ornaments are a smart way to use up scraps of stiffened felt, and make a fun project to do with kids. Add a few rhinestones for extra bling if you'd like!

Taste of Home Craft Editor Shalana Frisby

MATERIALS:

Patterns at right

Stiffened felt in choice of colors

Coordinating colored embroidery floss

Tapestry needle

DIRECTIONS (FOR ONE):

1. Choose a pattern design. Trace the pattern outline onto 2 different colors of stiffened felt. Cut out pattern shapes.

2. Following dotted lines as marked on pattern, cut interior line on one stiffened felt shape and exterior lines on the other stiffened felt shape.

3. Insert felt shape with exterior line cuts inside interior line cut on other felt shape. Overlap exterior line cuts onto solid ends of felt shape. Fold out sides of ornament to make it dimensional.

4. Cut a 10-in length of embroidery floss. Use tapestry needle to thread floss through top of ornament. Knot end of floss forming a hanging loop.

Circle, Tree and Star Patterns

Use a photocopier to enlarge each pattern 200%

Cut 2 each—stiffened felt

– – – – –	Interior cut lines
▬ ▬ ▬ ▬	Exterior cut lines
▬▬▬▬▬	Pattern outlines

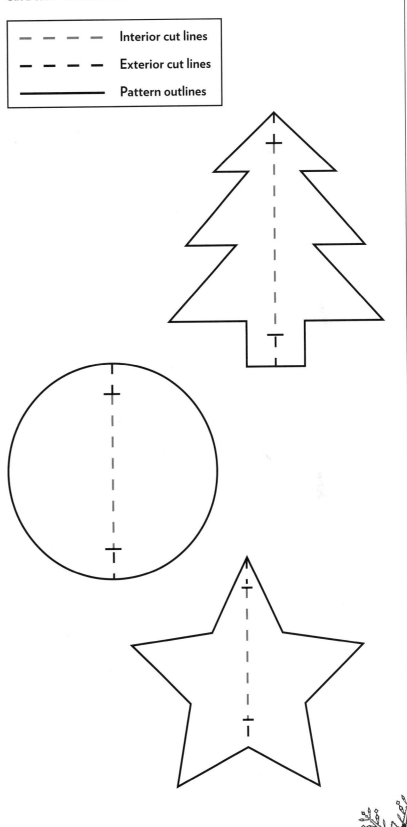

Felt Tree Skirt

CRAFT LEVEL: INTERMEDIATE

FINISHED SIZE: Skirt measures about 52 in. wide.

If you like a bit of whimsy in your Christmas décor, then our felt tree skirt is perfect for you! Use any two shades that work with your room or try two bright, electric colors that are sure to make a statement. The felt is easy to work with because the edges don't fray when cut.

Taste of Home Craft Editor Shalana Frisby

Contributing Crafter
Diane Coates ★ West Allis, Wisconsin

MATERIALS:

72-in.-wide premium felt–3/4 yd. each turquoise and dark gray

Scraps of felt in choice of colors for dots

22 in. length of 1/2-in.-wide Velcro

22-in. x 28-in. white poster board for pattern template

Standard sewing supplies

Iron with pressing cloth

Rotary cutter with cutting mat

Quilter's ruler or yardstick

Compass

DIRECTIONS:

Making the Pattern Template:
Refer to diagram on page 181 for cutting pattern template from poster board.

1. Draw a horizontal centerline on poster board dividing it into two 14-in. sections.

2. On one long side mark 13-1/2 in. out from centerline (or 1/2 in. from each corner). This side will be the bottom of the pattern template.

3. Measure 20 in. from bottom of template (or 2 in. from top) and draw a horizontal line. Line will be perpendicular to previously drawn centerline.

4. Measure and mark 2 in. out along horizontal line from the point where vertical centerline and horizontal line meet.

5. Draw two diagonal lines from the points marked at the bottom of the template to the points marked along the horizontal line.

6. Cut along diagonal lines and across horizontal line at top of template. This will make a flat top triangle for the pattern template.

Cutting:

1. Use the pattern template to cut three pieces each from the turquoise and the dark gray felt.

2. Use compass to make desired number of circles 2-5 in. across for dots. Cut out circles.

Assembly:

1. Using a 1/2-in. seam allowance and a straight stitch, sew the 6 felt pattern sections together alternating turquoise and dark gray colors. Do not join end sections. Sew Velcro strip to open end sections for closure. Use an iron with pressing cloth to press all seams open on the back.

2. Fold tree skirt in half and lay flat. Use compass to draw a 6-in. half circle at center creating an evenly rounded opening. Cut out circular opening. Sew a straight stitch 1/4 in. from inner edge on opening.

3. Randomly place felt dots on tree skirt. If desired, overlap smaller dots onto larger ones to create dimension. Pin dots in place. Edge stitch each dot in place.

Crafter's Note: Depending on the fiber content, some felt can melt when heat is applied. We recommend purchasing a premium quality felt and using a pressing cloth when ironing to avoid this problem.

Felt Tree Skirt Pattern

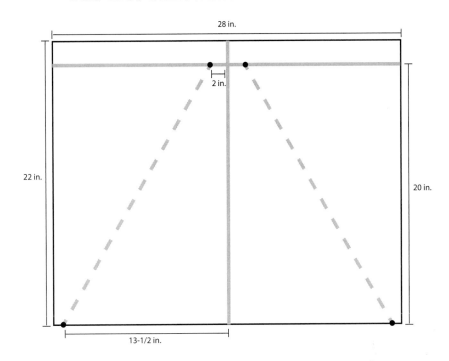

28 in.

2 in.

22 in.

20 in.

13-1/2 in.

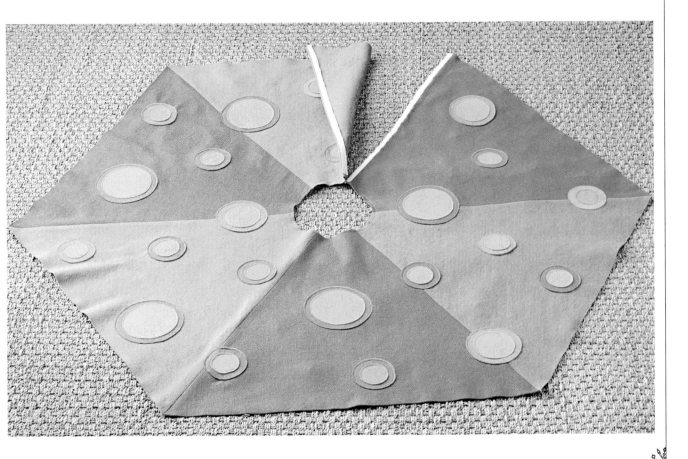

Rotary cutter with cutting mat

Quilter's ruler

Standard sewing supplies

Pinking shears

Iron with pressing cloth

DIRECTIONS:

Pockets:

1. Use iron and pressing cloth to press all fabric.

2. Use quilter's ruler and rotary cutter with cutting mat to cut four 3-3/4- x 4-3/4-in. fabric pieces from each of the 12 fat quarters. There will be 48 fabric pieces total used to create the 24 small pockets. From the remaining fabric cut two 15-3/4- x 7-3/4-in. pieces used to create the large pocket.

3. For all small pockets and one large pocket, pair matching fabric pieces laying them right sides together. Pin in place. Using a 3/8-in. seam allowance and a straight stitch sew each pair of fabric pieces together leaving a small opening for turning. Turn each sewn fabric pair right side out and press.

4. Arrange 8 small pockets horizontally on three of the placemats in 2 rows of 4 pockets. Each row should be a different color fabric. Pockets are placed about 1-1/2 in. from the placemat's outer edges. They are about 1 in. apart on each row with about 2 in. between the two rows. Place large pocket centered about 1-1/2 in. from bottom and side edges on the remaining placemat. Pin all pockets in place. Edge stitch along sides and bottom of each pocket leaving the top open.

Numbers:

1. Following manufacturer's instructions, use iron with pressing cloth to fuse brown felt to no-sew permanent adhesive.

2. Trace numbers pattern onto paper backing of fused brown felt. Cut out shapes. Remove paper backing.

3. Referring to photo for placement, put the appropriate number, adhesive side down, centered on each pocket.

Advent Calendar

CRAFT LEVEL: BEGINNER

FINISHED SIZE: Calendar measures about 18 in. wide x 52 in. long excluding hanger.

The whole family will have fun counting down the days to Christmas with this Advent calendar. Purchased placemats make it a cinch to put together.

Taste of Home Craft Editor Shalana Frisby

Contributing Crafter
Diane Coates ★ West Allis, Wisconsin

MATERIALS:

Number patterns on page 183

Four 13- x 18-in. cloth placemats

Twelve 100% cotton fat quarters–3 colors, 4 different prints per color

8-in. square scrap of brown felt

8-in. square no-sew permanent iron-on adhesive

24 in. length of 1-in.-wide grosgrain ribbon

2-in. x 16-in. piece of scrap fabric

20 in. length of 1/2-in.-wide dowel rod

4. Following manufacturer's instructions, use iron with pressing cloth to fuse brown felt numbers to pockets. Let cool before hanging.

Finishing:

1. With open pockets facing upward, arrange placemats side by side vertically with large pocket placemat last. Use a zigzag stitch to join placemats together.

2. Turn calendar to backside. Use pinking shears to cut edges of 2- x 16-in. scrap fabric. Place scrap fabric centered lengthwise about 1/2 in. from top and pin in place. Edge stitch along each long side creating a pocket. Insert dowel rod into pocket. Tie ribbon to each end of rod creating a looped hanger.

Number Patterns

Patterns are shown at 100%. Patterns are in reverse for tracing.

Winter Wonderland Coasters

CRAFT LEVEL: QUICK & EASY

FINISHED SIZE: Tile measures about **4-1/4 in. square.**

Go green this year by turning old holiday greeting cards into coasters. We chose black and white winter scenes for a contemporary feel, but any cards will work just fine. What a fun way for hostesses to add a touch of Christmas cheer to winter get-togethers!

Taste of Home Craft Editor Shalana Frisby

MATERIALS (FOR ONE):

Ceramic tile about 4-1/4 in. square

Recycled cards or decorative papers

Paper trimmer

Sticky back stiffened felt

Decoupage glue

Sponge brush

Clear acrylic sealer

DIRECTIONS:

1. From recycled cards or decorative papers, cut a 4-in. square.

2. Use sponge to apply a thin coat of decoupage glue to top surface of tile and adhere paper square centered on tile. Let glue dry.

3. Apply a thin layer of decoupage glue covering paper and edges of tile. Let glue dry.

4. Following manufacturer's instructions, apply a coat of clear acrylic sealer to make the tile water-resistant. Let sealer dry.

5. Cut a 4-in. square piece of sticky back stiffened felt. Adhere centered on back of tile coaster.

6. Repeat steps 1-5 for desired number of tile coasters to create a complete set.

Golden Angel

CRAFT LEVEL: QUICK & EASY

FINISHED SIZE: The angel measures about 7-1/2 in. wide x 8 in. tall.

Let this sweet angel be your joyous inspiration throughout the holiday season. The perfect height for tabletops or mantels, she's simple to make and wonderful to share with friends. Prepare the parts ahead of time, and let little ones help with the overall assembly.

Taste of Home Craft Editor Shalana Frisby

MATERIALS:

2-7/8- x 5-7/8-in. Styrofoam cone

2-in. Styrofoam ball

12-in.-square sheet of patterned card stock

8-1/2- x 11-in. sheet of textured gold paper

Paper trimmer

18-in. length of 1/4-in.-wide wired ribbon

Extra fine gold glitter

Tacky glue

Low temperature hot glue gun and glue sticks

Sponge brush

2 toothpicks

Clear acrylic spray sealer

Paper plate

DIRECTIONS:

Angel Body:

1. Wrap cone in gold paper. Fold paper edges over top and bottom of cone about 1/2 in. and trim excess. Secure paper to cone with hot glue.

2. Insert a toothpick halfway into the Styrofoam ball. Using toothpick to hold ball, apply a thin layer of tacky glue with the sponge brush. Pour glitter onto a paper plate. Roll glue-coated Styrofoam ball in glitter, shaking off excess. Cover completely in glitter and let dry. Spray with clear acrylic sealer and let dry. Remove toothpick and set ball aside.

3. Insert a toothpick halfway into the top center of paper-covered cone. Secure in place with hot glue. Insert other end of toothpick centered all the way into the glitter-covered ball forming the head. If needed, secure in place with hot glue.

4. Wrap wired ribbon around the neck of cone body. Tie into a bow. Trim ends as desired.

Angel Wings:

1. Cut 12-in. card stock into six 3-in. square pieces. For each piece, fold in two opposite corners overlapping them until a cone is formed. Adhere edges of each cone with hot glue; secure in place.

2. Using hot glue, adhere cones to back of paper cone body. Begin by placing 1 bottom cone about 3-1/2 in. from the head on each side. Stack 2 more cones on each side, forming wings made of 3 cones each.

3. From leftover card stock, cut a small oval shape. Glue at base of wings to cover where the cone ends meet.

front

back

Yuletide Shadow Box

CRAFT LEVEL: QUICK & EASY

FINISHED SIZE: Shadow box measures
10 in. high x 12 in. wide.

*Think outside the box this year and
let your creative juices flow! The
possibilities are endless with a purchased
shadow box, some holiday-themed
scrapbook papers and a few cute craft
embellishments. Feel free to add photos or
miniature treasures, too. It is a quick and
easy way to add a touch of the holidays
anywhere in your home.*

Taste of Home Associate Editor
Amy Glander

MATERIALS (FOR ONE):

One 10- x 12-in. shadow box or letterblock
tray

Holiday-themed scrapbook patterned
papers

Scissors or paper trimmer

Double-sided tape or scrapbook adhesive

Metallic letter stickers

Star stickers, snowflake stickers and holly
stickers

Buttons, self-adhesive rhinestones and
additional embellishments of your choice

Crafter's glue (optional)

Ribbon

DIRECTIONS:

1. Trim a variety of coordinating
patterned papers to fit into each box of
the letterblock tray. Adhere the papers
to tray using double-sided tape or
scrapbook adhesive.

2. Add letters, stickers, buttons,
rhinestones and other embellishments
of your choice.

3. Glue 2 pieces of ribbon to the back
of the shadow box and tie into a bow,
or tie the ribbon to the handle of the
letterbox tray.

Crafter's Note: The letterblock tray pictured is
from 7gypsies, www.sevengypsies.com

Scissors or paper trimmer

Ruler

Pencil

Double-sided tape or glue dots

Glue gun and glue sticks

DIRECTIONS:

1. Cut dowel rod to about 18 in. high or to the desired tree height.

2. Use spray paint to basecoat the dowel rod, wooden spool and wooden base. Let dry.

3. Once completely dry, apply a thin layer of wood glue to the bottom and no more than 1 in. up the side of the dowel rod; insert dowel rod into opening of spool. Let dry. Once dry, glue the spool to the center of the wooden base. Set aside and let dry.

4. Trim patterned papers into squares of varying sizes – one 12-in. square; one 10-in. square; one 8-in. square; one 6-in. square.

5. Place each square pattern side down. Using a ruler and pencil, mark the center of one side on each square. Using the mark as a starting point, roll each square into a cone. Adhere with double-sided tape or glue dots on the inside of the cone so adhesive is not visible.

6. Trim the pointed tops off the three largest cones so they easily slide over the dowel rod. Beginning with the largest cone, slide each one onto the dowel rod and position as desired for a topsy-turvy look. Use a glue gun and glue sticks to adhere each cone to the dowel rod permanently. Put a small dot of glue on top of the dowel rod and place the final cone. Repeat steps for desired number of trees.

Crafter's Note: When selecting a dowel rod and wooden spool, be sure that the diameter of dowel rod and the opening of the spool are a perfect fit.

Paper Cone Trees

CRAFT LEVEL: QUICK & EASY

FINISHED SIZE: Each holiday tree measures about 18 in. high.

Made of no-fuss paper cones, these merry mini trees boast a playful topsy-turvy appeal. Make just one as a single adornment or fashion a fun forest of trees for a welcoming window display.

Taste of Home Associate Editor
Amy Glander

MATERIALS (FOR ONE):
One 36-inch x 1/8-inch dowel rod

One 1-inch wooden spool with 1/8-inch opening (see Crafter's Note)

One circular wooden base

Spray paint (brown, white or color of your choice)

Wood glue (Gorilla Glue)

12-in. square coordinating scrapbook patterned papers

Framed Santa Silhouettes

CRAFT LEVEL: QUICK & EASY

FINISHED SIZE: Varies depending on frame surface size.

Santa's coming! This effortless project will take minutes to construct, quickly dressing up any wall with whimsical illustrations. Use them in sequence or choose your favorite one to hang alone.

Taste of Home Craft Editor Shalana Frisby

MATERIALS:

Illustrations below

3 frames with 8-in. x 10-in. openings

Photocopier

White copy paper

Paper trimmer

DIRECTIONS:

1. Photocopy each image onto white paper. Enlarge as indicated on illustrations.

2. Use paper trimmer to cut each image to the marked 8-in. x 10-in. area.

3. Remove backing from each frame opening. If desired, remove glass also.

4. Insert an image into each frame and replace backing.

5. When hanging, arrange frames in sequence order as shown in photo.

SANTA SILHOUETTES

Use a photocopier to enlarge each illustration 400%.

Christmas Card Box

CRAFT LEVEL: BEGINNER

FINISHED SIZE: Box measures about 11 in. long x 8 in. wide x 4 in. tall.

Store your precious holiday cards from years past in this decorative box. Or fill with photos or other mementos to make a sentimental gift for a loved one.

Taste of Home Craft Editor Shalana Frisby

MATERIALS:

Unfinished wooden box with lid about 11 in. long x 8 in. wide x 4 in. tall

Metallic acrylic craft paint in choice of color

Flat paintbrush

2-in.-square punch

Several recycled cards or scraps of decorative card stock

1-3/4-in.-tall dimensional sticker letters spelling "MEMORIES"

Two 1/2- x 8-in. border strips

Decorative dimensional sticker embellishments (optional)

Decoupage glue

Sponge brush

DIRECTIONS:

1. Use flat paintbrush and choice of metallic craft paint to basecoat interior and exterior of wooden box. Apply as many coats as needed for complete coverage, letting box dry between coats.

2. Using square punch, make 12 squares from the recycled cards or scraps of decorative card stock. Vary the design of each square.

3. Lay out the squares side by side and centered on the lid surface in 3 rows of 4 squares each. Lightly mark the position of each square for reference.

4. Using the sponge brush apply a thin coat of decoupage glue to the back of each square and adhere to the surface of the lid. Use the previously made marks as a guide when gluing down squares.

5. After all squares are glued in place, apply a thin coat of decoupage glue to the entire surface area of the grouped squares. Let glue dry.

6. Use decoupage glue to adhere a border strip to the top and bottom of the grouped squares. Let glue dry.

7. Adhere sticker letters "MEMORIES" centered on front side of box. If desired, add other dimensional sticker embellishments to side and top of box. If needed, use decoupage glue to secure stickers in place.

Letter Tiles Message Board

CRAFT LEVEL: BEGINNER
FINISHED SIZE: Varies.

Brighten up any room with this playful magnet board. Perfect for the kitchen, living room or even playroom, use it to spread some holiday cheer, display Christmas cards and more. Best of all, you can keep it up after the season and use it for the family bulletin board.

Taste of Home Craft Editor Shalana Frisby

MATERIALS:

Choice of metal or wooden frame

Thin sheet metal sized to fit frame opening

Spray paint in choice of color (optional)

Desired number of wooden Scrabble tiles

1/2-in round craft magnets

Dimensional chipboard or card stock embellishments

Foam adhesive

DIRECTIONS:

1. If desired, spray paint one side of the sheet metal following manufacturer's instructions. Apply as many coats as needed for complete coverage. Let dry.

2. Remove backing and glass from frame opening. Insert sheet metal into frame opening. (Do not reinsert the glass.) Put on frame backing and secure in place.

3. Use foam adhesive to adhere a round magnet to the back of each Scrabble tile and each dimensional chipboard or card stock embellishment. For larger embellishments, you may need to use 2 to 3 magnets as needed.

4. Arrange tiles and embellishments on framed sheet metal as desired.

Crafter's Note: Due to the weight of the sheet metal, we recommend using a sturdy frame that is 11- x 14-in. or smaller. If hanging the framed sheet metal use heavy-duty hardware.

Countdown-to-Christmas Blocks

CRAFT LEVEL: BEGINNER

FINISHED SIZE: Block set measures about 5-1/2 in. wide x 3 in. tall.

Little ones will enjoy counting down the days to Christmas with these colorful numbered blocks. Change them each day and watch how quickly the time passes until the big day finally arrives!

Taste of Home Craft Editor Shalana Frisby

MATERIALS:

Medium flat paintbrush

Red acrylic paint

5-in. x 3-in. wooden base

Glitter varnish

Paper trimmer

Patterned scrapbook paper

Red card stock

Decorative corner punch

Decoupage or tacky glue

Small sponge brush

Two 2-in. wooden blocks

1-in. white sticker numbers

DIRECTIONS:

1. With medium flat brush and red acrylic paint, apply base coat to wooden base. Let dry and repeat as needed for complete coverage. Apply a coat of glitter varnish as a sealer.

2. Use paper trimmer to cut twelve 2-in. squares from patterned paper and twelve 1-1/2-in. squares from the red card stock.

3. Use decorative corner punch on each corner of the 1-1/2-in. squares of red card stock.

4. With sponge brush and decoupage or tacky glue, adhere a patterned square to each side of the blocks; let dry. Glue a red square centered on each patterned square. Let dry.

5. On one block, center and adhere one of the number stickers on each red square: 0, 1, 2, 3, 4 and 5. On the other block adhere these numbers: 0, 1, 2, 6, 7 and 8.

6. Set blocks side-by-side on wooden base. Position blocks to count the days until Christmas, from 25 to 1.

DIRECTIONS:

1. Using the ruler, measure and mark Styrofoam into four 2- x 11-15/16- x 15/16-in. sections. Use serrated knife to cut marked sections.

2. Assemble Styrofoam rectangle pieces into an open square. (See placement diagram below.) Join pieces with hot glue and secure corners with pins.

3. Wrap interior and exterior sides with 7/8-in. metallic gold ribbon to hide roughly cut edges. Secure ribbon in place with greening pins and hot glue.

4. Use holly leaf punch on gold papers and design area of Christmas cards to make several cutout leaves. Use circle punch on red paper scraps to make several circle cutouts for berries.

5. Use hot glue to adhere a layer of gold leaves to entire surface on one side of the wreath base. Overlap leaves and extend from edges randomly.

6. Use hot glue to adhere a layer of leaves punched from Christmas cards. Leave room between card leaves for gold leaves to show through. Overlap some of the leaves with gold leaves. Place randomly.

7. For hanging ribbon, cut a 24-in. length of sheer gold ribbon. Use pins to attach each end of the ribbon on opposite corners on the back of one side of wreath. Cut another 24-in. length of sheer gold ribbon and tie into a bow. Attach to top center of hanging ribbon with wire. Trim ends as desired.

PLACEMENT DIAGRAM

Glue at corners between ends.

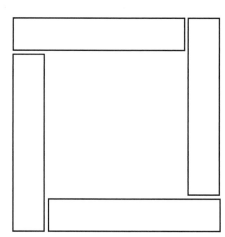

Recycled Card Wreath

CRAFT LEVEL: BEGINNER

FINISHED SIZE: Wreath measures about 16-in. square excluding ribbon.

Do you save your Christmas greeting cards every year? If so, here's a lovely way to recycle them into a wreath you'll proudly display year after year. Paper punches speed up the project, but if you don't have any, feel free to cut the holly leaves and berries by hand.

Taste of Home Craft Editor Shalana Frisby

MATERIALS:

8- x 11-15/16- x 15/16-in. piece of Styrofoam

Florist greening pins

3-in. length of 18-gauge wire

4 sheets of 12-in. square gold paper

10-15 Christmas cards

Scraps of red paper

5/8-in. circle punch

1-7/8-in. holly leaf punch

7/8-in.-wide metallic gold ribbon

1-1/2-in.-wide sheer gold wire ribbon

Low temperature glue gun and glue sticks

Ruler

Serrated knife

Berry Tree Bulbs

CRAFT LEVEL: QUICK & EASY

FINISHED SIZE: Each bulb measures about 2-1/2 in. across.

Give ordinary colored glass bulbs new life by embellishing them with a bit of paint! Consider the tree design at left or turn your imagination into a custom motif of your very own.

Taste of Home Craft Editor Shalana Frisby

MATERIALS:

2-1/2 in. wide glass bulb ornament in choice of color

Liner paintbrush

1/4-in. round pouncer sponge

Acrylic craft paint in red and metallic gold

DIRECTIONS:

1. Using a pencil, lightly freehand sketch a tree trunk with branches onto one side of the glass bulb ornament. Draw a 3-in. centerline first for the trunk base.

2. Add 6-8 curved branches from the centerline. Continue to add smaller branches as desired.

3. Using metallic gold paint and the liner paintbrush, paint on top of the pencil drawn tree trunk and branches. Load brush heavily and begin from the bottom of trunk and inner part of branch lines painting outward for each one. Let dry.

4. Using red paint and round pouncer sponge, create small berries and place randomly on the tree trunk and branches. Load sponge, dabbing off excess, then pressing evenly onto glass bulb surface to create a dot. Repeat for each berry. Let dry.

Hanging Ribbon Decor

CRAFT LEVEL: QUICK & EASY

FINISHED SIZE: Display measures about 18 in. wide x 24 in. long.

Add a festive flair to your home in a few minutes with this lovely treatment. Hang the ribbons from door or window frames.

Taste of Home Craft Editor Shalana Frisby

MATERIALS:

Coordinating colors of 1-1/2-in. sheer ribbon

A variety of 10-12 ornaments and jingle bells

Glue dots or double-sided tape

DIRECTIONS:

1. Cut a length of ribbon for each of the ornaments or jingle bells. Vary the ribbon lengths between 18-24 in.

2. Secure an ornament or jingle bell to one end of each ribbon length with a knot. Trim the excess ribbon to base of the knot.

3. Hang ribbons side by side on the back of a door. Secure ends of ribbon to top of doorframe with glue dots or double sided tape.

Berry and Moss Centerpiece

CRAFT LEVEL: QUICK & EASY

FINISHED SIZE: Varies.

Anyone can bring a little holiday glamour to the table with this Berry and Moss Centerpiece. We used branches with red berries, but for a more sophisticated look, use a silver or gold container with glittery berries in metallic tones.

Taste of Home Craft Editor Shalana Frisby

MATERIALS:

Metal container about 4 in. tall x 12 in. wide

Floral foam to fit container

Artificial moss

Several wire stem berries

Serrated knife

Wire cutters (optional)

DIRECTIONS:

1. Use serrated knife to cut floral foam to fit snugly into the bottom of metal container. Put floral foam in container leaving about 1 in. of space between foam and top of container.

2. Place a thin layer of moss on top of the floral foam.

3. Randomly insert wire stem berries securely into foam base. Place stems about 2-3 in. apart. Bend stems to create dimension. If desired, use wire cutters to shorten some stems before inserting into foam.

4. Once stems are placed where desired, add more moss between the base of the stems to create depth.

Festive Stamped Luminaries

CRAFT LEVEL: BEGINNER

FINISHED SIZE: Each luminary measures about 4 in. wide x 7 in. tall.

It's a snap to set the mood with these lovely luminaries. Whether your holiday style is fun and silly or fancy and sophisticated, these pretty accessories are sure to enhance any living space. Scraps of extra card stock, decorative punches and battery-operated tea light candles make this project a delightfully bright idea for any crafter.

Taste of Home Craft Editor Shalana Frisby

MATERIALS (FOR ONE):

One 12-in. square of textured card stock in choice of color

Two 8-1/2- x 11-in. sheets of vellum paper

Decorative edger punch in choice of design

Paper trimmer

Glue dots

Clear tape

Inkpad in choice of color

Holiday stamp about 3-1/2 in. tall x 2-1/2 in. wide

One 4- x 4- x 1-in. piece of white Styrofoam

Battery-operated, flameless tea light candle

DIRECTIONS:

1. Using a paper trimmer, cut one 12- x 3-in. piece of card stock and one 4- x 3-in. piece of card stock. Also cut two 8-in. square pieces of vellum.

2. Use decorative edger punch on one long side of each piece of card stock. Fold the 12-in. long piece of card stock into three equal 4-in. sections.

3. Use decorative edger punch on one side of each transparent paper square. Fold each square in half with the decorative punched edge at the top.

4. Use inkpad to stamp the holiday image onto one of the folded transparent paper pieces. Lay the transparent paper piece flat with the long folded edge to the left and the decorative punch at the top.

5. Gently place the inked stamp centered about 1 in. from the decorative punched top and press to transfer the image. Remove stamp and let image dry.

6. Unfold both transparent paper pieces to form 90° angles. Place their bases at opposite corners around the 4-in. Styrofoam square, forming a cube-shaped wall. Use glue dots around the base and clear tape along the edges to secure the transparent paper pieces to the Styrofoam.

7. Unfold the 12-in. length of card stock and wrap it around the bottom of the transparent paper wall. Center the middle section below the stamped image. Use glue dots to secure in place. Place the 4-in. piece of card stock on the open back and secure in place with glue dots.

8. Put a battery-operated, flameless tea light candle in the center on top of the Styrofoam base.

Christmas Tree Stamped Collage

CRAFT LEVEL: BEGINNER

FINISHED SIZE: Frame measures about 10 in. wide x 12 in. high.

Take a breather from the seasonal rush and spend some time crafting this charming piece of wall art. We used various Christmas tree stamps to design the casual collage, but feel free to try any stamps you wish. Choose colors that best match your space.

Taste of Home Craft Editor Shalana Frisby

MATERIALS:

Choice of frame with 8- x 10-in. opening

Four 1-3/8-in. or smaller Christmas tree stamps

Inkpads – red and green

1/4-in.-wide satin ribbon in red and green

Letter-size white card stock

Glue dots or scrapbook adhesive

Paper trimmer

Ruler and pencil

DIRECTIONS:

1. Use paper trimmer to cut an 8- x 10-in. piece of white card stock.

2. Using the ruler and pencil, lightly mark 2-in. square sections on the card stock making 5 rows of 4 squares each.

3. Alternating green and red ink colors and the 4 stamp designs, stamp a tree centered in each marked square section. Let ink dry between stamping. The odd rows will begin with green, while the even rows will begin with red. Use a different tree stamp design at the beginning of each row, rotating designs consistently throughout each row.

4. Cut three 10-in. lengths and four 8-in. lengths of red ribbon. Use glue dots or scrapbook adhesives to adhere a 10-in. ribbon length vertically centered between each of the 4 columns of stamped trees. Adhere an 8-in. length horizontally centered between each of the 5 rows of stamped trees.

5. Remove backing from frame opening. If desired, also remove glass. Insert card stock with stamped collage. Replace frame backing.

6. If desired, cut lengths of green and red ribbon to fit on front sides of frame surface for decoration. Use glue dots or scrapbook adhesive to adhere ribbon.

Crafter's Note: Customize your stamped collage by choosing any four holiday stamps that are about 1-3/8 in. or smaller.

Two 8-1/2-in. lengths of 1/2-in. decorative trim

Two 15-in. lengths of 1/2-in. sheer ribbon

Low temperature hot glue gun and glue sticks

DIRECTIONS:

1. Place fusible interfacing centered between patterned fabrics. Using iron with pressing cloth and following the manufacturer's instructions, fuse all layers together.

2. Using a circle cut quilting template or compass, draw a 12-in. diameter circle centered on one side of the fused fabric. Draw a line through the circle center.

3. Use the rotary cutter with mat to cut around edge of circle and on centerline to create two equal size half circles.

4. For each half circle, fold the straight edge from each corner until it overlaps onto itself forming a cone shape. Use tapestry needle and floss to tack side seam in place. Trim top edge evenly. Whipstitch the overlapping edge from bottom to top to secure side seam. (See Fig. 1 for stitch illustration.)

5. Use hot glue to adhere decorative trim around each cone top perimeter. Trim the excess. For each cone, use hot glue to adhere ends of the 15-in. sheer ribbon on opposite sides of the cone interior top edge, forming a hanging loop.

Fig. 1 Whipstitch

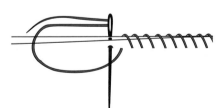

Fabric Cornucopias

CRAFT LEVEL: BEGINNER

FINISHED SIZE: Each cone measures about 2-3/4 in. wide x 5 in. tall, excluding the ribbon hanger.

Give your tree a hint of Victorian sophistication with these eye-catching cornucopia ornaments. Fill the cones with small silk flowers or tiny ornaments—or you can even add candy or potpourri.

Taste of Home Craft Editor Shalana Frisby

MATERIALS (FOR TWO):

13-in. square each of two patterned fabrics

12-1/2-in. square heavyweight double-sided stiff fusible interfacing

Iron with pressing cloth

Rotary cutter with mat

Quilting ruler

Circle cut quilting template or compass

Tapestry needle

Coordinating colored floss

Checkerboard Votive Candles

CRAFT LEVEL: QUICK & EASY

FINISHED SIZE: Display measures about 8 in. wide x 10 in. long.

Light up your party with this super-easy candle display. It takes literally minutes to put together. Vary the candle colors to complement your space.

Taste of Home Craft Editor Shalana Frisby

MATERIALS:

20 frosted-glass 2-in. square votives

20 votive candles–10 each red and green

DIRECTIONS:

1. If needed, clean the glass votives and let dry. Place them side-by-side on a flat surface forming 5 rows of 4 votives each.

2. Beginning at the upper left corner, alternate red and green votive candles, forming a checkerboard pattern.

Glistening Holiday Votive

CRAFT LEVEL: BEGINNER

FINISHED SIZE: Each luminary measures about 3 to 4 in. high x 3 to 4 in. across.

Bring a soft, warm glow to your home this season with sparkling handmade accents you attach to votive candle holders. Polymer clay is a unique medium that is easy to work with, and its translucent nature adds a lovely touch of radiance to your holiday décor.

Taste of Home Associate Editor
Amy Glander

MATERIALS (FOR ONE):

1-2 packages of translucent polymer clay

8-in. clear acrylic clay roller

Rubber molding mat (optional)

3-in. to 4-in. holiday-themed cookie cutter

Iridescent embossing powder

Cookie sheet

Aluminum foil

Metal spatula

2-in. square glass votive

Glue dots

DIRECTIONS:

1. On a clean, smooth surface, flatten polymer clay to approximately 1/8 in. thick, using acrylic roller. If desired, place rubber molding mat texture side down on top of smooth clay. Roll acrylic roller firmly over molding mat to imprint a textured design onto clay.

2. Using a cookie cutter, cut desired shape from clay.

3. Place iridescent embossing powder in a small bowl. Dip an index finger into powder and lightly tap or rub powder over clay cutout and in grooves of textured design for a shimmer effect.

4. Gently place clay cutout on a foil-lined baking sheet.

5. Bake according to manufacturer's instructions. Watch clay near end of baking time to avoid overbaking.

6. Remove clay from oven and allow to cool for about 15 minutes. Using metal spatula, remove cutout to a clean, cool surface. Allow clay to harden for about 45 minutes.

7. Carefully brush off any excess embossing powder that did not bake onto the surface.

8. Add cutout to the front of a glass votive using a large glue dot. Repeat steps for desired number of luminaries.

Crafter's Note: You can typically bake three to four clay cutouts at one time depending on the size of your cookie cutters and baking sheet.

Outdoor Sled

CRAFT LEVEL: QUICK & EASY

FINISHED SIZE: The sled measures about 22 in. wide x 42 in. high.

Do you have a cherished wooden sled from your childhood hidden away in the basement or garage? Well, 'tis the season to show it off! With a few basic items, you can easily dress it up for a merry outdoor display. If you don't have an antique sled, use a new wooden one and give it a distressed look with a little paint and sand paper.

Taste of Home Craft Editor Shalana Frisby

MATERIALS:

Choice of wooden sled

24-in. long artificial evergreen swag

20-gauge or larger floral wire

Wire cutters

2-1/2-in.-wide wired ribbon

Jingle bells 3 in., 2 in. and 1-1/2 in. wide

DIRECTIONS:

1. Using floral wire, attach the swag to the top of the seat base on the sled.

2. If not already joined, use floral wire to join the three jingle bells in order of descending size. Use floral wire to attach the bells to top center of swag.

3. Use hot glue to adhere artificial berries to top of swag above the bells.

4. Tie a large bow with the wired ribbon. Use floral wire to attach to the sled frame directly above the artificial berries.

Noel Banner

CRAFT LEVEL: BEGINNER

FINISHED SIZE: Banner measures about 12 in. wide x 29-1/2 in. long.

Welcome holiday guests and neighbors with this simple but elegant statement. Sewable iron-on adhesive and outdoor canvas fabric make this an ideal project for beginning crafters.

Taste of Home Craft Editor Shalana Frisby

Contributing Crafter
Diane Coates ★ West Allis, Wisconsin

MATERIALS:

Outdoor canvas fabric: 1 yd. light green print, 1/2 yd. solid red and 1/4 yd. solid green

3/4 yd. sewable iron-on adhesive

1 yd. heavyweight fusible interfacing

24 in. length of 1-in.-wide grosgrain ribbon

Standard sewing supplies

Iron with pressing cloth

Rotary cutter with cutting mat

Quilter's ruler

14-in. length of 1/2-in.-wide dowel rod

DIRECTIONS:

Banner base:

1. Use iron and pressing cloth to press all fabric.

2. Use quilter's ruler and rotary cutter with cutting mat to cut two 13- x 32-in. pieces from the light green print fabric for the front and back of banner. Cut one 12- x 31-in. piece of fusible interfacing.

3. Following manufacturer's instructions, use iron with pressing cloth to fuse interfacing centered on the wrong side of one fabric piece.

4. Lay fabric pieces right sides together with edges matching and pin in place. Using a 1/2-in. seam allowance and straight stitch, sew two long sides and one short side leaving a short side open for turning. (Stitching should be next to the fused interfacing edges.) Turn banner right side out with interfacing on the interior. Fold in about 1/4 in. of the top edges on open side and press in place.

5. Fold open end about 1-1/4 in. so that it overlaps onto surface of banner, forming a flap, and press in place. Edge stitch flap down forming a pocket for the hanging rod to be inserted later.

Letters and holly leaves and berries:
1. Following manufacturer's instructions, use iron with pressing cloth to fuse red and green solid fabrics to sewable iron-on adhesive. To conserve fabric, only fuse enough to accommodate the pattern sizes.

2. Trace letter and holly berry patterns onto paper backing of fused red fabric. Trace holly leaf patterns onto paper backing of fused green fabric. Cut out shapes. Remove paper backing.

3. Lay banner on a flat surface right side up with rod pocket at top. Referring to photo for placement, put the letters adhesive side down vertically centered on the banner beginning about 1-3/4-in. from the top. Place letters in the correct order spelling "NOEL" with each letter about 1-1/4 in. apart. Put holly berries and leaves adhesive side down centered below the last letter on the banner bottom.

4. Following manufacturer's instructions, use iron with pressing cloth to fuse letters and holly leaves and berries to banner. Let cool.

Finishing:
1. Insert dowel rod into pocket at top of banner.

2. Tie the ribbon into a bow at one end forming a loop. Wrap loop around ends of the rod for hanging.

Crafter's Note: Be sure to choose an outdoor canvas fabric that can withstand the weather. Outdoor canvas is usually made of polyester that can melt when ironed. We recommend using a pressing cloth to avoid this.

Noel Letters and Holly Leaf and Berry Pattern

Use photocopier to enlarge patterns 200%.

Patterns are in reverse for tracing.

Peppermint Candy Candleholder

CRAFT LEVEL: QUICK & EASY

FINISHED SIZE: Candleholder size varies.

Need a simple but stylish holiday decoration? Try your hand at these peppermint candleholders. In just minutes, you can dress up any table setting, bookcase or mantle.

Taste of Home Craft Editor Shalana Frisby

MATERIALS:

Choice of clear glass vases

Choice of candle(s)

Epsom salts

Round peppermint candies

DIRECTIONS (FOR ONE):

1. Clean glass vase and let dry.

2. Pour a layer of Epsom salts in the bottom of the vase about half way to the top.

3. Place a layer of round peppermint candies stopping about an inch from top.

4. Put the candle(s) centered in the vase. Slightly embed the candle base in the peppermints.

5. Fill in around the candle with more peppermints until reaching the top of the vase.

Crafter's Note: You can also make these with green peppermint candies.

Gifts
TO GIVE

Lavender Spa Basket

CRAFT LEVEL: BEGINNER

FINISHED SIZE: Varies.

Who wouldn't be thrilled to receive a spa basket at this hectic time of year? So why not try crafting one or all of the following items for a truly one-of-a-kind gift?

Taste of Home Craft Editor Shalana Frisby

MATERIALS (FOR ALL):

Waxed paper or newspaper

Microwave-safe bowls

Measuring cups and spoons

Plastic spoons for mixing

(FOR LOTION BARS):

2 oz. shea butter

2 oz. cocoa butter

4 oz. grape seed oil

4 oz. bee's wax

2 Tbsp. lavender essential oil

Double-boiler and stovetop

Choice of flexible silicone mold

Choice of lidded container(s)

(FOR SUGAR SCRUB):

2-1/2 cups raw washed sugar

1/2 cup coconut oil

2 Tbsp. grape seed oil

20-30 drops lavender essential oil

Choice of lidded container(s)

(FOR SOAPS):

2 lbs. clear glycerin soap

20-30 drops lavender soap fragrance

3 drops liquid soap dye in purple

2 Tbsp. dried lavender buds (optional)

Choice of plastic soap mold

Clear cellophane (optional)

Choice of ribbon (optional)

(FOR CANDLES):

4 cups white microwaveable soy wax chips

1/4 cup lavender colored and scented soy wax beads

1/2 tsp. lavender candle scent

Extra large soy wax wicks

Clothespin

Choice of glass candle jars

1 Tbsp. dried lavender buds (optional)

Holly leaf and round punches (optional)

1/8-in. hole punch (optional)

Choice of paper scraps (optional)

Choice of ribbon or string (optional)

DIRECTIONS:

To protect surfaces, cover area with waxed paper or newspaper. After using bowls, utensils and molds for making spa basket items, do not use for food.

Lotion Bars (makes about ten 1-1/2 oz. bars):

1. Combine shea butter, cocoa butter and grape seed oil in bowl. Melt in microwave in 1-minute intervals, stirring after every minute until completely liquefied.

2. Use a double-boiler to melt bee's wax over low heat on stovetop. Stir continually until completely liquefied.

3. Combine melted ingredients and add lavender essential oil. Stir thoroughly to mix all ingredients.

4. Pour mixture into desired silicone mold. Let set for 2 hours or until cool and solid. Remove from mold and place in container(s). Embellish as desired.

Sugar Scrub (makes about 20 oz.):

1. Place coconut oil in bowl. Microwave in 30-second intervals, stirring between, until completely liquefied.

2. Add sugar, grape seed oil and lavender essential oil to melted coconut oil. Stir thoroughly to mix all ingredients. The mixture should have a course, sticky texture.

3. Put sugar scrub mixture into container(s). Shake gently before each use.

Soaps (makes about eight 4-oz. bars):

1. Following manufacturer's instructions, use microwave to melt clear glycerin soap in bowl.

2. Add lavender soap fragrance and purple soap dye to melted glycerin. Stir thoroughly to mix all ingredients.

3. For plain soap bars, fill each soap mold to about 1/8 in. from the top edge. For soap bars with lavender buds, fill each soap mold about 2/3 full. Let glycerin set until firm (about 30 min.) then add a thin layer of dried lavender buds and cover with melted glycerin to about 1/8 in. from the top edge.

4. Let soap bars dry until completely firm. Remove from molds.

5. If desired, wrap bars in clear cellophane and tie closed with choice of ribbon.

Candles (makes about four 8-oz. candles):

1. Combine white soy wax chips and lavender soy wax beads in bowl. Following manufacturer's instructions, use microwave to melt wax.

2. Add lavender candle scent to melted wax. Stir thoroughly.

3. Place metal tab end of wick centered in glass candle jar. While holding wick in place, pour desired amount of melted wax into jar. If needed, use a clothespin to prop wick in place until wax begins to harden.

4. If desired, add a few sprinkles of dried lavender buds to the top of the candle once the wax begins to harden. Be sure to place lavender buds an inch or more away from the base of the wick.

5. Let candle cool and harden completely. Trim wick to desired length.

6. For tags, punch holly leaves and circles from scraps of paper. Use 1/8-in. hole punch to make a hole at the top edge of each. Thread ribbon or string through the holes and tie around top.

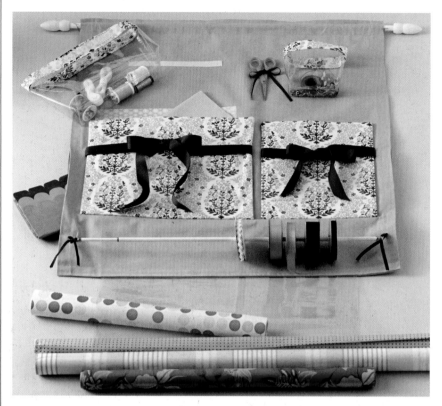

Gift-Wrap Organizer

CRAFT LEVEL: INTERMEDIATE

FINISHED SIZE: Gift-wrap organizer measures about 27-in. wide x 40-1/2 in. long.

For the friend who has everything, just consider this organizer for wrapping or crafting supplies. Give it as a gift or make it for yourself and keep any New Year's resolutions to get organized!

Jane Craig ★ Big Bend, Wisconsin

MATERIALS:

60-in.-wide upholstery fabric: 1 yd. of solid for background and 1/2 yd. of print for pockets and trim

1 yd. of 54-in.-wide 4-gauge clear vinyl

12-1/2-in. length of 5/8-in.-wide hook-and-loop tape

Coordinating grosgrain ribbon: 3-1/2 yds. of 7/8-in.-wide ribbon for trim on pockets and 1-1/2 yds. of 1/4-in.-wide ribbon for spool and scissors holders

All-purpose thread to match fabrics and ribbon

Two 10-1/2- x 13-1/2-in. pieces of clear plastic canvas

21-40-in. adjustable sash rod for ribbon holder

27-in.-long curtain rod for hanger

Standard sewing supplies

DIRECTIONS:

1. From solid upholstery fabric, cut two 29-in.-wide x 30-in.-long pieces for front and back of organizer. Overcast all edges of each piece. Fold 1 in. along each 30-in. side of each piece to wrong side. Topstitch close to raw edges and 1/4 in. from fold for hem. Set one piece aside for back.

2. From print upholstery fabric, cut two 14-in.-wide x 12-in.-long pieces for gift-wrap pocket and two 9-3/4-in.-wide x 12-in.-long pieces for tissue pocket. Also cut a 2-1/2-in.-wide x 25-1/2-in.-long piece for trim on bow container and a 2-1/2-in.-wide x 13-1/2-in.-long piece for trim on tape container.

3. From vinyl, cut one 8- x 12-in. piece for pocket on front of gift-wrap pocket, one 6- x 7-3/4-in. piece for pocket on front of tissue pocket, two 7-1/2- x 13-in. pieces for bow container and two 5- x 7-in. pieces for tape container. Also cut one 20- x 24-in. piece for gift-wrap rolls.

Gift-Wrap Pocket:

1. Center 8- x 12-in. vinyl pocket piece on right side of one 14-in.-wide x 12-in.-long gift-wrap pocket piece. Sew 1/4 in. from the two short edges and one long edge. Sew down center to make two pockets on the front. Place the two gift-wrap pocket pieces together with right sides facing and edges matching. Sew top and side edges together with a 1/4-in. seam. Turn right side out. Insert 13-1/2-in. x 10-1/2-in. plastic canvas piece inside pocket.

2. Slide plastic canvas up to top of pocket and sew close to plastic canvas to close pocket. Trim, leaving a 1/4-in. seam allowance. Overcast the raw edges together.

3. Referring to layout diagram on page 209 for position, place gift-wrap pocket on front piece with vinyl pocket facing right side of front piece. Sew bottom edge of gift-wrap pocket to front of organizer with a 1/4-in. seam.

Ribbon Trim:

1. Flip pocket up. Mark top edge and sides of pocket. Flip pocket down again.

2. Center and sew a 2-yd. length of 7/8-in.-wide grosgrain ribbon 3 in. from marked line. Flip pocket up and tie ends of ribbon to secure pocket. Trim ribbon ends as desired.

Tissue Pocket:

1. Center 6-in. x 7-in. piece of vinyl pocket piece on right side of one tissue pocket piece. Sew 1/4 in. from two long edges and one short edge. Place the two tissue pocket pieces together with right sides facing and edges matching. Sew top and side edges together with a 1/4-in. seam. Turn right side out.

2. Cut piece of plastic canvas to fit and insert plastic canvas piece inside pocket. Slide plastic canvas piece up to top of pocket piece and sew close to plastic canvas piece to close pocket. Trim, leaving a 1/4-in. seam allowance. Overcast raw edges together.

3. Referring to layout diagram below for position place tissue pocket on front piece with vinyl pocket facing right side of front piece. Sew bottom edge of tissue pocket to front of organizer with a 1/4-in. seam.

Ribbon Trim:

1. Following instructions above for gift-wrap pocket, sew a 1-1/2-yd. length of the 7/8-in.-wide ribbon to the front of organizer.

Bow Container:

1. Place the two 7-1/2- x 13-in. pieces of vinyl together with edges matching.

2. Sew the 7-1/2-in. edges together with a 1/4-in. seam for the sides.

3. Sew the 13-in. edges together with a 1/4-in. seam for the bottom.

4. Finger-press seams in opposite direction. Align side seams with bottom seam (as shown in Fig. 1 below). Sew 1-1/2 in. from point of triangle on each side. Trim leaving a 1/4-in. seam allowance.

5. Turn right side out.

Trim:

1. Sew short ends of 2-1/2-in. x 25-1/2-in. piece of trim together with a 1/4-in. seam. Press seam open. Fold the trim piece in half lengthwise to make a 1-1/2-in.-wide piece.

2. Cut an 8-1/2-in. length of hook-and-loop tape. Sew hook side of tape centered over seam on trim.

3. Slip trim piece over top edge of bow container with hook side of tape facing the outside of the bow container and raw edges matching. Sew in place with a 1/4-in. seam. Flip trim piece up so tape is on the outside.

4. Referring to layout diagram below for position, sew matching piece of hook-and-loop tape to front of organizer.

Tape Container:

1. Place two 5-in. x 7-in. pieces of vinyl together with edges matching.

2. Sew the 5-in. edges together with a 1/4-in. seam for the sides.

3. Sew the 7-in. edges together with a 1/4-in. seam for the bottom.

4. Finger-press seams in opposite direction. Flatten corners to make triangular points. Align the bottom seam and side seam as shown in Fig. 1 below. Sew 1 in. from point of triangle on each side. Trim seam to 1/4 in.

5. Turn right side out.

Trim:

1. Sew short ends of 2-1/2 x 13-1/2-in. piece of trim together with a 1/4-in.

seam. Press seam open and fold trim piece in half lengthwise to make a 1-1/4-in.-wide piece.

2. Cut a 4-in. length of hook-and-loop tape. Sew hook side of tape centered over seam of trim.

3. Slip trim piece over top edge of bow container with hook side of tape facing the outside of the tape container and raw edges matching. Sew in place with a 1/4-in. seam. Flip trim piece up so tape is on the outside.

4. Referring to layout diagram on page 209 for position, sew matching piece of hook-and-loop tape to front of organizer.

(continued on page 210)

Layout Diagram

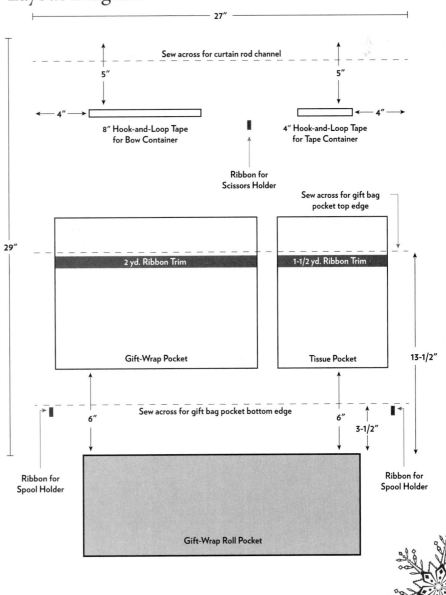

Sew across for curtain rod channel

5"   5"

4"   4"

8" Hook-and-Loop Tape for Bow Container

4" Hook-and-Loop Tape for Tape Container

Ribbon for Scissors Holder

Sew across for gift bag pocket top edge

27"

29"

2 yd. Ribbon Trim

1-1/2 yd. Ribbon Trim

Gift-Wrap Pocket

Tissue Pocket

13-1/2"

Sew across for gift bag pocket bottom edge

6"   6"

3-1/2"

Ribbon for Spool Holder

Ribbon for Spool Holder

Gift-Wrap Roll Pocket

FIG. 1
(Bottom view of bag)

Cut 1/4-in. from seam.

Sew on inner dotted lines.

(continued from page 209)

Scissors Holder:

1. Cut a 12-in. length of 3/8-in.-wide grosgrain ribbon.

2. Referring to layout diagram for position, sew center of ribbon to front of organizer.

Spool Holder:

1. Cut two 18-in. lengths of the 3/8-in.-wide grosgrain.

2. Referring to layout diagram for position, sew center of each ribbon piece to front of organizer.

Gift-Wrap Roll Pocket:

1. Fold 20- x 24-in. piece of vinyl in half crosswise to make a 12- x 20-in. rectangle.

2. Sew raw edges opposite fold together with a 1/4-in. seam.

3. With all raw edges matching, center vinyl rectangle along bottom edge of the front of organizer. Sew vinyl to front of organizer with a 1/2-in. seam.

Assembly:

1. Pin front and back pieces of organizer together with right sides facing and edges matching. Gift roll vinyl pocket will be sandwiched between the front and back pieces.

2. Sew along bottom and top edges with a 1/2-in. seam. Turn right side out. Press along seam lines, making sure side edges are aligned. Topstitch through all layers 1/4 in. from seam and again 1 in. from bottom seam. Topstitch through all layers 1/4 in. from top seam and again to form a channel for the curtain rod.

3. Sew through front and back pieces from side to side about 3-1/2 and 13-1/2 in. from bottom edge to make an interior pocket for gift bags. Be careful not to sew through gift-wrap and tissue pockets.

4. Press hook-and-loop tape on bow and tape containers to front of organizer to hold.

5. Place scissors over ribbon and knot to hold. Tie ribbon ends in a small bow. Trim ribbon ends as desired.

6. Slip spools of ribbon onto adjustable curtain rod. Thread one end of each grosgrain ribbon piece through the hole on the ends of the curtain rod. Tie ends together in a small bow to hold. Trim ribbon ends as desired.

7. Insert curtain rod in top channel.

8. Place flat-fold paper, tissue paper, gift tags and cards into pockets on front. Slip gift bag into openings between front and back layers.

Crafter's Tips for Sewing on Clear Vinyl:

To increase visibility, cut a paper pattern for each piece and slip it under the vinyl.

Use a rotary cutter and quilter's ruler when cutting.

Use a roller presser foot or a Teflon foot. If you don't have either of these, place gift-wrap transparent tape on the bottom of your presser foot and cut an opening in it for thread. Or cut strips of tissue and place them over seam lines as you sew to reduce drag. Remove paper after stitching.

Use a long stitch (3.0) and tie threads off rather than backstitching.

Creases and wrinkles can be removed by warming the vinyl with a blow dryer.

Knit Hat and Mitten Set

CRAFT LEVEL: BEGINNER

FINISHED SIZES: Hat measures about 8 in. wide x 8 in. high and fits a 20-in. head circumference. Each mitten measures about 7-1/2 in. long x 3 in. wide.

GAUGES: For Hat, 18 sts and 24 rounds = 4-in. in stockinette stitch. For Mittens, 22 sts and 30 rounds = 4-in. in stockinette stitch. Make sure to check your gauge and adjust needle size to match gauge.

Looking for a cap and mitten set for a special little one in your life? This pattern is very flexible and easy enough for beginning knitters. To change sizes, use larger or smaller needles. Play with colors, textures or pattern stitches, and create your own style.

Hat pattern by
Catherine Smith ★ Rochester, New York

Mittens pattern by
Nancy M. Harrington ★ Rochester, New York

MATERIALS (FOR BOTH):

Stitch marker

Contrasting scrap yarn

Yarn or tapestry needle

Scissors

MATERIALS (FOR HAT):

1 skein or 4 oz. worsted-weight yarn in choice of color (Sample knitted in Red Heart Soft Baby Steps, 100% acrylic.)

16-in. size 8 (5.0 mm) circular knitting needle

One double-pointed size 6 (4.0 mm) knitting needle

Size G/7 (4.5 mm) crochet hook

MATERIALS (FOR MITTENS):

1 skein or 4 oz. worsted-weight yarn in choice of color (Sample knitted in Red Heart Soft Baby Steps, 100% acrylic.)

Set of 4 size 6 (4.0 mm) double-pointed knitting needles

DIRECTIONS (FOR HAT):

Cast on 90 sts on circular needle; making sure work is not twisted, join to work in rounds. Place marker on needle at beginning of round. Also attach a short piece of contrasting yarn to the first stitch of the round.

Ribbing:

Rounds 1-36: [K1, p1] around: 90 sts. Tuck the ribbing to the inside, aligning the cast-on edge with the stitches on the needle. Starting at the first stitch marked with the contrasting yarn, use the dpn to pick up 10 sts along the cast-on edge. Knit the picked-up sts together with the first 10 sts on the needle. Repeat this process 8 more times until all stitches have been joined.

Body:

Rounds 1-18: K around: 90 sts.

Round 19: K 43, k2tog, k 43, k2tog: 88 sts.

Crown:

Rounds 1-3: [K1, p1] around: 88 sts.

Round 4 (Eyelet Row): [K1, p1, k2tog, yo] around.

Rounds 5-7: [K1, p1] around.

Rounds 8-13: K around.

Bind off all stitches. Cut yarn and weave in ends.

Crochet I cord:

Using the crochet hook, chain 76 sts. Make a slip stitch in the second loop from hook and the next 75 crochet chains. Cut thread and tie off.

Weave the I cord through the eyelet row. Pull tight and tie in a bow.

DIRECTIONS (FOR ONE MITTEN):

Cuff:

Cast on 32 sts and divide on 3 needles (8, 12, 12). Making sure work is not twisted, join to work in rounds. Place marker at beginning of round.

Rounds 1-18: [K2, p2] around: 32 sts.

Hand:

Rounds 1-3: K around: 32 sts.

Round 4: Kfb, k1, kfb, k to end of round: 34 sts. This begins the thumb gusset.

Rounds 5: K around.

Round 6: Kfb, k3, kfb, k to end of round: 36 sts.

Rounds 7: K around.

Round 8: Kfb, k5, kfb, k to end of round: 38 sts.

Rounds 9: K around.

Round 10: Kfb, k7, kfb, k to end of round: 40 sts.

Rounds 11: K around.

Round 12: Slip the first 11 sts onto a length of scrap yarn—these are the thumb sts. Cast on 2 sts onto needle and k around to beginning of round: 31 sts.

Rounds 13-30: K around.

Round 31: K8, k2tog, k8, k2tog, k9, k2tog: 28 sts.

Round 32: K around.

Round 33: [K2, k2tog] around: 21 sts.

Round 34: K around.

Round 35: [K1, k2tog] around: 14 sts.

Round 36: K2tog around: 7 sts.

Break off yarn, leaving an 8-inch tail. Thread yarn or tapestry needle with tail yarn and insert needle through all sts, removing them from the knitting needles. Pull tight and thread needle through sts again. Fasten off on the inside.

Thumb:

Slip the 11 sts onto 2 needles.

With a third needle, pick up and k on the 2 cast-on sts: 13 sts.

Rounds 1-9: Join the sts and k around: 13 sts.

Round 10: K5, k2tog, k6: 12 sts.

Round 11: [K1, k2tog] around: 8 sts.

Round 12: K around.

Round 13: [K2tog] around: 4 sts.

Break off yarn, leaving an 8-inch tail. Thread yarn or tapestry needle with tail yarn and insert needle through all sts, removing them from the knitting needles. Pull tight and thread needle through sts again. Fasten off on the inside.

Follow above directions to make second mitten.

ABBREVIATIONS

k	knit
p	purl
yo	yarn over
k2tog	knit 2 stitches together (decrease)
kfb	knit into the front and back of stitch (increase)
st(s)	stitch(es)
dpn	double-pointed needle
[ ]	Instructions between brackets are repeated as directed

Christmas Star Cross-Stitch

CRAFT LEVEL: INTERMEDIATE

FINISHED SIZE: Design area is 99 stitches high 70 stitches wide. Excluding frame, design is about 7 in. high x 5 in. wide.

A heartwarming wintery scene is always at hand when you stitch this treasured gift for a loved one. The cross-stitch piece makes a lovely heirloom when matted and framed for the holidays.

Ronda Bryce
North Augusta, South Carolina

MATERIALS:

Chart on page 213

One 8- x 10-in. piece of white 14-count Aida cloth

DMC six-strand embroidery floss in colors listed on color key

Size 26 tapestry needle

Choice of 8- x 10-in. mat with 4-1/2- x 6-1/2-in. opening

Choice of 8- x 10-in. frame with 6-1/2- x 8-1/2-in. opening

Standard sewing supplies

DIRECTIONS:

Cross-Stitching:

1. Zigzag or overcast edges of Aida cloth to prevent fraying.

2. Fold cloth in half lengthwise, then fold it in half crosswise and mark where folds intersect.

3. Using arrows, draw centerlines across chart. Begin counting where lines intersect to locate first stitch of top row, then locate same spot on the Aida cloth and begin stitching there for a centered design.

4. Each square on the chart represents one set of fabric threads surrounded by four holes. Each stitch is worked over one set of threads with the needle passing through the holes.

5. The color and/or symbol inside each square, along with the color key, tells which color of six-strand embroidery floss to use for the cross-stitch. Wide lines on charts show where to work backstitches. (See Fig 1 on page 213 for stitch illustrations.)

6. Use 18-in. lengths of six-strand floss.

Chart & Color Key

FIG. 1 Cross-stitch

Backstitch

Longer strands tend to tangle and fray.

7. Separate the strands, then thread the tapestry needle with two strands for all cross-stitches, one strand for 310, 500 and 3021 backstitches and two strands for 444 backstitch.

8. To begin stitching, leave a 1-in.-long tail of thread on back of work and hold it in place while working the first few stitches around it.

9. To end stitching, run needle under a few stitches in back before clipping the embroidery floss close to work.

Assembly:

1. Remove backing from frame. Insert mat right side down on top of glass. If necessary, trim exterior edges of mat to fit frame.

2. Place stitched piece right side down centered on mat. Design area should show through mat opening. Replace backing on frame.

MATERIALS:

Three pieces fleece in choice of color— 6 x 28 in., 6 x 22 in. and 6 x 15 in.

Three 1-1/2-in. buttons

Coordinating colored floss

Three 1-in. lengths of 1/2-in. wide Velcro

Tapestry needle

Standard sewing supplies

Rotary cutter with mat

Compass

DIRECTIONS:

1. Fold each piece of fleece leaving about 5 in. on the end of the longest pieces and about 3-1/2 in. on the end of the shortest piece for closing flaps. Pin each folded fleece in place. Using a ¼-in. seam, stitch side edges together forming the sack pocket.

2. Use compass to draw a half circle on each open-end flap. Cut around edges. Turn sacks right side out.

3. Use coordinating colored floss and a tapestry needle to blanket stitch around the edge of each flap. (Refer to Fig. 1 for stitch illustration.)

4. For each sack, sew Velcro centered on interior of flap and opposite on pocket to form closures. Sew a button centered on each flap for decoration.

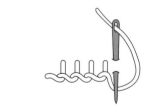

FIG. 1 Blanket stitch

Fleece Gift Sacks

CRAFT LEVEL: QUICK & EASY

FINISHED SIZE: Small sack measures about 5 in. wide x 6 in. high. Medium size measures about 5 in. wide x 8-1/2 in. high. Large size measures about 5 in. wide x 12 in. high.

Create your own special gift bags with just a few supplies. Pictured above are solid fleece colors, but for a quirky look, try the printed fleece ideal for children's gifts. Use the bags for candy, jewelry or cologne. Or slip a gift card or cash into them. The bags make a keepsake that can be used over and over again.

Taste of Home Craft Editor Shalana Frisby

Silver and Gray Necklace

CRAFT LEVEL: BEGINNER

FINISHED SIZE: Necklace measures about 42 in. long.

Make a gift that your girlfriends are sure to treasure! I use silver, gray and black beads so the necklace works with many different outfits; however, feel free to customize it as you see fit.

Sarah Farley, Menomonee Falls, Wisconsin

MATERIALS:

40 eye pins

Twelve 8mm light gray glass pearls

Twelve 10mm dark gray glass pearls

Eight 6mm translucent gray beads

Four 20mm silver foil beads

Four 10mm black beads

3 ft. medium linked chain

Flat and round nose pliers

Wire cutters

DIRECTIONS:

1. String each bead onto an eye pin. Using the round nose pliers make a matching loop at the open wire end. To make the loop, bend the wire at a right angle against the bead surface and grip the wire with the round nose pliers about 1/4 in. away from the bead. Turn the wire inward toward the bead making a full circle for the loop. Use wire cutters to trim excess wire.

2. Link four sets of beads in the following pattern: dark gray glass pearl, light gray glass pearl and dark gray glass pearl. Link another four sets of beads in the following pattern: light gray glass pearl, dark gray glass pearl and light gray glass pearl. To make the linked bead sets, first use the flat nose pliers to slightly open the loop on each end of the designated center bead. Slide a closed loop of each of the end beads onto an open loop of the center bead. Use flat nose pliers to close the loops

on the center bead joining the set of three beads. There should be four each of dark-light-dark gray linked bead sets and light-dark-light gray linked bead sets.

3. Use wire cutters to cut 8 each of the following lengths of chain: 3/8-in., 1/2-in. and 1-3/8-in.-long pieces.

4. Join the linked bead sets together with the cut lengths of medium linked chain. Use flat nose pliers to open and close wire loops on end of beads to attach to the chain lengths. Join the beads and chain lengths alternating in the following order: dark-light-dark gray linked bead set, 3/4-in. length of chain, 6mm translucent gray bead, 1/2-in. length of chain, 10mm black bead, 1/2-in. length of chain, 6mm translucent gray bead, 3/4-in. length of chain, light-dark-light gray linked bead set, 1-3/8-in. length of chain, 20mm silver foil bead and 1-3/8-in. length of chain.

5. Repeat joining the sequence of alternating beads and chain lengths in Step 4 three more times. Connect ends to form a necklace.

Felt Bird Ornament

CRAFT LEVEL: BEGINNER

FINISHED SIZE: Ornament measures about 4 in. wide x 2-1/4 in. high excluding hanging ribbon.

Check your craft materials for leftover felt scraps, and then make a set of these cute tree trimmings for anyone on your Christmas list. Whether you use bold colors or classic tones, the friendly flyers are sure to garner smiles.

Taste of Home Craft Editor Shalana Frisby

MATERIALS (FOR ONE):

Pattern below right

5-in. square piece of felt in choice of color

Felt scraps in two other coordinating colors

Embroidery floss in choice of color

1/2-in. wide button in choice of color

8-in. length of 1/8-in.-wide satin ribbon in choice of color

Tapestry and sewing needles

Straight pins

Polyester fiberfill

Low temperature hot glue gun and glue sticks

DIRECTIONS (FOR ONE):

1. From the 5-in. square felt piece cut two body pattern shapes. From felt scraps cut one each of the beak, inner wing and outer wing pattern shapes. Be sure the inner and outer wing shapes are cut from two different colors of felt.

2. Place body pattern shapes together with edges matching. Insert beak between body pieces at front of face. Fold ribbon in half and insert about 1/2 in. of each end between body pieces at top center forming a hanging loop. Pin pieces in place. If needed use a small dot of hot glue on each to tack beak and ribbon in place.

3. Using embroidery floss and tapestry needle backstitch about 1/4 in. from edge to join body pieces together. Begin stitching at tail. Stitch over inserted beak and ribbon ends to secure each in place. Stop stitching about an inch from the end, stuff body with fiberfill and stitch opening closed. (Refer to Fig. 1 for backstitch illustration.)

4. Use embroidery floss and sewing needle to stitch button to face for eye. Refer to pattern for placement.

5. Use hot glue to adhere inner wing felt piece centered on outer wing felt piece. Then adhere outer wing to body. Refer to pattern for placement.

Right-Facing Felt Bird Ornament

(For left-facing bird, reverse pattern.)
Cut 1 each from felt—beak, inner wing and outer wing
Cut 2 from each from felt—body
Use photocopier to enlarge pattern 200%

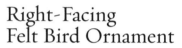

——————	**Pattern cut lines**
– – – – –	**Backstitch line**
●	**Button eye placement**

FIG. 1 Backstitch

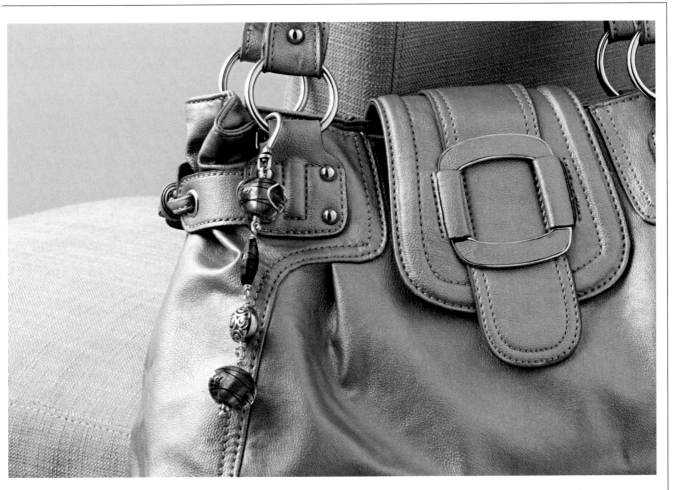

Beaded Purse Charm

CRAFT LEVEL: BEGINNER

FINISHED SIZE: Charm measures about
6 in. long. (Size will vary depending on bead
sizes.)

*Just the right size for a stocking stuffer,
this no-fuss charm promises to add
some bling to any handbag. Best of all,
it can be assembled in moments. Create
several in different colors—one for each
of your girlfriends.*

Sarah Farley ★ Menomonee Falls, Wisconsin

MATERIALS:

Choice of key chain base

Choice of glass beads—2 large round and
1 large oval

Choice of large metal bead

Choice of very small clear bead

20-gauge aluminum wire

Wire cutters

Needle and round nose pliers

DIRECTIONS:

1. Use wire cutters to cut a 5-in. length
of wire. Use round nose pliers to make a
loop about 1/4-in. from one end. String
on one large round glass bead. Use
round nose pliers to make a double loop
about 1/4-in. from the end securing the
bead loosely in place on the wire. Trim
excess wire with wire cutters.

2. To wrap the bead in wire, first use
wire cutters to cut a 6-1/2-in. length of
wire. Starting at the single loop end of
the base wire wrap the length of wire a
couple times around the space of wire
between the single loop and the bead.
Wrap the wire around the bead in a
swirl design. Then wrap the wire end a
couple times around the space of wire
between the double loop and the bead.
Wrap tightly so the wire fits snugly
around the bead.

3. For the next bead, use wire cutters
to cut a 5-in. length of wire. First string
one end of the wire through the double

loop on the previous bead. To connect
the beads use round nose pliers to make
a single loop about 1/2-in. from the end
of the wire around the double loop on
the previous bead. Wrap the remaining wire around the single loop base a
couple times and trim excess short end.
String choice of bead on remaining
wire. Use round nose pliers to make a
double loop about 1/8-in. from the end
securing the bead in place on the wire.
Wrap remaining wire around base of
double loop a couple times and trim
excess wire.

4. Repeat Step 3 to connect two
remaining beads. At base of last bead,
slip on small clear bead. Then make
a double loop next to bead bottom to
secure snugly in place. Trim excess wire.

5. On first bead use needle nose pliers
to open the single loop slightly. Slip
opened loop onto key chain base and
reclose loop.

Cute Little Sock Critters

CRAFT LEVEL: BEGINNER

FINISHED SIZE: Bunny measures about 5 in. wide x 14 in. tall. Cat measures about 3 in. wide x 10 in. long. Dog measures about 5 in. wide x 12 in. long.

Pick a pretty patterned knee-high sock and create a lovable pet. Each animal is made from just one sock, and they all come together easily. Make one or craft all three for a cuddly Christmas surprise.

Taste of Home Craft Editor Shalana Frisby

MATERIALS (FOR ONE):
Pattern diagrams on page 219

One knee-high knit sock

Standard sewing supplies

18mm black plastic nose with screw-on washer

Two 12mm (for Bunny and Cat) or 15mm (for Dog) black plastic eyes with screw-on washer

Polyester fiberfill

Tacky glue (optional)

DIRECTIONS:
For all sewing use a 1/4-in. seam allowance and coordinating colored thread. Refer to photo and pattern diagrams for cutting and assembly.

Bunny:
1. Turn sock wrong side out. Mark cutting lines according to pattern diagram. Cut out all pieces.

2. For arms, fold each piece in half wrong side out forming two squares. Sew two of the open sides on each square and turn right side out. Stuff each arm with fiberfill, stitch openings closed and set aside.

3. For legs, fold each piece in half wrong side out forming two long rectangles. Sew one short side and the open long side leaving only a short side open on each. Stuff each leg with fiberfill, stitch openings closed and set aside.

4. For head, with wrong side out sew ends and inner edges of ears. Turn right side out. Mark placement of eyes and nose according to pattern diagram. Following manufacturer's instructions, attach eyes and nose. If desired, use a drop of tacky glue on the back of each before screwing on washer to secure in place. Let glue dry. Stuff head with fiberfill and set aside, leaving open at base.

5. For tail, with wrong side out sew sides leaving a 1/2-in. opening forming a triangle. Turn right side out. Stuff with fiberfill, stitch opening closed and set aside.

6. For body, while wrong side out sew the two diagonal cut lines leaving small neck opening unstitched. Turn right side out. Stuff with fiberfill and set aside, leaving neck area open.

7. To join head to body, overlap head base opening about 1/4 in. over neck opening on body. Fold bottom sides of open head base in at an angle as shown on diagram. Hand stitch head base to body.

8. Hand stitch arms, legs and tail to body. Refer to photo for placement.

Cat:
1. Turn sock wrong side out. Mark cutting lines according to pattern diagram. Cut out all pieces.

2. For body, with wrong side out sew ends and inner edges of legs leaving about an inch opening at the inner edge of one leg. Turn right side out. Stuff body with fiberfill, stitch opening closed and set aside.

3. For head, with right side out mark placement of eyes and nose according to pattern diagram. Following manufacturer's instructions, attach eyes and nose. If desired, use a drop of tacky glue on the back of each before screwing on washer to secure in place. Let glue dry. Turn wrong side out and sew inner edges of ears leaving about an inch opening their base. Turn right side out. Stuff head with fiberfill, stitch opening closed and set aside.

4. For tail, while wrong side out sew sides leaving a 1/2-in. opening forming a long, skinny triangle. Turn right side out. Stuff with fiberfill, stitch opening closed and set aside.

5. Hand stitch head with ears and tail to body. Refer to photo for placement.

Dog:

1. Turn sock wrong side out. Mark cutting lines according to pattern diagram. Cut out all pieces.

2. For legs, fold each piece in half wrong side out forming four rectangles. Sew one short side and the open long side leaving only a short side open on each. Stuff each leg with fiberfill, stitch openings closed and set aside.

3. For body and head, turn right side out. Mark placement of eyes and nose according to pattern diagram. Turn wrong side out. Sew diagonal edge on head, leaving the back end open. Turn right side out. Following manufacturer's instructions, attach eyes and nose. If desired, use a drop of tacky glue on the back of each before screwing on washer to secure in place. Let glue dry. Stuff head and body with fiberfill, stitch back end opening leaving about an inch open at top to insert tail. (Refer to pattern diagram.)

4. For each ear, with wrong side out sew sides leaving a 1/2-in. opening, forming two triangles. Turn each right side out.

Stuff with fiberfill, stitch opening closed and set aside.

5. For tail, with wrong side out sew sides leaving a 1/2-in. opening, forming a long rectangle. Turn right side out. Stuff with fiberfill, stitch opening closed and set aside.

6. Hand stitch legs to bottom of body. Refer to photo for placement. Insert tail into opening on back end of body and hand stitch to join.

Crafter's Note: Due to small parts, these are not recommended for very young children. They may pose a choking hazard.

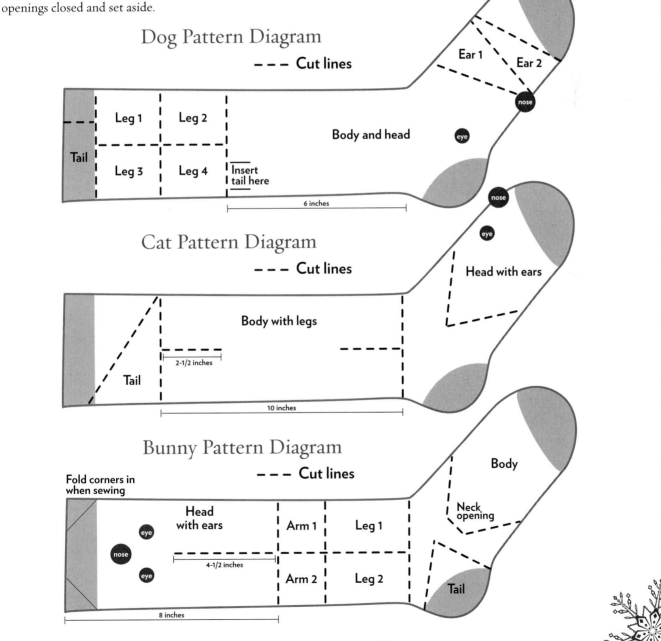

Dog Pattern Diagram

– – – **Cut lines**

Ear 1 · Ear 2 · nose · Body and head · eye · Leg 1 · Leg 2 · Tail · Leg 3 · Leg 4 · Insert tail here · 6 inches

Cat Pattern Diagram

– – – **Cut lines**

nose · eye · Head with ears · Body with legs · Tail · 2-1/2 inches · 10 inches

Bunny Pattern Diagram

– – – **Cut lines**

Fold corners in when sewing · Body · Head with ears · Arm 1 · Leg 1 · Neck opening · eye · nose · eye · 4-1/2 inches · Arm 2 · Leg 2 · Tail · 8 inches

Crocheted Afghan

CRAFT LEVEL: BEGINNER

FINISHED SIZE: Afghan measures about 36 in. wide x 58 in. long.

This lap-size afghan is perfect to curl up with on chilly winter nights. It crochets up quickly, too, so you can make several to give as gifts. Customize the color for friends and family.

Original pattern by
Rebecca Marvin ★ Waseca, Minnesota

Pattern adapted by
Joanne Wied ★ Greendale, Wisconsin

MATERIALS:

36 oz. 4-ply worsted weight yarn in choice of color (Sample afghan made with Caron's Simply Soft yarn.)

Size I/9 (5.5mm) crochet hook

GAUGE: 8 dc or post stitches = 4 in.

SPECIAL STITCHES:

Front Post Stitch (FP): yo, insert hook from front to back around post of next st on last row, (yo, draw through 2 loops on hook) 2 times. Skip next st on last row behind FP.

Back Post Stitch (BP): yo, insert hook from back to front around post of next st on last row, (yo, draw through 2 loops on hook) 2 times. Skip next st on last row behind BP.

DIRECTIONS:

Interior:

Row 1: Loosely ch 87, dc in fourth ch from hk, dc in each ch across, turn.

Row 2: Ch 3 (counts as first dc), dc in each st across, ch 3, turn.

Row 3: [FP around next st in last row, dc in next st] across, ch 3, turn.

Row 4: [BP around next st in last row, dc in next st] across.

Row 5: Dc in each st across.

Repeat Rows 2-5 24 more times.
Do not turn work.

Border:

Round 1: Ch 1, work 3 sc in corner st, work sc down side, spacing sts evenly and using as many sts needed to keep area flat. Work 3 sc in next corner, work sc in each unused loop of beginning ch. Work 3 sc in next corner, work sc down side, spacing sts evenly and using as many sts needed to keep area flat. Work 3 sc in last corner, work sc in each st across. Join with sl st in first sc. Ch 1 (do not turn).

Round 2-4: Work first sc in same st as joining. Work 3 sc in second corner st, work sc in each st down side. Work 3 sc in second st of next corner, work sc in each st across. Work 3 sc in second st of next corner, work sc in each st down side. Work 3 sc in second st of last corner, work sc in each st across. Join with sl st at end of each Round. For Round 2-3, ch 1 (do not turn). For Round 4, ch 3 (do not turn).

Round 5-7: Dc in each st around, working 3 dc in second st of each corner. Join with sl st at end of each Round. For Round 5-6, ch 3 (do not turn). For Round 7, ch 1 (do not turn).

Round 8: Sc in same st as joining, [ch 3, skip 1 st, sc in next st] around. Join to first sc. Fasten off and weave in ends.

ABBREVIATIONS

ch(s)	chain(s)
sc(s)	single crochet(s)
dc	double crochet(s)
sl st	slip stitch
st(s)	stitch(es)
hk	hook
[ ]	Instructions between brackets are repeated as directed.

Elf Party Favors

CRAFT LEVEL: QUICK & EASY

FINISHED SIZE: Each elf measures about 3 in. wide x 8 in. tall.

Turn Santa's helpers into your personal Christmas collaborators! These adorable elves can be used as decorations, gift boxes or even candy-filled party favors. Repurposed plastic gum containers make the bodies, and colorful felt and tiny embellishments give each gnome a unique personality!

Taste of Home Craft Editor Shalana Frisby

MATERIALS (FOR ONE):

3-1/2- x 2-1/4-in. plastic gum container

8- x 3/4-in. piece of felt in choice of color for belt

8- x 2-3/4-in. piece of felt in choice of color for body

7-in. square piece of felt in choice of color for hat

1/2-in. button in choice of color

3/4-in. pompom in choice of color

Two 20mm wiggle eyes

Low temperature hot glue gun and glue sticks

Standard sewing supplies

DIRECTIONS:

1. Thoroughly wash and dry container. Hot glue eyes side-by-side to rim of container lid just below the snap opening. Adhere pompom on container base centered below the eyes.

2. Wrap 8- x 2-3/4-in. piece of felt horizontally around perimeter of body. Overlap ends under the eyes and nose. Glue in place along overlapping seam. Leave open at eyes and nose. Fold top corners down forming a collar.

3. Wrap 8- x 3/4-in. piece of felt about 3/4 in. from bottom of container on top of body felt piece. Overlap ends at body felt seam and glue in place. Adhere button on top of overlapping belt ends.

4. For hat, fold 7-in. square piece of felt in half diagonally forming a triangle. Sew one open edge of the triangle. Cut straight from end of sewn edge at opening to center of opposite folded edge. Slightly fold up edge opposite of sewn side to form a brim on the hat.

5. Use hot glue to attach bottom of hat seam to top of body felt on the opposite side of eyes and nose. Hat should be loose everywhere else so that it can be flipped back when opening container lid.

One-of-a-Kind Gift Tags

CRAFT LEVEL: QUICK & EASY

FINISHED SIZE: Varies.

Dress up ordinary packages with eye-fetching handmade tags. The tags are a cinch to create using a basic punch or die cut, and you can spin your creative wheels by mixing and matching a variety of elegant, sparkly embellishments.

Taste of Home Associate Editor
Amy Glander

MATERIALS (FOR ALL):

Textured specialty papers

Glittered specialty papers

Tag punch or tag die-cut

Rub-on letters or journaling pen

Paper or fabric flowers, brads, rhinestones, metal charms and other embellishments of your choice

Crafter's glue (optional)

Ribbon or lace trim

Hole punch (optional)

DIRECTIONS:

1. Using a tag punch or a tag die cut, trim specialty papers into a variety of tag shapes.

2. Add gift recipients' names using rub-on letters or a journaling pen.

3. Add flowers, brads and additional embellishments as desired.

4. Tie ribbon through hole in tag for hanging. (If your tag does not have a hole, add one with a hole punch).

Christmas Tree Apron

CRAFT LEVEL: QUICK & EASY

FINISHED SIZE: Apron measures about 20 in. wide x 27 in. long.

The cook who goes all out for Christmas deserves to look festive while in the kitchen! Surprise them with this decked-out apron.

Taste of Home Craft Editor Shalana Frisby

MATERIALS:

Patterns below right

Choice of canvas apron

Three patterned cotton fabrics: 9- x 4-in., 8- x 4-in. and 7- x 6-in. pieces

2-1/2-in.-square piece brown felt

1/4 yd. no-sew permanent iron-on adhesive

Iron with pressing cloth

Three 5-in. lengths of 5/8-in. ribbon

3/4-in. jingle bell

Standard sewing supplies

DIRECTIONS:

1. Prewash apron and cotton fabric pieces. Iron each with pressing cloth.

2. Following manufacturer's instructions, fuse iron-on adhesive to wrong side of fabric and felt pieces. Trace tree shape patterns on paper back of corresponding size pieces and cut out. Cut felt piece to a 2- x 2-1/4-in. rectangle for the trunk.

3. Remove paper backing from fabric and felt pieces. Center tree shape pieces right side up on apron overlapping edges slightly. Refer to photo for placement. Center felt trunk under bottom tree piece adjacent to edge.

4. Using iron with pressing cloth and following manufacturer's instructions, fuse tree and trunk pieces to apron.

5. Fold each ribbon length into a loop overlapping ends in the center. Stack pieces diagonally in a circular shape to form a bow. Stitch center. Sew jingle bell centered on bow. Sew bow with jingle bell on apron treetop.

Tree Patterns

Trace 1 each—fused fabric paper backing
Cut 1 each—fused fabric pieces
Use photocopier to enlarge pattern 400%

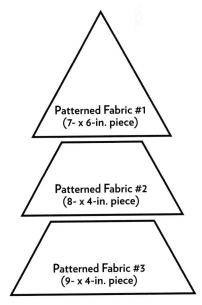

Patterned Fabric #1
(7- x 6-in. piece)

Patterned Fabric #2
(8- x 4-in. piece)

Patterned Fabric #3
(9- x 4-in. piece)

Holly Leaf Glitter Card

CRAFT LEVEL: QUICK & EASY

FINISHED SIZE: Card measures about 4-in. wide x 6-in. tall.

Let Mother Nature lend you a hand, or in this case a leaf, when you create holiday cards for special friends. Holly leaves were the inspiration for the glittery cards that come together in no time. In fact, they're a playful project for family fun!

Taste of Home Craft Editor Shalana Frisby

MATERIALS (FOR ONE):

4- x 6-in. card with envelope in choice of color

Fine glitter in choice of green and brown colors

Merry Christmas stamp about 2-in. wide x 3-in. tall

Inkpad in brown or choice of color

Tacky glue

Small square foam brush

1/2-in.-round sponge pouncer

Toothpicks

Real or artificial holly leaves

DIRECTIONS:

1. Use square foam brush to apply a thin coat of tacky glue to the back of a holly leaf. Press coated side of leaf onto card face. Refer to photo for positioning. Press gently to transfer tacky glue to paper. Remove leaf and set aside. Use toothpick to remove lines of glue defining center veins.

2. Sprinkle green glitter onto glue coated area of card. Cover completely and shake off excess glitter.

3. Repeat Steps 1 and 2 for second glitter leaf.

4. Dip round sponge pouncer into tacky glue. Press gently onto card face to form a round berry shape at base of leaves. Repeat twice more for three berries total.

5. Sprinkle brown glitter onto round berry shapes being careful not to get glitter on the leaves. Cover completely and shake off excess glitter.

6. Use inkpad to stamp Merry Christmas image onto card face about ¼ in. from bottom right corner. Let ink dry.

Crystal Shimmers

CRAFT LEVEL: BEGINNER

FINISHED SIZE: The ornament measures about 5-1/2 in. long.

Embellish your tree with the sparkle that accompanies these lovely Crystal Shimmers. The handcrafted ornaments twinkle against brilliant tree lights.

Sarah Farley, Menomonee Falls, Wisconsin

MATERIALS (FOR ONE):

Four 18-in. lengths of Fireline braided bead thread

4mm beads in choice of colors (about 160 needed)

4-in. length of thin wire

Small metal cone

Wire cutters and round nose pliers

DIRECTIONS:

1. String a bead centered on a length of Fireline. Fold in half at centered bead. With ends together, string about 40 beads onto strand in desired pattern. Repeat with remaining Fireline.

2. Gather the ends of all beaded strands together. Wrap about an inch of wire tightly around the gathered strand ends as close to the beads as possible. Trim excess strand ends to about 1/8-in. long. Place cone snugly onto remaining wire covering strand ends and top of beads.

3. At top of cone hole, bend wire to a right angle. Use the round pliers to make a loop. Place pliers on wire about 1/4 in. from the cone top and turn pliers inward toward the cone making a full circle. Wrap remaining wire end around the loop stem tightly to secure loop in place. Use wire cutters to trim excess wire.

DIRECTIONS:

1. Using iron with pressing cloth and following manufacturer's instructions, fuse iron-on adhesive to back of denim. Trace reindeer pattern centered on iron-on adhesive paper backing. Cut out reindeer shape.

2. Press 18-in. square fabric and lay right side up. Remove paper backing from reindeer shape. Place reindeer fabric side up about 3 in. from the bottom right corner of the fabric piece. Refer to photo for placement. Using iron with pressing cloth and following manufacturer's instructions, fuse denim reindeer to patterned fabric.

3. Lay fused fabric centered on top of canvas. Adjust placement of reindeer to match photo example. Carefully flip canvas and fabric over so canvas is facedown on the backside of fabric.

4. Beginning on one side, fold fabric over canvas back and staple a few times on outer edge to secure in place. Next staple the opposite side stretching tightly in place. Then staple the other sides stretching tightly in place each time. Finally turn each corner fabric in and staple in place.

Reindeer Pattern

Trace 1—iron-on adhesive backing
Cut 1—fused denim
Use photocopier to enlarge pattern 400%

Reindeer Fabric Mural

CRAFT LEVEL: QUICK & EASY

FINISHED SIZE: Mural measures 12-in. square.

In just one evening, you can create this charming one-of-a kind wall hanging. Start with a wintry patterned cotton fabric and then choose a solid denim or other sturdy cotton fabric. Before you know it, you'll be able to cross someone off your Christmas list!

Taste of Home Craft Editor Shalana Frisby

MATERIALS:

Pattern at right

12- x 12- x 1-1/2-in. canvas

18-in. square patterned 100% cotton fabric

10- x 12-in. piece solid colored denim, duck cloth or outdoor canvas

10- x 12-in. piece no-sew permanent iron-on adhesive

Rotary cutter with mat

Quilter's ruler

Iron with pressing cloth

Staple gun with 3/8-in. staples

Hanging Topiary

CRAFT LEVEL: QUICK & EASY

FINISHED SIZE: Topiary hangs about 26 in. long.

Jazz up any door in your home with this simple holiday decoration. Lengthen or shorten the ribbons to fit your space, and make it your own with vine or moss balls if you'd like.

Taste of Home Craft Editor Shalana Frisby

MATERIALS:

4-in. topiary seed ball

6-in. topiary seed ball

Choice of 4-in. gold ornament

Wired artificial berries

Florist greening pins

Low temperature hot glue gun with glue sticks

1-1/2-in. wide sheer wire ribbon

6-in. wide ribbon

2-1/2-in. gold metal ring

DIRECTIONS:

1. Insert wired artificial berries randomly into topiary balls.

2. From 1-1/2-in. sheer wire ribbon, cut 10-in., 16-in. and 24-in. lengths. Place gold ornament centered on 10-in. length and fold ribbon in half forming a loop. Use greening pins to secure ribbon ends to 4-in. ball allowing ornament to hang. Fold 16-in. ribbon length in half. Use greening pins to secure ribbon ends to 6-in. ball. Then secure folded end to the 4-in. ball opposite the other ribbon to connect both topiary balls. Fold 24-in. length ribbon in half. Use greening pins to secure ribbon ends to 6-in. ball opposite the other ribbon.

3. Use 6-in. ribbon to tie a large bow onto end of folded 24-in. ribbon. Insert metal ring into back of bow to use for hanging.

DIRECTIONS:

1. Use spray adhesive to attach sheet cork centered on cardboard. Trim edges to fit frame opening if needed. Then attach fabric centered on top of cork. Overlap fabric edges onto back of cardboard.

2. Remove backing and glass from frame opening. Insert layered cardboard, cork and fabric board, fabric side up into frame opening. Put backing on and secure in place.

3. (Optional) Use a staple gun to attach ribbon ends to opposite sides on the top edge of frame back forming a hanging loop.

4. Add an assortment of tacks and pins to hold photos and other lightweight items.

Crafter's Note: To make buttons into usable tacks, simply cut off shank if necessary and add a flathead tack to the back with dimensional foam adhesive.

Cork Bulletin Board

CRAFT LEVEL: QUICK & EASY

FINISHED SIZE: Measurement varies depending on choice of frame size.

Here's a fun idea that can be made to appeal to anyone on your gift list. Make a memory board for teens, or add a few hooks so your girlfriends can hang necklaces and bracelets. Since it's made of cork, families can use the board to post notes, shopping lists and more. Choose fabrics and frames to match specific rooms and decorating styles.

Taste of Home Craft Editor Shalana Frisby

MATERIALS:

Sturdy wooden or metal frame in choice of size

Cardboard and sheet cork to fit frame size

Fabric scrap 1-in. larger around than frame size

Spray glue

Choice of tacks and pins

24-in. length of 1-in. wide satin ribbon (optional)

Staple gun with 3/8-in. staples (optional)

Felt Trees

CRAFT LEVEL: BEGINNER

FINISHED SIZE: Large size tree measures about 8 in. wide x 14 in. high. Medium size tree measures about 6 in. wide x 11 in. high. Small size tree measures about 5 in. wide x 8 in. high.

Add some merriment to any room with these adorable trees. Try them in bright colors or traditional green, or mix up the colors and let your imagination flow.

Taste of Home Craft Editor Shalana Frisby

MATERIALS (FOR ALL):

Low temperature glue gun and glue sticks

Several small beads or choice of other embellishments

Acrylic craft paint in choice of color

Flat paintbrush

Compass with pencil

(FOR LARGE TREE):

10 sheets each craft felt–coordinating light and dark colors

7-in.-wide round wooden plaque

12-in. long x 3/4-in.-wide dowel rod

1-in.-wide bead in choice of color

(FOR MEDIUM TREE):

6 sheets each craft felt–coordinating light and dark colors

5-in.-wide round wooden plaque

9-in.-long x 3/4-in-wide dowel rod

5/8-in.-wide bead in choice of color

(FOR SMALL TREE):

4 sheets each craft felt–coordinating light and dark colors

4-in.-wide round wooden plaque

6-in.-long x 3/4-in.-wide dowel rod

1/2-in.-wide bead in choice of color

DIRECTIONS:

Making the Tree Base:

1. Use hot glue to adhere the dowel rod centered on the topside of the round wooden plaque.

2. Use choice of acrylic paint and the flat paintbrush to basecoat exterior of dowel rod and round wooden plaque. Add coats of paint as needed for complete coverage, letting paint dry after each application.

Cutting the Large Tree Felt Circles:

1. Use the compass with pencil to mark 2 each of the following width circles onto the light and dark coordinating colored felt sheets: 8-1/2-in., 8-in., 7-1/2-in. 7-in., 6-1/2-in., 6-in., 5-1/2-in., 5-in., 4-1/2-in., 4-in., 3-1/2-in., 3-in., 2-1/2-in., 2-in. and 1-1/2-in. wide.

2. Cut out each circle. There will be 30 circles from each color felt (2 of each size circle) totaling 60 circles in all.

Cutting the Medium Tree Felt Circles:

1. Use the compass with pencil to mark 2 each of the following width circles onto the light and dark coordinating colored felt sheets: 6-1/2-in., 6-in.,

5-1/2-in., 5-in., 4-1/2-in., 4-in.,
3-1/2-in., 3-in., 2-1/2-in., 2-in. and
1-1/2-in. wide.

2. Cut out each circle. There will be
22 circles from each color felt (2 of each
size circle) totaling 44 circles in all.

Cutting the Small Tree Felt Circles:

1. Use the compass with pencil to mark
2 each of the following width circles
onto the light and dark coordinating
colored felt sheets: 5-1/2-in.,
5-in., 4-1/2-in., 4-in., 3-1/2-in., 3-in.,
2-1/2-in., 2-in. and 1-1/2-in. wide.

2. Cut out each circle. There will be 18
circles from each color felt (2 of each
size circle) totaling 36 circles in all.

Assembling the Tree:

1. Cut a small X shape about 1/2 in.
wide in the center of each felt circle. For
easier assembly, organize the felt circles
in a stack from smallest to largest.

2. Place one of the largest dark
colored felt circles onto the dowel
rod by inserting the rod end into the
X-shape cutout. Slide the felt circle to
the base of the dowel rod. Then place
a same-sized light-colored felt circle
on the rod in the same manner. Continue placing alternating light- and
dark-colored felt circles onto the rod in
decreasing size order. Position each felt
circle about 1/8 in. from the previous
felt circle. Secure each in place with a
small amount of hot glue where the felt
circle X-shape cutout and rod meet.
The stacked felt circles should lay with
slightly wavy edges.

3. At the top of the dowel rod, use
hot glue to adhere the last small circle
directly to the top of the rod covering
the flat end.

4. Use hot glue to adhere the large bead
centered on top of the last small circle.

5. Use hot glue to adhere several small
beads or other embellishments randomly placed on the stacked felt circles.

Crafter's Note: If needed, use a hand-held hack-
saw or electrical saw to cut the appropriate length
of dowel rod before beginning and smooth end
with sandpaper.

Wine Cork Tray

CRAFT LEVEL: BEGINNER

FINISHED SIZE: Tray measures about
11 in. wide x 17 in. long.

*Put wine corks to good use with this
elegant tray. Perfect for the wine and
cheese connoisseur on your list, the tray
comes together with just a few supplies.*

Taste of Home Craft Editor Shalana Frisby

MATERIALS:

Choice of 11- x 17-in. wooden tray

About 120 natural wine corks

Clear acrylic sheet sized to fit tray interior

Tacky glue

Sponge brush

Serrated knife

DIRECTIONS:

1. Place tray vertically on a flat surface.
Beginning at the top left corner, use the
sponge brush to apply a 2-in.-tall strip
of tacky glue across the tray width.

2. First place two wine corks vertically
side by side. Then place two wine corks
horizontally side by side. Repeat vertical
and horizontal wine cork pattern across
tray width in a row. Place wine corks
close together for a snug fit. If needed,
cut wine corks with serrated knife to fit.

3. Repeat Steps 1-2 for 8-9 more rows,
applying glue and placing wine cork
pattern. (Wine corks on the last row
may need to be cut to fit remaining area
on tray.) When finished, let glue dry.

4. Prior to use place clear acrylic sheet
on top of wine corks to protect surface.

Crafter's Note: Wondering where to find wine
corks? Natural craft corks can be found in small
quantities at craft stores. For larger quantities, try
looking online at craft sites like Etsy.

RECIPE & CRAFT INDEXES

We've included three indexes for your convenience. The first is a complete alphabetical listing of all the recipes in this book. If you know the name of the recipe you need, simply turn to this index. The second index, the General Recipe Index, lists every recipe by food category, major ingredient and/or cooking method. For example, if you're looking for an appetizer recipe or one that uses beef, use this index. The last index can be used to find a craft. They're listed by title and type of craft.

Alphabetical Recipe Index

General Recipe Index

Craft Index

Share the Magic of Christmas

Do you have a special recipe that has become part of your family's Christmas tradition? Do you have a special flair for decorating on a budget or make the most superb, original gifts? Those are the types of recipes, ideas and crafts we'd like to include in future Taste of Home Christmas books.

To submit a cherished recipe, craft or decorating idea, print or type the information on a standard sheet of paper. Please be thorough and include directions, measurements and sizes of materials or equipment. Also include your name, address and daytime phone number, photo if available and add a few words about yourself and your submission.

Send to "Taste of Home Christmas Annual", 5400 S. 60th Street, Greendale WI 53129 (with a self-addressed stamped envelope if you'd like your materials returned). Or email your submissions and photos to bookeditors@reimanpub.com (write "Taste of Home Christmas Annual" on the subject line).